PUNISHMENT AND POLITICAL THEORY

Punishment and Political Theory

Edited by
MATT MATRAVERS

OXFORD and PORTLAND, OREGON
1999

Hart Publishing
Oxford and Portland, Oregon

Published in North America (US and Canada) by
Hart Publishing c/o
International Specialized Book Services
5804 NE Hassalo Street
Portland, Oregon
97213-3644
USA

Distributed in the Netherlands, Belgium and Luxembourg by
Intersentia, Churchillaan 108
B2900 Schoten
Antwerpen
Belgium

Distributed in Australia and New Zealand by
Federation Press
John St
Leichhardt
NSW 2000

© The contributors severally 1999

Hart Publishing is a specialist legal publisher based in Oxford, England.
To order further copies of this book or to request a list of other
publications please write to:

Hart Publishing, 19 Whitehouse Road, Oxford, OX1 4PA
Telephone: +44 (0)1865 434459 or Fax: +44 (0)1865 794882
e-mail: hartpub@janep.demon.co.uk

British Library Cataloguing in Publication Data
Data Available
ISBN 1 901362–88–4

Typeset in 10pt Sabon
by Hope Services (Abingdon) Ltd.
Printed in Great Britain on acid-free paper
by Biddles Ltd, Guildford and King's Lynn.

Contents

Acknowledgements	vii
Notes on Contributors	ix
Introduction Matt Matravers	1
1 Punishment in a Kantian Framework Tom Sorell	10
2 Punishment and Rights Dudley Knowles	28
3 Punishment, Communication, and Community R. A. Duff	48
4 Punishment, Penance, and the State: A Reply to Duff Andrew von Hirsch	69
Response to von Hirsch R. A. Duff	83
5 Justifying Punishment in Intercultural Contexts: Whose Norms? Which Values? Duncan Ivison	88
6 "What to Say?": The Communicative Element in Punishment and Moral Theory Matt Matravers	108
7 Punishment, Communication, and Resentment Thomas Baldwin	124
8 Albert Speer, Guilt, and "The Space Between" Alan Norrie	133
9 Penal Practices and Political Theory: An Agenda for Dialogue Nicola Lacey	152
Index	165

Acknowledgements

Most of the papers in this volume were given at a conference on political theory and punishment at the University of York in September 1997. The editor wishes to acknowledge his gratitude to the trustees of the C. and J. B. Morrell Trust for their financial support of the conference, and for their continuing support of the study of political theory in the Department of Politics at York. I am also grateful to the contributors, to many of them for making the conference such a memorable event and to all for the swiftness of their responses to editorial pleas; to Antony Duff, additionally, for his advice throughout; to my colleagues here in the Department of Politics at York; to Richard Hart for his support and patience as an editor; and to Gill Pulpher for her help in organising the conference. Katy Fellows provided invaluable assistance in preparing the manuscript and dealt with my frantic demands with great patience and efficiency. My colleague Duncan Ivison provided the kind of support and assistance that one dreams of from a colleague, and I am very grateful to him. Finally, I would like most especially to thank another colleague, Sue Mendus, for the advice, kindness and support that she has unfailingly given me since my arrival in York and that has contributed in many ways to this volume.

Notes on Contributors

Thomas Baldwin is currently Professor of Philosophy at the University of York. He has previously been a Lecturer in Philosophy at Makere Univeristy, Uganda, and at Cambridge University. He is the author of *G E Moore* (Routledge), editor of some of Moore's works, and among other things writes about the foundations of analytical philosophy.

R A Duff has taught in the Department of Philosophy, University of Stirling, since 1990. He is the author of *Trials and Punishments* (1986), *Intention, Agency and Criminal Liability* (1990), and *Criminal Attempts* (1996). He is currently working on a new book on the philosophy of punishment.

Andrew von Hirsch is Honorary Professor of Penal Theory and Penal Law and Fellow of Fitzwilliam College, Cambridge University. He is author of *Censure and Sanctions* (1993) and other writings on the thory of punishment and on sentencing policy.

Duncan Ivison is Lecturer in the School of Philosophy at the University of Sydney. He was previously Lecturer in political theory at the University of York. He is the author of *The Self at Liberty* (Cornell, 1979), and various articles on the history of political thought and contemporary political theory.

Dudley Knowles is Lecturer in Philosophy at theUniversity of Glasgow. He has published articles in moral and political theory as well as the history of these subjects. He has a special interest in Hegel's political philosophy.

Nicola Lacey is Professor of Criminal Law at the London School of Economics and Political Science; she was formerly Professor of Law at Birkbeck College and, before that, Fellow and Tutor in Law at New College, Oxford.

Matt Matravers is lecturer in the Department of Politics at the University of York. He is the author, with Brian Barry, of the entries on Justice and International Justice in the *Routledge Encyclopedia of Philosophy* and of a number of papers on justice and punishment. He is currently completing a book entitled *Justice and Punishment* to be published by Oxford University Press.

Alan Norrie is Edmund Davies Professor of Criminal Law and Criminal Justice at King's College London. He is author of *Crime, Reason and History* (Butterworth, 1993) and *Law, Ideology and Punishment* (Kluwer, 1991). He is presently working to complete a book provisionally entitled *After Kant: Dialectic, Criminal Justice and the Blaming Relation*.

Tom Sorrell is Professor of Philosophy at the University of Essex. He is author of *Hobbs* (1986), *Descartes* (1987), *Moral Theory and Capital Punishment* (1987), *Scientism* (1991), *Business Ethics* (1994), and *Moral Theory and Anomaly* (forthcoming).

Introduction

MATT MATRAVERS

The problem of punishment is one of the most enduring in the political theory corpus. Whilst other problems—political obligation, power, democracy, and the like—go in and out of fashion, there is a seemingly constant and substantial stream of contributions to the discussion of punishment.[1] Ordinarily, the debate surrounding the justification of punishment is presented as occurring between consequentialism and retributivism. Consequentialist theory defends punishment as a means to secure greater utility, typically through individual and general deterrence. Retributivism, in contrast, justifies punishment through the notion of desert. The criminal is said to deserve to suffer for his past act of wrongdoing. Whether this picture of the debate was ever accurate is open to question, but it certainly now fails to capture the subtle and sophisticated ways in which punishment theory has developed. This has happened not merely through the flourishing of so-called "mixed theories", but also because of developments within the consequentialist and retributive traditions.[2]

As with any substantial body of work it is risky to try to characterise what is a diverse and disparate literature in terms of movements or to try to tell a "recent history" of punishment theory. However, that said, it is possible to discern some themes in contemporary penal philosophy. In the 1970s the consequentialist orthodoxy in penal theory was challenged by a revival in retributivism. The consequentialism that had held sway was not simple deterrence theory, but promoted punishment as the means of achieving a number of objectives including those of incapacitating offenders until they were reformed and rehabilitated. The retributivist revival developed not merely from a dissatisfaction with these consequentialist goals, but also from the re-emergence of rights based and contractualist political theory more generally. The "new retributivists" focussed not merely on the failures of consequentialism, but also—to borrow the Kantian parlance of many such theorists—on the right of the offender to be treated as an "end" and not merely as a "means" to some further end.[3]

---

[1] I have not attempted to provide an overview of this literature. For two relatively recent attempts to do so see, R. A. Duff and D. Garland, "Introduction" in their *A Reader on Punishment* (Oxford, Oxford University Press, 1994); R. A. Duff, "Penal Communications: Recent Work in the Philosophy of Punishment", (1996) 20 *Crime and Justice: A Review of Research* 1–97.

[2] So much so that the labels "consequentialist" and "retributive" are of increasingly little use as the theories that they are meant to group together have become so diverse.

[3] This had a political as well as a philosophical dimension. Indeterminate sentencing had (especially in the USA) given great power to bodies such as parole boards and prison officials and there

Of course, the new versions of retributivism still have to face the old problem of how to find in the past act of the offender a justification for his present punishment. That is, of how to make sense of the idea of desert. Furthermore, emphasis on the rights of the offender (and of the community) seemingly makes the problem of punishment more intractable insofar as punishment involves the infliction of suffering.[4] In response to these (and other) problems one strand of retributivism looks to the social contract tradition both to explain the idea of desert (as contained within a general theory of the distribution of the benefits and burdens of social co-operation) and to find an idea of consent so as to explain away the apparent rights violations that occur in the infliction of penal hard treatment.[5] The other main strand in contemporary retributivism also developed from the focus on the offender, but concentrated on the offender's guilt and on the need to express or communicate proportionate censure. On such a theory punishment is understood primarily as the expression or communication of condemnation. This account is discussed below and in a number of the essays in this volume.

Recently the philosophy of punishment has become, if anything, more fragmented. The various new retributive theories have come under close examination and in some cases sustained criticism. In addition, consequentialist theorists have proposed more sophisticated versions of that theory both in defence (against the argument that consequentialism is blind to claims of justice, specifically to the rights of the offender) and in the development of their own justifications of punishment.[6] In addition to further developments within the two traditions, there has also been something of a change in the way that the questions of penal philosophy are addressed. In part this is a result of a general scepticism about "grand theorising" and of a certain engagement with postmodern thought. Increasingly in punishment theory, as in political theory more widely, there is a concentration on the local and particular rather than the general and universal.

Despite the development of punishment theory it has remained relatively isolated from moral and political philosophy more generally. In part perhaps, because the literature on punishment is substantial enough for it to be considered a distinct sub-discipline of political, moral and legal theory, and this status is protected and affirmed by punishment journals and in the book review sections of other periodicals. Although the situation is changing, the discussion of what justifies punishment is often presented independently from questions of the justification of political or legal authority, of moral judgements of wrong-

was widespread evidence of the abuse of such power to discriminate on racial and political grounds. Not, it must be said, that the adoption of more retributive penal practices has done much to change the situation. (See, for example, S. Donziger (ed.), *The Real War on Crime: The Report of the National Criminal Justice Commission*, New York, HarperCollins, 1996.)

[4] Cf. Knowles's essay in this volume.

[5] For discussion of some of these issues see *ibid.* and n.8 below.

[6] See, for example, J. Braithwaite and P. Pettit, *Not Just Deserts: A Republican Theory of Criminal Justice* (Oxford, Clarendon Press, 1990).

doing, of having laws that threaten sanctions if contravened, and so on.[7] Moreover, whilst few would deny that "justice" has been the dominant concern of political theory for almost three decades what is meant is "distributive justice". With a small number of exceptions the advances made in the study of distributive justice since the 1970s have not had much direct influence on the study of punishment and there has been no boom in the study of retributive justice to accompany that which has taken place in the distributive sphere.[8]

Yet, even if few punishment theorists consciously locate their accounts of the justification of punishment within broader moral or political theories, it is clear from the recent developments in the literature on punishment that penal philosophy has mirrored (and sometimes contributed to) changes in the prevailing theoretical climate. The abandoning of consequentialism and the renewed emphasis on rights that occurred in the 1970s, for example, coincided with the change in the overall Anglo-American theoretical climate that accompanied publication of Rawls's *A Theory of Justice*. More important to the themes of the essays in this collection, the literature on punishment is beginning to mirror the way in which the neo-Kantianism of Rawlsian political theory has come under attack from communitarian and post-modern theorists. Put crudely, one of the achievements of Rawls's theory was to show how an impartialist, procedural account of justice could incorporate a concern for consequences.[9] To a degree this has meant that the traditional way of presenting moral and political theory as a debate between consequentialism and deontology has been replaced by a series of debates between liberalism and various critics: communitarians; post-modernists; feminists; environmentalists; and so on.

The essays collected below in various ways address the relationship of punishment theory to political and moral philosophy. Each is an example of the way in which addressing broad questions of moral and political philosophy can illuminate the study of punishment and in which consideration of the problem of justifying punishment can be used as a lens through which to examine particular moral, metaphysical, and political theories. As noted above, one of the main debates in recent political theory has been between liberals and communitarians and the issues that are central to that discussion emerge here in the different

[7] It is also true, as Nicola Lacey points out in her contribution to this volume, that the theoretical and philosophical literature on punishment has paid too little attention to empirical data and the concerns of penal theory.

[8] There have been few explicit attempts to apply Rawlsian techniques to the problem of punishment (for one such see D. Hoekema, "The Right to Punish and the Right to be Punished" in H. G. Blocker and E. Smith (eds.), *Rawls' Theory of Social Justice: An Introduction*, Athens, Ohio, Ohio University Press, 1980). More general attempts to discuss punishment as part of the problem of the distribution of the benefits and burdens of social co-operation can be found in W. Sadurski, "Theory of Punishment, Social Justice, and Liberal Neutrality", (1989) 7 *Law and Philosophy* 351–73 and in the account of punishment as "fair play" (for discussion and references see Matravers's essay in this volume at n.9 and the surrounding text).

[9] Indeed, arguably the best interpretation of utilitarianism (as a decision procedure in which each individual's interests are represented equally) is that it is one version of impartialist theory (see B. Barry, *Justice as Impartiality: Volume II of a Treatise on Social Justice*, Oxford, Oxford University Press, 1995).

emphasis given by the contributors to the autonomy of the individual and the role of the community in the justification of punishment.

In the opening essay, Tom Sorell uses the problems of coercion and punishment to explore the relationship of Kant's ethics and politics and in so doing offers an interpretation of Kant's theory of punishment. Sorell offers the striking claim that paternalistic coercion is compatible with Kant's injunction to treat people as ends and never as merely means. He grounds this in human fallibility, in the idea that human beings can choose badly. Coercion, according to Sorell, is Kant's response to human failure; failures of practical reason and of motivation. Without it the possibility of reversion to the state of nature would arise and with that the loss of the conditions in which autonomy is possible.

The problem of how to integrate Kant's ethics and his politics is a troubling one and Sorell makes an interesting contribution to this debate. His argument also has implications for others. In grounding his account in what he describes as Kant's "error theory of choice" he poses a challenge for those who wish to claim Kant for contemporary liberalism. As Sorell notes, contemporary liberals value the capacity of choice and forgo judgement of the content of people's choices. Typically, it is only when what a person chooses conflicts with or harms another that liberals think it a matter for public intervention. Once one admits that what a person chooses, even where the choice has little to do with any other, can be defective or misconceived, the case for intervention is considerably strengthened. Almost in passing Sorell makes a contribution to another debate, one that is discussed at length in a number of the other papers. In arguing that Kant justifies the use of coercion as a way of securing civil society and thus the conditions of autonomous choice, Sorell remarks that such coercion does not reduce choice. His argument is that those who obey the law because of the threat of the penalty for not doing so do not obey for "ideal reasons". But for those who obey the law because it is right to do so the penalty clause in the law is "idle". This speaks to the relationship between prudential and moral reason and, as is discussed below, to that between "hard treatment" and "censure" in contemporary accounts of punishment.

Ultimately Sorell finds Kant's justification of punishment coherent, but defective. By justifying punishment as a response to those who do not constrain their wills in accordance with the demands of civil society Sorell argues that Kant is pushed towards thinking of every crime as, first and foremost, a harming of the commonwealth. This mirrors a familiar debate in the discussion of "fair play" theories of punishment.[10]

In his contribution Dudley Knowles investigates the apparent tension between rights based accounts of morality and punishment. Punishment is, of course, thought to be particularly problematic because it involves the doing to people of things that would normally be thought to be paradigmatic rights violations—the taking of their life, liberty or property. Knowles looks at both a

---

[10] This is hardly surprising. One of the founders of the "fair play" school, Jeffrie Murphy, developed his account as an interpretation of Kant's theory.

consequentialist and a contractualist account of rights and concludes that this paradox can be dissolved in both cases. This conclusion, of course, leaves open the question of which account is better and this may disconcert some. However, in developing his argument for how it is that both the consequentialist and contractualist traditions can cope with punishment he offers a sophisticated version of each. Proponents of the argument on both sides will undoubtedly think that his defence of each is insufficient, but what is revealed is that even if this is right the arguments that need to be made to show this will have to be far less dismissive and far more elaborate than those that often appear in the literature.

Sorell's and Knowles's contributions are primarily to a liberal or Kantian debate. Their language is individualist and their concern is with the possibility of an account of punishment that is consistent with a rights or autonomy based individualism. The papers of Duff, von Hirsch, Ivison, Matravers, Baldwin, and (in a different way) Norrie revolve around the idea of punishment as a form of communication; as the outcome of a judgement of guilt and culpability. Duff's penitential account of punishment is important to a number of these and is described briefly in the first section of his paper. For Duff, as for von Hirsch, punishment is grounded in the appropriate censure that is deserved by the offender for his conduct. Punishment conveys to the offender the judgement of blame and gives the offender the chance of responding. This is an account that is more firmly embedded in the community yet both Duff and von Hirsch claim that one advantage of this account is that it treats the offender as a rational human being deserving of respect. It does not try to manipulate, intimidate or condition. This combination of a Kantian respect for persons and a communitarian understanding of the locus of the individual's self-understanding raises (at least) two interesting questions, both addressed in these papers: How thick a notion of community is needed for a communicative account to do the work required of it? And, what is the role of the state in communicative theories of punishment?

Much of the debate between Duff and von Hirsch concerns the question of "hard treatment" and its integration into a communicative theory of punishment. Duff argues that hard treatment is a form of secular penance. It forces the attention of the offender onto the message being delivered and, crucially, it provides a vehicle for the offender. A vehicle through which he can "strengthen or deepen his repentant understanding of his wrongdoing", and through which he can express that understanding to others. For von Hirsch the element of hard treatment is a "prudential supplement" designed to reduce offending by offering to those who do not find the law's moral appeal compelling an additional, prudential reason to obey.

This argument is not merely one of how to integrate hard treatment and communicative theories of punishment. Rather, it goes directly to the debate over the nature and function of the state. For Duff, the penitential account of punishment presupposes a communitarian understanding of the state. One in which there is a rich shared language of values; in which those in whose name punishment is carried out have a legitimate interest in the moral character of the offender's actions; and in which the community has the moral standing to judge and censure the offender. Nevertheless, Duff argues this can be a liberal-communitarianism, because the shared values around which it is organised can be liberal ones. Although it should be noted that even if Duff's argument is successful at this point and his account can be shown to be compatible with a respect for autonomy understood as a basic substantive value of liberalism, this is not the same as saying that his account is compatible with the kind of liberalism that tries to remain neutral with respect to different accounts of value.

Von Hirsch is sceptical even of Duff's limited claim that the penitential account is compatible with a substantive liberalism. For von Hirsch, Duff simply gives to the state functions that are inappropriate to it. The reform of the individual is not illegitimate and may be a welcome by product of punishment, but it should not be a constitutive function of punishment. To make it so is to empower the state with the functions of an abbott and that is incompatible with its proper function. Duff, of course, disagrees and replies to some of von Hirsch's criticisms in a brief appendix to the latter's paper.

The importance of this debate is hard to overestimate and it has implications for a number of other questions raised in this group of papers. The questions of proportionality in punishments and of the moral standing of those who punish are addressed directly by both Duff and von Hirsch and their different approaches to these stem from their contrasting communitarian and liberal views of the state.

Although Duff's and von Hirsch's disagreement, then, extends beyond how hard treatment and communication are to be integrated in an account of punishment, their accounts presuppose a stable, fixed community that has, or could have, the moral standing to condemn. Ivison and Matravers, both sympathetic to the communicative approach, put this supposition into question. Ivison uses the example of post-colonial societies, primarily Australia, to examine whether a communicative theory of punishment can coexist with legal pluralism and in doing so develops this latter notion further. As the title of his paper indicates, Ivison asks of communicative theories "whose norms and which values" should underpin, and provide the content of, penal communications in societies where there are competing traditions and understandings of moral value. Matravers questions the source of the authority of the community. That is, even if the problem of individuating the community that is posed by Ivison can be resolved, it remains necessary to establish the grounds of the norms to which the community gives expression.

The (post-) colonial societies discussed by Ivison pose a significant problem for communicative theorists. Not only because of the likelihood that the offender may "hear" the penal communication as an alien imposition, but also because the existence of such pluralism may cause those who punish to question the validity of their imposing their judgements on others who avow very different beliefs. Ivison focuses on the combination of a Kantian respect for persons with a communitarian understanding of the source of those persons' self-understandings and conceptions of value and argues that this combination is unstable. He poses directly the question of how thin the communitarian element can be given the heterogeneity of modern states without it becoming so thin as to undermine the possibility of a viable communicative account of punishment.

Whereas for Ivison the problem is essentially one of there being a "relative abundance" of moral norms, for Matravers the problem is one of absence. In a sense, Ivison understands the problem for communicative accounts of "which values" as a political problem, Matravers understands it as meta-ethical. Communicative accounts of punishment, whether as broad as Duff's or as narrow as von Hirsch's, require not only that the offender's act be condemned as wrong, but also that the offender be given reasons (of the right kind) that (at least in principle) allow her to understand what she has done as wrong and why its being wrong should matter to her. Matravers argues that meeting this demand cannot be isolated from the challenge of pluralism or, more seriously, scepticism. Insofar as the theorist of communicative punishment relies on the understandings and practices of the relevant community to provide the content of penal communications, she opens herself up to the charge of conventionalism as well as to the kinds of problems discussed in Ivison's paper. However, the alternative is to attempt to offer an account of the values contained in the communication that is independent of the local understandings of those who do the punishing and those who are being punished. This is a serious challenge; one that many take to be impossible. However, even if this is so the argument is that theorists of communicative punishments need to say more about the source and motivational force of the values contained in penal communications.

Whereas Duff, von Hirsch, Ivison and Matravers all allow that punishment may have an essential communicative element Thomas Baldwin finds the idea unconvincing. In part Baldwin, like von Hirsch, objects that Duff's advocacy of hard treatment as a vehicle for penitence is incompatible with the demand to treat people as autonomous agents deserving of equal respect. He begins by questioning Duff's integration of hard treatment and communication. Baldwin argues that Duff makes room for hard treatment through the idea of reforming the individual, but that this introduces a tension in the account. The more Duff emphasises the sincere and open communication of reasons the less compelling is his account of hard treatment. Similarly, insofar as it is the reform of the individual that is sought, it seems that communication becomes merely instrumental to this end. Baldwin illustrates this tension using J. L. Austin's theory of speech acts. Conceiving of communication as locutionary and illocutionary captures the condemnation, but cannot make room for hard treatment. Conceiving of it as perlocutionary allows the incorporation of hard treatment, but is, Baldwin argues, "wholly unacceptable" because it is incompatible with treating the offender as an autonomous agent deserving of respect.

Nevertheless, Baldwin thinks that there is something worth rescuing in communicative theory. Returning to a more expressivist tradition he argues that punishment includes the communication of resentment. It cannot be just this, and merely citing the feeling of resentment cannot itself justify punishment, but Baldwin indicates how he thinks that the theory can be developed by being located in a general theory of the function of the state to protect the life, liberty, and possessions of its citizens.

Alan Norrie's paper raises a number of questions about the nature of the community and of the self in conditions of late modernity. His argument concerns blame and its relation both to the self and to the community (or communities) that self inhabits. As such it contributes to the debate over the relation of the individual to the community and is significant for all theories of punishment, including those based on communication. Beginning with the work of Anthony Giddens, Norrie argues that guilt is to be understood in the relation between individuals and particular normative communities. Whereas for Giddens late modernity is characterised by the erosion of such communities and consequently a turning away from guilt, Norrie is interested in the fragmentation of communities and the implication of this for judgements of guilt and for the self. In addition, Norrie focuses on the way in which individuals construct themselves through biographical narratives and on the fluidity of late modern selfhood. His argument is, in part, about the crucial role of the community—of those who do the judging—in "fixing" responsibility, although, as he indicates at the end of his paper, this is not to embrace a necessarily conventionalist or relativist position. Judgements of responsibility can be correct even if they are located in the "space between" the individual and the self who is judged.

Norrie illustrates some of this argument through a reading of the life of Albert Speer as retold in a recent biography. The biography, Norrie argues, reveals a curiously ambiguous figure. To reduce a sophisticated argument to a crude claim: Norrie's reading is that the ambiguity stems from the radically different communities to which Speer is oriented in the course of his life as a Nazi leader and subsequently a reviled prisoner. The narratives that Speer tells to make sense of his life are incompletely brought together by him. The fluidity of his self allows a narrative in which he escapes guilt, but never completely as his attempt to bring the stories of his life together requires that he confront himself in relation to the post war liberal democratic community that condemned him.

Of course, Speer is an exceptional case, and few (Norrie is not one such) would claim that he is not guilty or that the later Speer who tried to come to terms with his earlier life was a different person from the Nazi leader. Nevertheless, Norrie argues that there are conclusions to be drawn from this analysis for the philosophy of punishment generally and certainly his discussion of the two communities (pre and post war) can be compared with Ivison's discussion of the two communities in post-colonial societies. Norrie's location of the "site" of judgement requires a complex understanding of the relationship of individuals and communities. More complex, he claims, than is provided by traditional liberal and communitarian approaches.

Introduction   9

In the final paper Nicola Lacey contributes to the debate over the relationship of individual to community, and provides something of a future research agenda that is at the same time a plea for interdisciplinary study. It is a fitting end to a collection dedicated to exploring such interconnections. Lacey draws attention to two areas that have not commanded sufficient attention amongst philosophers of punishment. First, the analysis of power offered by Michel Foucault and especially the notion of disciplinary power. Second, the tendency amongst political and punishment theorists to identify the political and the public with the state. Lacey argues that Foucault's notion of disciplinary power constitutes an important aspect of contemporary practices of punishment. Of course, the questions of how punishment works and of what justifies it are different, but insofar as penal philosophers wish to assess the practices of punishment and to recommend changes to those practices Lacey argues that they need the richer notion of power offered by Foucault (or at least need to engage in the debate), just as sociologists of punishment require normative concepts to understand fully the functions and practices of punishment.

In the second part of her paper, Lacey once more brings the question of the state into focus. The attention of penal philosophers on the nation state is, she claims, unduly narrow and distorts the accounts that are subsequently developed. Lacey's point is not merely that a great deal of punishment is not inflicted by the State, but that the fragmentation of penal power raises fundamental questions about the nature of the political and of the public private divide. Thus a richer notion of power, as suggested in the first part of the paper, should inform a better analysis of "the political and the personal, the public and the private". Like the essays that precede it, Lacey's contribution warns against the use of too simplistic a notion of community and (connectedly) of power. And like them, it is an example of how the study of punishment can illuminate broader political and ethical issues. Issues that themselves need to be addressed if a satisfactory theory of punishment is to be developed.[11]

---

[11] I would like to thank my colleague Susan Mendus for her very helpful comments and advice on this introduction.

1
Punishment in a Kantian Framework

TOM SORELL

Many people who are attracted to Kant's ethics are repelled by his politics. The same writer who conjures up the ideal of a kingdom of ends and of respect for persons also condemns rebellion against regimes that show no respect for persons and that seem to be the antithesis of the kingdom of ends. The same writer who says that people cannot be treated merely as means endorses coercive institutions within the state. And it comes as a surprise to some that Kant is a retributivist about punishment and a believer in the death penalty for certain crimes. There is a natural, but also incorrect, interpretation of Kant on the relation between ethics and politics that would make sense of this position. According to this incorrect interpretation, ethics is about how people should ideally treat one another, if they are rationally motivated, while the institutions of the state reflect the ways people actually treat one another. The interpretation goes on to say that as things actually are, even an unjust state may make people behave better than no state at all, which is why rebellion is always outlawed. Similarly, coercive institutions, including a regime of capital punishment, may be necessary to keep under control people who are not rationally motivated, who are a far cry from the mutually respectful legislators whom Kant conjures up to elucidate the categorical imperative.

I say that this interpretation is wrong, because Kant's ethics is not all idealisation, and Kant's politics not all worldliness and disillusionment. The *Metaphysics of Morals*[1] gives reasons why any political order is better than none, but it also sketches an ideal political order—a kind of civic republicanism, toward which even the imperfect regimes of Kant's day could evolve. That is how the book is able to condemn rebellion, without implying that the political world as we have it, or as Kant had it, is the best we can hope for. Again, the *Groundwork*[2] is not a book about holy beings or beings with special rational powers. It is a book about human beings and other finitely rational agents. This and other writings acknowledge some motivating forces in people that are not moral, though they lead to actions that are consistent with morality, and other forces that are flatly immoral, like self-love and the evil or bad will. Moral

---

[1] I. Kant, *Metaphysics of Morals*, (trans. Mary Gregor) Cambridge, Cambridge University Press, 1991.

[2] I. Kant, *Foundations of the Metaphysics of Morals*, (trans. L.W. Beck) New York, Liberal Arts Press, 1959).

development is all about disciplining a will that is highly receptive to non-moral influences, disciplining it in such a way that it is more directly under the control of practical reason.

Is there a better interpretation of the relation between ethics and politics in Kant that reconciles the permissibility of coercion in the political sphere with the treatment of people as ends in the ethical sphere? In the first section of this chapter I shall outline one. I shall suggest that while coercion is never desirable for Kant, it is sometimes permissible—namely when it removes some obstacle to autonomy. The obstacle may be internal and pathological, as in the case of a compulsion or addiction that force may succeed in breaking, or it may be external and a matter of a bad will, as when one agent is compromised by another's policy of putting his interests above everyone else's. Coercive laws and penal institutions discourage people from putting themselves first and restricting the freedom of others. In particular they counteract the invitation to aggressively self-interested action provided by the state of nature—where each person is the sole judge of what it is right to do. Kant thinks it is permissible to force people out of the state of nature, because when each person is their own judge of right there is no standard of right, and so no basis for autonomy. By the same token it is permissible to use force to keep people from reverting to the state of nature, which is where coercive penal laws and institutions come in. Punishment in Kant's political framework is at least in keeping with Kant's ethics (sections 2–4). But Kant's framework is not the only Kantian one, and perhaps there are others that not only make political institutions consistent with mutual respect among autonomous agents, but which make penal institutions reflect a different conception of penal justice from a retributive one. In section 5 this suggestion is considered, but with a certain amount of scepticism. I myself doubt that a reorientation in this area is either straightforward or desirable. Or, to put it another way, I doubt that the alignment of liberalism with Kantianism is perfect. Partly this is because of the considerable and proper allowance that Kant's theory makes for defective practical judgement and bad motivation. Coercion is a way of compensating for the bad impulses, both psychological and social, that lead people to make bad choices. Retribution only carries out what coercive laws and institutions threaten and what parties to the social contract promise to bear.

1. KANT AND THE MORAL PERMISSIBILITY OF COERCION

There is no inconsistency between Kant's handling of coercion in his ethics and his handling of coercion in his politics. But there may *seem* to be an inconsistency. According to a standard reading of one of Kant's formulations of the categorical imperative, coercion is morally wrong; whereas according to the *Metaphysics of Morals* coercion is right. There is no real inconsistency here, because according to Kant coercion is *juridically* right, and the juridical and the moral or ethical are distinguishable spheres. The background for what is maintained in the *Metaphysics of Morals*[3] is that ethics is all about the adoption of ends, and no one can be forced by someone else to adopt ends. For an end to be mine it has to be freely adopted by me. Someone else can perhaps compel me to *behave* as if I adopt a certain end, but unless I choose the end, all my behaviour indicates is the pretence of adopting an end. If I do genuinely *choose* the end, on the other hand, the choice cannot result from coercion. Coercion is a possibility in the case of actions rather than in the adoption of ends our actions are supposed to serve. But actions in this sense are the province of a subject other than ethics, namely what Kant calls the doctrine of right. And according to the doctrine of right, force may sometimes legitimately be exerted to get people to discharge certain strict juridical duties in so-called "external actions". So coercion is possible and sometimes necessary outside ethics, but impossible within ethics.

That is the argument in the *Metaphysics of Morals*. The *Groundwork* runs along quite different lines. There it is less clear that coercion is not a possibility in ethics. For one of Kant's formulations of the categorical imperative—the so-called Principle of Humanity—seems to say that morally right actions never serve ends that deny or give insufficient weight to the human capacity to choose. And this principle both appears to belong to ethics and to have a bearing on coercion, at least as coercion is ordinarily understood, since when one agent coerces another, he tries to subject not only himself but another to his own power to choose. The other's power to choose, or at least the other's exercise of that power, is an obstacle to be overcome rather than a background fact that the coercer agrees to live with. And the Principle of Humanity seems to call for actions that accept the other's power to choose, that do not regard it as an obstacle.

When we consider in detail Kant's formulation and application of the Principle of Humanity, however, it is not so clear that it does rule out all kinds of coercion. The principle calls on us to:

> "Act so that you treat humanity, whether in your own person or in that of another, always as an end and never as a means only".[4]

Kant gives false promising as an example of a violation of the principle. What makes a false promise a clear case of treating someone as means is that the person on the receiving end cannot possibly adopt the end the lying agent has, cannot possibly assent to the lying promise. Following Korsgaard,[5] we may infer from Kant's treatment of the lying promise that it is always a sufficient condition of violating the principle of humanity that the one at the receiving end of the treatment cannot endorse the agent's end in meting out that treatment.

Now if we take the "cannot" seriously, quite a lot of prima facie objectionable treatment turns out to be insufficient for violating the principle of human-

---

[3] I. Kant, n.1 above, at p. 381.
[4] I. Kant, n.2, above at p. 429.
[5] C. Korsgaard, "The Right to Lie: Kant on Dealing with Evil", reprinted in Korsgaard's *Creating the Kingdom of Ends* (Cambridge, Cambridge University Press, 1996), pp. 133–58.

ity. Suppose that you are a smoker who knows the health risks of cigarettes but refuses to quit smoking. If I make it my life's work to shadow you and take way any cigarettes you acquire; if I handcuff you to keep you from lighting up, I certainly seem to be in the business of forcing you to give up. But if I do it for the sake of your health, do I have an end you *couldn't* share? The answer is "No". You could share it if you gave greater weight to protecting your health than to the enjoyment you get from smoking. Not only could my end conceivably be adopted by you; it might be irrational for you not to adopt it. To put it another way, you *ought* to (choose to) stop smoking. And if you ought to, you *could*, choose to stop smoking (choosing to stop smoking is not the same as stopping itself.) Or, if you realise you couldn't do it by will-power alone, you could choose to have the habit broken by something (a drug) or someone else (a hypnotist). Against this background my taking away your cigarettes and handcuffing you is not necessarily a case of treating you as a means; or, if it is, what makes it wrong is not the same as what makes a lying promise wrong.

The example of coercing the smoker is one of a range where compulsion or an intervention that someone would or does resist is driven by an end that the one on the receiving end *could* reasonably share. Another case in the range would be the forced feeding of anorexics. Another would be throwing someone who is on the point of being able to swim into the deep end. Korsgaard claims[6] that coercion is never something that could be agreed to by the one on the receiving end, because coercion involves not giving the coerced person a chance to assent. But this claim is wrong twice over. Coercion can follow upon, and be explained by, refusal to assent; so it is compatible with giving the relevant agent a chance to assent. Secondly, the impossibility of assent which seems to be involved in the case of deception seems to flow from the concept of a lying promise and the position that the conditions for success of a lying promise put the other person in. The impossibility does not seem to have anything to do with being given or not being given the opportunity to assent.

The interpretation I am putting forward does not make coercion in general, or the typical forms of coercion, compatible with Kant's Principle of Humanity. But it does seem to find room under the Principle for what might be called paternalistic coercion. Not treating another as a means does not mean going along with everything the agent has chosen, especially if some of those choices reduce the power of choice by leading to addiction, illness, or premature death. And acting for purposes the agent could have chosen, especially when the purposes are ones he ought rationally to pursue (in discharging a duty of perfecting oneself, for example) may be permissible, even when it means hindering actions that the agent takes (although mistakenly) to contribute to his happiness, such as smoking or injecting himself with drugs. It is true that some of the means adopted by the paternalistic agent, such as taking away cigarettes that the smoker has legally acquired, may be prohibited for reasons other than the

---

[6] *Ibid.*, at p. 138.

Principle of Humanity, reasons that come from the doctrine of right. But what is in question here is whether coercing people for their own good is ruled out by that Principle. It does not seem to be.

It might be thought that paternalistic coercion is ruled out by another element of Kant's ethics. Kant thinks that there is an ethical duty, a duty of virtue, to help others to promote the happiness of others. Does this duty rule out paternalistic coercion? It would if helping others to pursue their happiness meant helping them to do just anything that (they think) would make them happy. But this is not what Kant means. The relevant passage in this connection reads:

> "When it comes to my promoting happiness as an end that is also a duty, this must therefore be the happiness of *other* men, *whose* (permitted) *end I thus* make *my own end as well*. It is for them to decide what they count as belonging to their happiness; but it is open to me to refuse them many things that *they* think will make them happy, but that I do not, as long as they have no right to demand them from me as what is theirs".[7]

Kant seems to be saying that there can be legitimate disagreements between you and me as to what will make me happy, and that you are not obliged to defer to my opinion just because it is *my* happiness that is in question. The strong implication is that the pursuer of happiness is not necessarily authoritative about what will make him happy, and that even if he were, other agents would be entitled to use their judgement in discharging their duty to help. An even stronger restriction on what other agents can be expected to do to make me happy is introduced when Kant says that only my *permitted* ends need be promoted. "Permitted" is a defined term in both the doctrine of right and the doctrine of virtue:

> "That action is permitted (*licitum*) which is not contrary to obligation" (p. 222),

and

> "*Obligation* is the necessity of a free action under the categorical imperative of reason" (p. 222).

Putting these together, we can read Kant as saying that only those ends of agents that do not conflict with duties can be made the ends of other agents. The anorexic's end of getting slimmer and slimmer might conflict with a duty of people to look after themselves or to keep up their physical capacities;[8] so might the end of maximising enjoyment from smoking. If that is right, then the passage about other people's happiness suggests that we would be justified in not making these ends our own. Thus, we could refuse requests to buy the anorexic weight-reducing drugs or we could refuse to buy the smoker cigarettes, or refuse to keep a look out while he lights up in a no-smoking zone. Admittedly, we do not get from the passage an argument for all-out paternalistic intervention in

---

[7] I. Kant, n.1 above, at p. 388.
[8] cf. e.g. *ibid.*, at p. 427.

another's pursuit of happiness by smoking or starvation; we are only given reasons for a certain kind of omission. But the omission, like the coercion discussed earlier, looks paternalistic. Kant seems to be saying that to the extent *my* efforts are channelled into another person's happiness, I may judge what that happiness requires.

Perhaps talk of paternalism does not strike quite the right note. Perhaps what we are alerted to by the detail of the Principle of Humanity and by the explanation of our duty to contribute to the happiness of others is really human fallibility about what ends are worth pursuing, and not the need for paternalism as a response to fallibility. The reason why treating people as ends is a matter of giving value to the faculty of choice rather than actual choices; the reason why we only have a duty within limits to pursue the happiness of others, is that people can easily adopt the wrong ends. Kant has a theory of human nature to explain why the wrong ends are likely to be chosen by people as they actually are; he has a theory of human possibility to explain how the faculty of choice can be redirected to better ends; and he has a philosophy of history which makes intelligible how a process that has led to human behaviour and institutions as they actually are could lead beyond that to the realisation of more attractive possibilities.

2. KANTIAN POLITICS AS A CONDITION OF IMPROVED HUMAN CHOICE

Citizenship in a republic is a key means of redirecting the natural choices of human beings toward higher ends, according to Kant. The creation of civil society makes possible standards of public right, standards which limit what may be done by each in the pursuit of happiness. In civil society, people may do what they like, so long as what they do is in keeping with a law that could govern *everyone's* free actions. This is the antithesis of being a law unto oneself, of acting as if what is right is whatever one judges to promote one's own well-being. But being a law unto oneself is the mark of pre-political life. Before there is civil society there is only the disunity of wills of the state of nature, each steered by his own lights. Each may compete for physical possession of things they won't or can't share, and as each is the sole judge of what to do and take, there is nothing to prevent the competition from becoming violent. These conditions are not sufficient for genuine possession of anything by anyone, and so defeat the pursuit of happiness. Where each is free in the sense of being a law unto himself, there is no genuine possession or property, according to Kant, for even if someone manages to take over something and to fend off for the time being others who wish to take it over, possession is only possession when there is a general willingness by the many not to take over what is already occupied by the individual. Such general willingness is the key to the effective pursuit of happiness, which for Kant is the pursuit of happiness within a civil society.

The mechanisms for entering civil society, and the institutions through which legislation is made and enforced, all make possible and encourage a detachment from narrow self-interest in the pursuit of happiness. But though there is a detachment from narrow self-interest and an acceptance of universal law, still it is *happiness* that is being pursued, inclination that is being served by universal laws governing behaviour. There remains the possibility of further detachment, this time from inclination itself. Here is where the cultivation of virtue takes over from conformity with public right. Ends may be adopted in one's treatment of oneself or others that are worthwhile in their own right and that could be adopted by anyone, irrespective of the ingredients of personal happiness in their case. With the cultivation of virtue, one emancipates oneself from the pursuit of happiness in the adoption of ends and takes further the moral development that starts with the aspiration to the rightful pursuit of happiness. Before the rightful pursuit of happiness, before civil society, the pursuit of happiness is guided only by the succession of personal desires. The frustration of some of those desires by other people leads to the general agreement to rein in acting on desires within limits set by universal laws. This reining in yields a kind of freedom of action, but one that is still subservient to the play of personal desire. A more thoroughgoing freedom comes from the adoption of ends independently of inclination and personal desire.

The error theory of human choice that goes with this account is readily stated. At the lowest or animal stage of human moral development habitual pleasure determines a range of choice. In that case, there is no insurance against excess except the pain (if any) of overindulgence, and perhaps no conceptual background in an agent for consciousness of excess *as* excess, still less of the need to guard against excess. There is no insurance either against the conflict that ensues from people acting on pleasure alone. Insurance against excess and against violence becomes available when choice is determined not only by sense and intellect but law. Even at this level of moral development, however, the overarching end is happiness, albeit not mere animal happiness. And Kant's point is that it is easy to be wrong about what makes one happy. So long as happiness is one's ultimate end, choice is likely to be mistaken, since it takes a great deal of experience for each person to find out what will make him happy.[9]

Now at least one choice is compatible with the effective personal pursuit of happiness in *any* form, and that is the choice of civil society over the state of nature. Kant reinterprets both the idea of the state of nature and the idea of civil society, but he does follow Hobbes in holding that the choice of civil society over the state of nature is highly rational. This is the choice that authorises coercion in civil society, that at the same time makes possible security of life, security of possession, and the free pursuit of happiness, while also making thinkable ways of life that go beyond the pursuit of happiness. Up to a point

---

[9] I. Kant, n.1 above, at p. 215; cf. I. Kant, n.2 above, at p. 418; I. Kant, *Critique of Judgement* (trans. J. Meredith) Oxford, Clarendon Press, 1952, §83.

Kant's claims for civil society echo Hobbes's. Civil society gives a sense to "mine" and "yours", "right" and "wrong", that is unbiased by the importance to each person of making this or that their personal property, and of implementing certain means to certain ends. The public standards of right and wrong are not tailored to the requirements of one person's personal projects, but to the requirement of reducing conflicts between personal projects without, as far as possible, reducing the freedom to pursue personal projects. Making oneself subject to the standards may be interpreted as creating an environment for improved personal choice, in which some of the distorting effect of personal bias is removed. In civil society it is no longer a decisive reason for one agent's being allowed to do something that it would give him a lot of gratification to do it. The permissibility of it would depend on its not interfering with others' plans. A good choice is no longer good just because it pleases me.

Creating and maintaining civil society is right, according to Kant, partly because its impersonal coercive mechanisms improve conditions for choice; paternalistic intervention may also be defended on these grounds, where the point of the intervention is to remove hindrances to choice, like addiction, or to get competences exercised, as when the person on the point of being able to swim is thrown in at the deep end. It does not follow from its being intervention that it extinguishes or reduces choice; and it does not follow from the fact that people are told by the law not to steal *or else* and told not to assault one another *or else* that they cannot be law-abiding perfectly freely, or that the "or else" introduces manipulation or denigration. People who would not dream of stealing or assault never have to engage with the law by means of thoughts about the penalties; neither do those who entertain the idea but find it repellent independent of the penalties. For them the specification of the penalty in the law is idle. On the other hand, those who need the thought of the penalties to refrain from stealing or assault are helped by the thought of the penalty. It is true that when the law gets them to refrain from stealing or assault by means of the thought of the penalties, the law does not get them to refrain from stealing or assault for ideal reasons. But it does get them to refrain or hesitate, and so increases the choices of people who would otherwise be their victims, while depriving the would-be criminals of no choices that are available to everyone else.

3. KANT'S JUSTIFICATION OF PUNISHMENT

I have been suggesting that Kant's error theory of choice is the key to the compatibility of freedom with coercion and of paternalistic intervention with treating people as ends. I pass on now from the justification of coercion in general to punishment in particular. The key to Kant's theory of punishment is the connection between what he calls "public crimes" and violence, and the connection between the institution and maintenance of civil society and the repudiation of violence. The unpunished public crime is a sort of counterpart of the violent act in a lawless state of nature. It is no more tolerable, given that people bargain for the end of violence when they enter civil society, than a wholesale return to the state of nature. That is why crimes must be punished. And except where to do so would itself bring on the end of the state, crimes and punishments must balance one another out.

Civil society comes about by a union of wills. The union aims at achieving a sort of harmony between agents who cannot avoid interacting with one another, and might come into conflict. By uniting wills individuals become a people, who are the source of legislative authority in a civil society. The reason the source of legislative authority is the people rather than something else, according to Kant, is that the people:

> "*cannot* do anyone wrong by its law. Now, when someone makes arrangements about *another*, it is always possible for him to do the other wrong; but he can never do wrong in what he decides upon with regard to himself (for *volenti non fit iniuria*). Therefore only the concurring and united will of all, insofar as each decides the same thing for all for each, and so only the united will of the people, can be legislative".[10]

The means by which individuals form themselves into a people is by first unanimously renouncing the freedom consisting of being a law unto oneself as an agent in the state of nature, and immediately taking up the freedom of action compatible with everyone being under the same universal law. It is possible for individuals to opt out of the renunciation of the freedom of the state of nature, but it is also morally reprehensible for them to do so, since it is way of endorsing a condition in which nothing and no one is secure against violence.[11] Indeed, Kant thinks opters-out can legitimately be forced to opt in.[12] Even if there were not this moral warrant for preventing it, opting out would be dangerous, since there is nothing to prevent anyone else's thinking it would be in their interest to make the opter-out a target of violence. If, on the other hand, one becomes party to a general legislative will, one cannot exempt oneself from the scope of its laws. Each legislates for all. Or at least, each votes for legislation that must be able to apply to all. Law-breaking against this background is always a renunciation of union of one's will with that of everyone else. One flouts legislation, including legislation specifying punishment for its violation, that one is responsible with others for making and that one is responsible with others for making oneself subject to. Not only that, but one takes advantage of the law-abidingness of others. The thief in civil society has relative security for his ill-gotten gains; the murderer, even if caught, is protected from the instant retaliation he might expect in the state of nature. Those who trust to an imperfectly enforced law and do not take their protection into their own hands are keeping to the spirit of maintaining a social contract and renouncing arbitrary violence. But

---

[10] I. Kant, n.1 above, at pp. 313–14.
[11] *Ibid.*, at pp. 307–8.
[12] *Ibid.*, at p. 313.

they also make themselves easier targets for those who unleash violence in the context of civil society.

The more a particular type of action disrupts the range and harmony of actions that are open to all when all are law abiding, the more it needs to be discouraged by the penalty for breaking it. Rebellion is particularly serious, because it threatens to reintroduce the state of nature with its unlimited and arbitrary violence. But other crimes can be understood as serious because they introduce into civil society slices of life from the state of nature—that is, episodes of arbitrary dispossession and assault—precisely what citizens hope to leave behind in return for universal constraint by law in civil society. The law against theft and assault or murder for gain are not just any old offences, because civil society itself is *fundamentally* a repudiation of the loss through violence of life and property. As Kant's distinction between public and private crimes suggests, the more an act looks like expressing a will to return, to what, in order to exist, a people have to repudiate, the more it is like an act of rebellion.

Private and public crimes correspond to cases tried by civil and criminal courts, respectively.[13] Public crimes, including counterfeiting of currency, robbery and theft are so-called, he says, because they threaten the commonwealth and not just an individual person.[14] Theft threatens the institution of property, interpreted as the stability of possession of the means of well-being, which makes its wrongness extend beyond the wrong done to the particular victim of theft. That is why it is supposed to be fair to punish the thief by depriving him of the right of property-owning and making him suffer a sort of legal slavery (imprisonment with forced labour) in order to survive.[15] By threatening one of the institutions that allows for the free pursuit of well-being, the thief casts himself entirely outside that institution. Murder can be treated similarly. It, too, can be interpreted as a direct attack on a condition for the existence of collective well-being. It not only takes away life, which as Kant defines it,[16] is a more fundamental condition of well-being even than desire; it shows the compatibility of extreme violence with institutions that are properly understood as excluding it; and so opens those institutions to contempt, or to competition from vigilante groups, which, as in the state of nature, make private judgement the measure of justice.

In short, in Kant's view, public criminality is politically subversive before it is victimising. No wonder he thinks that the worst thing that the sovereign—the public official in charge of punishment—can do to his subjects is simply to grant clemency to a criminal.[17] That is to become an accomplice in subversion. Crimes have to be punished, and the only standard of selecting punishments for crimes that is *a priori* defensible,[18] hence the only standard that belongs in a

[13] *Ibid.*, at p. 331.
[14] *Ibid.*, at p. 331.
[15] *Ibid.*, at p. 333.
[16] *Ibid.*, at p. 211.
[17] *Ibid.*, at p. 337.
[18] *Ibid.*, cf. at p. 363.

metaphysics of morals, is the law of equality of crime and punishment. In endorsing retribution as a philosophical standard of punishment,[19] however, Kant is not dictating to courts the details of sentencing, or even saying within the confines of the philosophy of punishment that in every case the punishment that typically fits murder or rebellion—namely death—must always be imposed. In unusual cases the death penalty would have to be carried out on such a scale that it would contribute to the dissolution of society,[20] making punishment itself subversive of the state. In other cases—Kant's examples are private crimes—the choice of penalty has to take account of facts about the criminal that may make the typical punishment for his crime inappropriate.[21] Kant's point seems to be that while there can be departures for a certain narrow range of reasons from the standard that underlies retributive justice, there is no standard other than retribution that would be both *a priori* defensible and admit of no exception. As for departures from the standard of retribution, these are not *ad hoc* departures, or departures justified by their consequences, but, on the contrary, departures justified by the tension between rigid retributivism and what it is supposed to be a means to, a permanent exit from the state of nature.

4. Problems with Kant's Theories of Punishment and the State

Kant's theory of punishment is coherent, I believe, but it is also defective, and some of what is wrong with it goes back to the sort of conception of civil society that it is embedded in. One problem arises from Kant's distinction between private and public crime. The public crimes that Kant's theory of punishment dwells on—robbery, theft, murder, and so on—are not, as his formulation of the private/public crime distinction implies, crimes against the commonwealth *as opposed to* crimes against individuals. Murder victims are relatively rarely

---

[19] In Thomas Hill's "Kant's Anti-Moralistic Strain" (reprinted in Hill's *Dignity and Practical Reason* (Ithaca N.Y, Cornell University Press, 1992) it is argued that if Kant is a retributivist at all, he is not a thoroughgoing one. According to Hill, Kant does not hold that punishment should be proportionate to the moral worth displayed by the criminal, and this is what one would expect of, so to speak, a "real" retributivist. But as Hill himself admits, some textual evidence does suggest that execution for murderer fits the viciousness of the criminal as well as the crime (Kant, n.1 above, at pp. 333–4), and it is unclear why the characteristic appeal of retributivists to *lex talionis* should not be sufficient for classifying Kant as one. In any case, it is unclear why reference to inner worth should be necessary or sufficient for being a retributivist in relation to criminality, since criminality, as opposed to immorality, is related by Kant to illegal action *whatever* the motivation. Hill claims that Kant's insistence in the *Groundwork* on the inscrutability of motives, even where they are one's own, lends weight to the interpretation of Kant as less than thoroughgoingly retributivist. But that is like saying that to acknowledge the difficulty of proving guilt up to the standard of the criminal law makes it hard for one consistently to prosecute those whom one has *some* evidence are guilty. It is actually possible to read Kant as saying in the *Groundwork* that the presence of factors such as self-love makes us inclined to be overcharitable to ourselves or self-deceiving about how noble our motives are. This is compatible with saying that our motives are scrutable, however, if there are ways of counteracting the influence of self-love, and of course Kant thinks there are such.
[20] I. Kant, n.1 above, at p. 334.
[21] *Ibid.*, at pp. 332–3.

strangers to their murderers, and the reasons for murders often arise from the detail of personal relationships. Murders committed from greed or jealously need not be committed by people who are murderous, and perhaps it is only serial killing or terrorist killing that really threatens the commonwealth. This does not mean that murders by killers other than serial ones are not serious, or that they do not deserve the death penalty. My point is that the reasons for retribution need to be drawn from the losses of the victims,[22] and not the threat to society that any murder supposedly carries with it. But if that is right, Kant's category of the public crime looks too comprehensive, lumping together violations of law that are readily seen as threats to the commonwealth with others that are serious for other reasons and are in a sense private crimes. It will not do to reply on Kant's behalf that in a sense any crime is a threat to the commonwealth, disrupting as it does the willed co-ordination of free pursuits that is supposed to constitute life in the commonwealth; for that would threaten to turn even crimes dealt with by the civil courts into public crimes, contrary to the intention behind the private/public distinction.

I labour the criticism of Kant's concept of the public crime, because it is through that concept that the rationale for civil society in general transfers to the justification for the execution for murderers and rebels, and imprisonment with hard labour for thieves. It may be less objectionable to maintain that the rationale for civil society justifies the existence of some penal laws and institutions or other, and that further grounding needs to be given for a particular collection of penal laws, or a certain design of penal institutions. The particular list of punishments for crimes may need to be justified by reference to the way different crimes harm people, and by reference to the weighting of different harms when the harms are considered together. This way of thinking would allow for retributivism, without necessarily bearing out Kant's claim the thief needs to be prevented from property-owning or that murderers deserve to die. Instead, it would imply that the most serious crimes—the ones that are responsible for the biggest harms—deserve the most serious penalties, and would leave open the question of whether death should be among the serious penalties. Arguments could then ensue about whether the scale of penalties was too narrow—e.g. by punishing fraud as if it were only slightly less severe than rape—or whether some punishments at the top of the scale were too severe, given reasonable interpretations of the constraint that no punishment can compromise the humanity of the criminal.

The framework just sketched, though different from Kant's, may still be regarded as Kantian. It is consistent with Kant's rationale for civil society, and with his idea that freedom in a civil society is everyone doing what they like within the confines of universal laws binding in the same way on all. It is consistent with constraining punishment with respect for humanity. It is consistent

---

[22] See my "Aggravated Murder and Capital Punishment", (1993) 10 *Journal of Applied Philosophy* 201.

with holding that it is a betrayal of those who agree to be law-abiding to let off those who are found by courts to be guilty of crimes. Perhaps, however, Kant's rationale for civil society is too unstable an amalgam of elements from non-Kantian theories and his own ethics to be acceptable. The framework for punishment is a framework within a framework, a framework within a framework for making sense of civil society, and perhaps Kant's wider framework needs revision, just as the narrower one does.

For a start, and as a number of recent commentaries make clear,[23] Kant's understanding of civil society is full of questionable dualisms. The noumenal/phenomenal dualism is one. Kant needs it to explain how a co-author of the civil law, a violator of it, and someone who is deprived of citizenship because he has committed a crime, can be in one sense the same person and in another not: the legislator is a noumenal being and the criminal phenomenal.[24] Another dualism, or perhaps a set of dualisms, is embedded in Kant's idea of an external action.

The idea of an external action is never freed of all of the unwanted associations it inherits from what I take to be its source: namely, Hobbes's idea of action *in foro externo*. Hobbes distinguishes between, on the one hand, acts of will, and on the other hand, pieces of observable behaviour. Acts of will are what we are unconditionally obliged to perform by a morality consisting of laws of nature. Hobbes's laws of nature call on us to seek peace, to be willing to transfer rights as a means to peace, to keep agreements, be forgiving, equitable and so on. To obey these laws is to be *inwardly* willing to follow them. Compliance is visible to ourselves and to a God who can see into a man's heart; it need not be visible to other men. When we *show* ourselves willing to obey the laws of nature, our morality does become visible to other men; but it also makes us easy prey for those who do not feel constrained to act morally in turn. Because it is by displaying different sorts of behaviours that we lay ourselves open to different sorts of treatment, some of it dangerous, our obligation to be outwardly forgiving, just, equitable and the rest is not absolute but conditional—conditional on the existence of a sovereign power strong enough to ensure that moral behaviour does *not* threaten personal security. In the state of nature, in the absence of a sovereign power, we are obliged to follow the laws of nature *in foro interno* but not *in foro externo*.

Now Kant's idea of external action is the descendent of Hobbes's idea of action *in foro externo*. Kant's idea of *juridical law* is also the descendent of Hobbes's idea of civil law. Hobbes's civil law calls for the omission by each subject in the commonwealth of behaviour that would threaten physical injury to another subject; and it calls for certain observable commissions. For example, it requires a certain form of religious ceremony if the sovereign commands it; it requires tax-paying and so on. In other words, civil law is the coercive law of observable action, just as in Kant juridical law is the coercive law of external

---

[23] See Howard Williams, *Kant's Political Philosophy* (Oxford, Blackwell, 1983), esp. ch. 3 and Allen D. Rosen, *Kant's Theory of the State* (Ithaca, N.Y, Cornell University Press, 1993), ch. 4.
[24] I. Kant, n.1 above, at p. 335.

action. And moral law is the law of the adoption of maxims just as in Hobbes moral law is the law of unobservable acts—acts of will. My complaint about the distinction between external action and the adoption of maxims is that it gives just as unsatisfactory a way of dividing the area of politics from the area of ethics as does the distinction between action *in foro interno* and action *in foro externo*. For Kant, *ethics* calls for consistency between universal laws of the will and the *premises* of practical syllogisms representing one person's practical reasoning; *politics* calls for the consistency of the *conclusions* of practical syllogisms with universal juridical laws, i.e. the consistency with universal juridical laws of the *actions* of a lot of interacting agents simultaneously pursuing happiness.

There is something odd about setting the dividing line between ethics and politics along the dividing line between the premises and conclusions of the practical syllogism. Whether something is ethical or political seems to have rather little to do with whether it is maxim or an action and a lot to do with whether the good or right being deliberated about is that of an individual or a circle of friends and acquaintances on the one hand, or a whole people on the other. The ethical is naturally understood to include the political. The ethical is naturally understood as concerned with right and wrong action in general; whereas the political is naturally understood as concerned with right and wrong actions on behalf of or for or toward a people. The ethical and the political do not coincide, because some morality is not public morality. In Kant the political is more to do with actions performed in public and by the public rather than to or for the public. The juridical duties do not regulate public life in the ordinary sense of "public life". At most they co-ordinate the open and simultaneous pursuit of a lot of private projects. It is true that the institutions of civil society come under politics in anyone's understanding, and that these and the division of powers between them is a concern of Kant's politics. It is even true that independent pursuers of personal projects necessarily double as legislators and citizens in Kant's civil society, so that the pursuit of personal projects is not carried out extrapolitically. Still, the problem that is supposed to be solved by fusing wills and fusing the roles of citizen is the Hobbesian one of conflict between different pursuers of happiness.

5. Kantianism Without Liberalism?

There are ways of conceiving the task of political philosophy that are more Kantian than Kant's, because they are less Hobbesian than Kant's. One way of formulating the task of a Kantian philosophy is by saying that it should specify ideals intermediate between the world as we have it and the kingdom of ends, ideals that it also gives us reason to think can be realised. The task of political philosophy would be to say what it would be to get closer to a world in which as many people as possible are equal, independent, self-ruling, and in which as many people as possible put these aspects of people foremost in their dealings with one another. Perhaps in such a world distributions of justly distributable goods would be subject to a difference principle;[25] perhaps in such a world institutions would be designed and run with a view to minimising avoidable injury;[26] perhaps in such a world the worst off would be benefited by substantial distributions of wealth from the best-off that even the best-off could be got by political persuasion to see as reasonable. [27]

Would one get closer to realising the kingdom of ends if fewer laws were penal, and if the means by which the actions of citizens were got to harmonise were not the threat of pain, but the prospect of criticism, or the prospect of being isolated in some non-violent way from the law-abiding? These arrangements for punishment may seem more humane than those that Kant endorses, but is humaneness the idea behind the kingdom of ends? I think not. I think that the idea behind the kingdom of ends, and the idea to which a political philosophy has to be geared if it is to be Kantian, is the idea of autonomy, of self-rule, where that means making one's organising goals, and the goals of institutions, ones that could be universalised—if not adopted unanimously, then unable reasonably to be rejected by anybody. Autonomy in these senses would obviate penal law. And if a political philosophy were to set out institutions that promoted autonomy in these senses, which took us closer to it, that political philosophy would have some claim to be Kantian.

Now in Kant's own political philosophy there is the ideal of legislative authority residing in a unity of the wills of all citizens, with these wills, or at least a majority of them, being lent to juridical laws that are understood and accepted by everyone to be binding on everyone. Since those who make and those who are subject to law are the same in some sense, if a law is enacted by the legislative authority, it is endorsed by the citizenry. In actual states in Kant's day those who were subject to law were rarely the makers of law. But in Kant's view that did not necessarily call the justice of the laws into question. If a whole people *could* have imposed the law on themselves, then the law, however enacted, was just. The "could have imposed" in question here is very similar to the "could consent to" in the formulation of the Principle of Humanity that I discussed much earlier. Kant does not claim that a law is just only if a people *are* willing retrospectively to endorse it, if they say to one another what a good thing the law is, and so on. Rather , he is maintaining that a law is just only if it *could* rationally be recognised to be consistent with what people come together in civil society to do, namely give themselves the opportunity to pursue as many conceptions of happiness as are simultaneously compatible with one another. Now a law may be consistent with the opportunity afforded by civil society even if particular people feel that the law interferes with their particular pursuit of happiness, and for that reason would refuse to impose the law on themselves. In

---

[25] J. Rawls, *A Theory of Justice* (Cambridge Mass., Harvard University Press, 1971).
[26] O. O'Neill, *Towards Justice and Virtue* (Cambridge, Cambridge University Press, 1996).
[27] T. Nagel, *Equality and Partiality* (Oxford, Oxford University Press, 1991).

other words, a law *could* be imposed by a people even if, as people actually are, they *wouldn't* impose it on themselves.

A law that could be endorsed by a people *would* only be endorsed by individuals concerned with their own happiness, if their own pursuit of happiness was regarded by them as counting for the same as everyone else's. If they thought their own happiness was more important than anyone else's, they would be preparing the ground for making themselves *exceptions* to laws binding on everyone, and this goes against the idea of Kantian autonomy—the imposition on the self of universalisable laws. Since people can be assumed naturally to put their happiness before the happiness of others, it is a question how one gets people in practice to trust that each will respect the other's happiness. One answer is, by everyone opening themselves to severe—in the sense of painful—penalties for actions that interfere with or undermine the pursuit of happiness by others. Agreeing to undergo the penalties is a token of one's will to refrain from the interference that would attract the penalties. Against this background, the endorsement of painful penal laws may be interpreted as a public sign of each person's stake in the next person's pursuit of happiness, and is consistent with promoting the autonomy of all pursuers of happiness.

Consider now *less* punitive institutions. Suppose that the punishment for a crime like assault is not imprisonment but instead widely broadcast solemn criticism of someone's failure to keep to the social contract. No fetters in sight; no prison walls. Just the disapproving public eye and the calm communication of public disapproval. This institution emphasises the anti-social nature of violent crime, and reminds the criminal of the way that the law he has broken is public. And it directs criticism, not scorn, or abuse, or ridicule, at the agent. Perhaps the criminal is invited to criticise himself, or to face as uncompromisingly as possible the consequences of his actions for his victims. Unattractive as it may seem—reminiscent to me of Maoist criticism and self-criticism sessions—the institution I am describing is designed to channel punishment not through the nerve-endings but through a civic persona, which is told that, and why, what the criminal has done is wrong. Is this institution an improvement on what is taken to be less humane? To me, it sounds like Orwell's *Nineteen Eighty Four*, but without the surveillance and the rats. Again, someone who endorses a law of assault carrying this sort of punishment and nothing more is apparently staking less on the importance of compliance than someone who is willing to undergo a more severe punishment.

There is something attractive about a social contract in which each is willing to stake a lot for the sake of the collective pursuit of happiness, and there is something *unattractive* about harsh penal regimes. Yet the big stake can *consist* of each contractor's being willing to submit to the harsh regime—as a token of commitment to freedom of external action. From the perspective of a law-abiding party to the social contract, an endorsement of the harsh penalties for crime is more symbolic than anything else; but for the innocent accused or the person who in a moment of weakness or anger uncharacteristically commits a crime, the threat of punishment is either an outrage or disproportionate. Kant writes for the well-meaning citizen and not for the criminal. Of course, Kant's theory agrees with intuition in holding the punishment of the innocent always to be an appalling injustice. But should his theory, or any Kantian theory, give more weight to the welfare of offenders who act in haste or in a moment of weakness? Should it allow the perspective of people at the receiving end of punishment to be on a level with the idea of contractors uprightly putting an end to life in the state of nature? If so, is such a theory recognisably a Kantian one? Does it not start to tip the balance toward welfare and away from autonomy as the organising value of the institution of the state and of punishment? I believe it does. I believe that so long as the value promoted by politics is autonomy in the sense of submission to universal law, the welfare of those who are enemies of autonomy—criminals—will always have relatively little weight.[28] People who complain of the harshness of Kant's retributive regime sometimes think they see a gratuitous authoritarianism. I think it is more likely that these readers are running up against the consequences of his choosing autonomy, and rejecting welfare, as the ultimate value.

There might be a better fit between autonomy and a crime-preventing system of moral *education* than between autonomy and a penal regime that protects or seeks to improve the welfare of offenders. For if the point of the education is to allow the agent to tell right from wrong and to get him to participate in developing his understanding of which choices to make, education creates the conditions for autonomy. The more education can implant in people a better sense of how their plans are only some among others; the more education can implant in people a frame of mind in which the agent cares that his organising goals are acceptable from many different points of view, the more the agent can be expected to accommodate his colleagues and not be a plaything of his self-regarding inclinations. But the task of outlining a theory of moral education should not be thought far more straightforward than the task of outlining a theory of punishment. The very idea of teaching another, especially a very young person, to choose freely, has paradoxical aspects, while the ethics of re-educating the anti-social when older, is controversial. And this to say nothing of dealing with the results of that education, when the results fall far short of what was intended. It is difficult to know whom to hold responsible for actions that reflect a character partly formed by others, or profoundly damaged by others. Perhaps, as already indicated, the difficulty with the ethics of moral education are more acute in a Kantian framework than in others. When education works,

---

[28] Unless, perhaps, increasing their welfare promotes a new-found will to reform on the part of the criminal. It is possible that there is an argument for improved welfare *from* the value of autonomy—an argument to the effect that unless the welfare of the criminal who can be returned to society is not at an acceptable minimum, his misery will prevent reform. (This parallels the slight moral argument Kant thinks there is for each person promoting his own happiness: see Kant, n.1 above, at p. 388.) But since Kant seems to conceive of criminality as flowing from an already fixed character (*ibid.*, at p. 331), perhaps someone who uncharacteristically commits a crime and then wishes to follow the straight and narrow is not really a criminal.

the source of the pupil's choice of the right ends is partly outside the pupil. So there is a question whether the choices are fully attributable to the pupil. Again, education can have coercive elements, which raises the question of whether choices based upon it are really free.

Perhaps the conclusion we are being led toward is that moral theories with a strict notion of autonomy as supreme organising value face very great difficulties. Yet autonomy is supposed to be the value that the ideal of the kingdom of ends embodies. In subjecting ourselves to universal laws, in respecting ourselves and others for this capacity to subject ourselves to universal laws, we make ourselves free—free from the tyranny of impulse, free from the lawlessness of the state of nature: free. Freedom in the relevant sense is an improved capacity to choose, improved because it allows us to overcome standing invitations to practical error in nature and in history. I think that the error theory of choice that provides the background in Kant for the pursuit of autonomy does not often register with those who seize upon the kingdom of ends as an expression of liberal values. But an error theory of choice sits uncomfortably with a certain type of liberalism, one that says that a person's goals are his business and not to be criticised unless they involve harming others. Kant was not this sort of liberal. And the larger question broached by this chapter is whether any Kantian can be: once there is an error theory of choice, there is a basis for second-guessing even choices that do not seem to have anything to do with anyone else: the private no longer set limits to morality.

I doubt that some error theory of choice or other can be omitted from a Kantian moral or political theory. Even if such a theory does not commit itself to a pure practical reason or a noumenal will, it makes pointed use of the concept of reason or of reasons or reasoning, and offers to show how authoritative judgements about right and wrong and about what to do are distinguished from others that are not authoritative. Kantian theories characteristically insist on the possibility of intellectual detachment from results of deliberation influenced by simple impulse or inclination or passion, and they lay very exacting conditions down for reasons to be objective or for practical judgements to be arrived at in ways that are as free as possible of bias. This sort of theory goes with a certain kind of realism, in the technical sense of "realism", about practical judgements. That is, the theory incorporates a strong version of the thesis that it does not follow from its seeming a good idea to an agent to do a thing that that thing ought categorically to be done. A strong version of this thesis implies that even people's strong preferences and projects can be misconceived and may need to be resisted. This thought is illiberal. But that does not mean it is wrong.

2

Punishment and Rights

DUDLEY KNOWLES

Nor must we underestimate the degree to which the mere sight of the judicial executive procedures inhibits the criminal himself from experiencing his act, his mode of conduct, as reprehensible *as such*; because he sees the same kind of action practised in the service of justice and given approval, practised with a good conscience: like spying, duping, bribing, setting traps, the whole intricate and wily skills of the policeman and prosecutor, as well as the most thorough robbery, violence, slander, imprisonment, torture and murder, carried out without even having emotion as an excuse, which are manifest in various kinds of punishment,—none of which is seen by his judges as a depraved and condemned act *as such*, but only in certain respects and applications.[1]

1. Introduction

What moral rights do we have? There are plenty of lists, no shortage of answers. How do we decide what moral rights we can legitimately claim? Philosophers and jurists are heir to a variety of different traditions purporting to answer this second question. And the questions are evidently related. If we had to hand a decision procedure which enabled us to test candidate rights, we could list the rights which passed the test and be satisfied with their authenticity. If we believed that no such decision procedure were available or that no candidates passed the test, we should have to become sceptics. At best, rights would be fictions, mere *façons de parler*.

It looks as though the dialectic can be entered at two different points. Dismissing sceptical doubts, students of these issues may find a core group of agreed rights and search, bottom-up, as it were, for the theory which best explains their agreement. Or one might work top-down, embracing a general normative theory and employing it to determine the validity of rights claims. The first strategy will be plausible where there is initial agreement on the detail of the rights claims; experience suggests, notoriously, that the more extensive the list or the more detailed the specification, the less likely it is that agreement

---

[1] F. Nietzsche, *On the Genealogy of Morals*, K. Ansell-Pearson (ed.), trans. C. Diethe (Cambridge, Cambridge University Press, 1994), Essay 2, §14, at p. 59.

can be found. The second strategy will work upon production of an adequate normative theory; one does not have to be a pessimist about philosophical progress to realise that the first-order items on the agenda may never be reached.

Fortunately there are other ways to proceed. We can test well-known theories, strong moral intuitions, and candidate rights for coherence. Whether theories remain unscathed, intuitions intact or rights endorsed, may not be settled, but sound argumentation may take us forward. We may hope to discover what combinations of claims cannot be advanced together, what repairs may be necessary to prevent a favoured structure of beliefs from collapse.

Philosophical issues concerning punishment are a promising site for this sort of investigation, since the phenomenon of punishment poses an immediate problem for the rights theorist. This can be stated bluntly: on most, if not all, accounts of moral rights we judge rights to be violated if their possessors are killed or physically injured, deprived of their liberty, have personal possessions confiscated. Schedules of punishment license behaviour of each of these kinds. Capital punishment takes lives and corporal punishment physically aggresses against the person. Imprisonment inhibits free movement, privacy, domesticity and much else. Fines command the surrender of private property. How can the rights theorist defend punishment?

This problem is striking enough if one believes that, for independent reasons, the institution of punishment is morally legitimate. It is all the more striking if one believes all citizens have a right to punish —"the executive right of the law of nature", in Locke's terminology. It is striking to the point of paradox if one claims, with Hegel, that punishment is "a *right for the criminal himself*".[2] Obvious questions arise: Can any doctrine of rights accommodate the systematic violation of rights which punishment in this world[3] promises? Can one have a right to violate rights? Can one claim a right to have one's rights violated?

In this chapter I shall concentrate on the first of these questions, broaching occasionally the second and third as relevant doctrines come into sight. I shall examine two very different accounts of rights, one consequentialist, the other contractarian. In each case, I shall argue, the threat of incoherence, not to mention the whiff of paradox, may be dissolved.[4] On the way, I hope to learn something about both punishment and rights.

2. Consequentialism and Rights

A caricature of this position will serve my purposes here, and Mill, as ever, gives us the best starting point:

---

[2] G. W. F. Hegel, *Elements of the Philosophy of Right*, A. W. Wood (ed.), trans. H. B. Nisbet, (Cambridge, Cambridge University Press 1991), at p. 100.

[3] "In this world" since I don't suppose it is analytic that penal regimes include as hard treatment practices which would generally be thought to violate rights.

[4] *Pace* Nietzsche, n.1 above.

"To have a right, then, is, I conceive, to have something which society ought to defend me in the possession of. If the objector goes on to ask, why it ought? I can give him no other reason than general utility".[5]

In other words, one has a right where utility dictates that citizens have a justified claim against their government for the protection or promotion of some interest. I phrase this re-working of Mill in political terms, mentioning citizens and government, because this is the central case, although it does not exhaust the field of rights talk. The utilitarian defence of rights amounts to a case by case justification of institutions which protect or promote specifiable interests on the basis that maximum well-being is served thereby. Suppose I claim a right to physical integrity of the sort that is violated by assault. The utilitarian will claim that he has vindicated that right when he has shown that a (no doubt complex) social practice involving the criminal law and its integral processes of trial and punishment, which effects the protection I require, serves utility. Institutional utilitarianism, of the variety defended by Rawls in "Two Concepts of Rules",[6] issues a formidable challenge to its opponents: describe in detail the social practices which acceptance of the rights you endorse requires. If it can be shown that utilitarian arguments support these practices, what is missing from the utilitarian account? David Lyons takes this point, but then insists that the utilitarian cannot capture the distinctive moral force of rights claims.[7] Where Lyons claims insight, I acknowledge a blind spot. The utilitarian theorist faces plenty of difficulties, but I am convinced that his treatment of rights is not one of them. This is how the dialectic goes: First, the utilitarian claims that utility requires just those institutions which the rights theorist demands. Secondly, the rights theorist insists that the utilitarian offers no more than "a promissory note"[8] that such institutions maximise utility. Thirdly, the utilitarian redeems the note: he offers such evidence as is available to support his endorsement of the institution.

Suppose all parties, the utilitarian as well as the rights theorist, agree on the facts of the matter: that whatever institutions best protect and promote the rights which are asserted, systematically maximise utility (and be sure, this is a factual matter). What does the rights theorist offer that the utilitarian cannot provide? At this point the rights theorist can speak rudely; he can question the credentials of "the promissory note". He cannot, *ex hypothesi*, dispute the facts of the matter, but he can claim that the coincidence of conclusions is a contin-

---

[5] J. S. Mill, "Utilitarianism", in *Utilitarianism, Liberty and Representative Government* (London, Dent, 1968), ch. V, at p. 50.

[6] J. Rawls, "Two Concepts of Rules", (1955) 64 *Philosophical Review* 3–32. Recent defenders of this position include R. Hardin, *Morality within the Limits of Reason* (Chicago, Chicago University Press, 1988) and R. Goodin, *Utilitarianism as a Public Philosophy* (Cambridge, Cambridge University Press, 1995).

[7] D. Lyons, "Utility and Rights" in J. R. Pennock and J. W. Chapman (eds.), *Ethics, Economics, and the Law: Nomos xxiv* (New York, New York University Press, 1982), pp. 107–38. Reprinted in Lyons, *Rights, Welfare and Mill's Moral Theory* (Oxford, Oxford University Press, 1994), pp. 155–61.

[8] *Ibid.*, at p. 166.

gency, fortuitous given the way the way the world is, whereas rights deserve a more solid anchor than this. They demand the sort of recognition of their "moral force" that the contingent facts of the matter cannot grant.

Rights, to be pejorative, have a halo, a normative brilliance, a transcendant aura of moral rectitude, to which considerations of mere utility are blind. Maybe . . . but the utilitarian, who demands that the debate be taken up at a level where more earthly considerations can register, has a point. My instincts suggest that the way to move forward is to examine the pros and cons of a specific dispute. So let us investigate, in appropriate detail, the utilitarian justification of punishment, and bring the discussion back to earth.

3. Utilitarianism and Punishment

What is your favourite right? What claims do your intuitions insist are bomb-proof rocket-stoppers? One will do. (Let me cheat a little: I don't want to discuss the right not to be killed or physically assaulted, since in the context of punishment these raise questions extraneous to the discussion I wish to engage). Suppose you claim the right to free movement: the right to wander without hindrance, up and down the streets (uncontroversial), over hills and moorland (controversial), across folks' private, productive, property (dubious). What does this claim amount to in utilitarian terms?

It is best represented as an argument that utility is maximised in jurisdictions which impose legal sanctions on those who prevent folks wandering unrestrictedly. Such an argument has no *a priori* credentials. It can be made good only upon the production of appropriate evidence. Suppose we do our homework and accept the first couple of kinds of wandering as pleasurable to participants and harmless to others. We accept that owners of moorland are not much damaged by happy wanderers, whereas corn-growers, horticulturalists and sunbathers on private lawns would be.

These facts gives us a preliminary prescription which characterises the right to wander: don't stop folks going about their business on public highways or private moorland. They also limit prospective freedoms: don't walk through fields of corn, tramp on beds of lettuce, or intrude on your neighbour's garden. In other words, the right to free movement will need to be spelled out in detail, and each detail will be justified in terms of some account of human well-being served by the appropriate rule.

Assume that the hard work has been done, the detail gathered in, the costs and benefits properly assessed. Have we done enough to delineate the utilitarian contours of the right to free movement? Of course not. Our work has issued in a variety of prescriptions. We cannot suppose that these, of themselves, bind those whose interests counsel transgression. The structure of rules which articulates the right needs supplementation in order that the demand for effective protection be met. Traditionally, it is supposed that punishment serves this purpose.

The right to free movement will now comprise the prescriptions demanded of government by its advocates together with institutional provision for punishing those who violate these prescriptions. The punitive measures which are sanctioned may include imprisonment, which, if effective, will itself inhibit free movement. Is there some sort of contradiction, paradox or incoherence in the scenario thus described? It looks as though we find ourselves describing a right of free movement which itself proscribes free movement on the part of some (disobedient) citizens. We have unearthed, in the context of rights, a thought familiar from discussions of freedom: my freedom to act in a specific fashion may require that others be unfree to act in ways that inhibit this freedom. The threatened contradiction here is evidently sharper, though, since the right is protected by measures which promise to impugn that very same right.[9]

The utilitarian has a direct response to this ostensive difficulty. He does not admit that there *is* a right to free movement in advance of the detail of institutional provision being spelled out. The language in which rights-claims are advanced is bedevilled by shorthand and simplicity—a tendency encouraged by the declarative mood in which rights are commonly registered. This has long been clear in discussions of the right to private property where it is common ground that the right in question needs to be spelled out as a complex structure of liberties, claim rights, immunities and privileges.[10] The right of free movement that we are discussing already admits of qualifications which imply that it is not violated by statutes that protect home-owners from trespass. The charge of contradiction assumes that we have a clear conception of what the right to free movement requires, which conception recognises imprisonment as a violation of that right. In particular, it assumes that such a right entails an immunity to imprisonment.

At this point the utilitarian can fairly insist that it does not. The content of the right to free movement is given by the full specification of the institutional dispensation which the argument from utility vindicates. Citizens *claim* the right to free movement when they demand such institutional provision. Citizens *possess* the right to free movement when institutions are in place which serve whichever interests underpin the judgement of utility. If, and it is a contingent matter, these institutions include procedures for trial and punishment which detail imprisonment (or curfew or injunction) as appropriate penalties, then the right to free movement demands that, in cases where such penalties are appropriate, free movement be inhibited.

---

[9] The threatened contradiction could be sharpened in the context of freedom, too. My freedom to roam, to be effective, may require to be protected by punitive measures which entail that those who limit my freedom have their own freedom of movement restricted.

[10] For details, see A. M. Honore, "Ownership" in A. G. Guest (ed.), *Oxford Essays in Jurisprudence* (Oxford, Oxford University Press, 1961) and J. Waldron, The *Right to Private Property* (Oxford, Oxford University Press, 1988), pp. 47–53.

4. PUNISHMENT AND INNOCENCE

Thus far I have argued that utilitarian accounts of rights are not vulnerable to the charge that the defence of rights calls for the treatment of criminals in ways that violate their rights. Many have thought that the utilitarian faces difficulties from a different quarter; it has frequently been held that the utilitarian account of punishment compromises the right of the innocent not to be punished. In broad terms I am satisfied by Rawls's treatment of these issues in "Two Concepts of Rules". This dwells on the details of an acceptable practice of punishment. Once we appreciate "the distinction between justifying a practice and justifying a particular action falling within it",[11] we can gauge the unlikelihood that a practice of punishment will seek to promote utility by granting officials a licence to punish the occasional scapegoat.

Nonetheless, it is worth asking directly about the rights of the innocent. What rights would be violated were innocents to be punished? And what account does the practice utilitarian give of these? In the first place, some will be rights of the kind we have discussed above: rights not to be put to death or physically assaulted, rights of privacy, domesticity and free movement, rights concerning private property. The specific structures of norms which comprise these rights would be violated by treating innocents as though they were guilty of crime. Such hard treatment as is required by the schedule of punishment incorporated into the delineation of the right is reserved for the guilty (although similar measures, e.g. custodial restraints may legitimately be imposed on those whose illness places themselves or others at severe risk; this provision, too, may qualify the right to free movement).[12]

Secondly, we can accept that those who defend the right of the innocent not to be punished have specific institutional procedures in mind which come under the heading of due process of law. Rules of evidence, principles such as the right to silence with impunity, provision for legal representation, rights of cross-examination: provisions of this sort are designed to reduce the incidence of innocents being convicted and punished. Again the utilitarian can plausibly defend such practices on grounds of general utility. Once they are in place, we can see exactly what the right of the innocent not to be punished amounts to. And again, there will be no prescription for this right antecedently to the facts of the matter being determined. No doubt the utilitarian has a well-founded hunch that disutility will be the product of corrupt or sloppy practices of criminal justice. *Pace* Lord Denning in the Court of Appeal,[13] nothing puts the law

---

[11] Rawls, n.6 above. Cited from P. Foot (ed.), *Theories of Ethics* (Oxford, Oxford University Press, 1967), at p. 144.
[12] M. Clark, "The Sanctions of the Criminal Law", (1997) XCVII *Proceedings of the Aristotelian Society*, 25–40.
[13] "If the six men fail [the "Birmingham Six"], it will mean that much time and money will have been expended by many people for no good purpose. If the six men win, it will mean that the police were guilty of perjury, that they were guilty of violence and threats, that the confessions were

into such disrepute as well-publicised cases of innocents being framed or convicted in error, as the citizens of the United Kingdom know to their cost. Nonetheless, the utilitarian will seek a compromise between procedures designed to prevent the conviction of innocents and procedures intended to secure the punishment of the guilty. Tighten the rules of evidence (commonsense suggests) and more of the guilty are found innocent. Relax the rules of evidence (commonsense suggests) and more innocents are found guilty. The scales of justice prescribe no principled balance. We need to appeal to matters of public policy, a.k.a. utility, the utilitarian craftily suggests, to settle the issue.

5. UTILITARIANISM AND CONTINGENCY

My concern here has not been to defend utilitarianism or some other variety of consequentialism as the optimal theory of normative ethics. Rather, I have been looking at the specific charge that the utilitarian cannot *both* incorporate a defence of rights *and* justify the practice of punishment. I have argued on two fronts, claiming first that the conception of rights which the utilitarian employs can disarm the suspicion that the practices of punishment systematically violate rights. Secondly, I have re-stated the familiar utilitarian defence against the claim that the doctrine violates the rights of innocents as it accommodates their occasional punishment. In both contexts I have helped myself to some convenient facts. In the first, I assumed that the facts concerning the optimal practices in respect of their utility would be congruent with an opponent's intuitions about rights. In the second, I assumed that the rights of the innocent could be grounded in utilitarian reflection and research.

Against such claims, it has been argued (in the particular case of the rights of the innocent, though the point may be generalised) that it is a mistake to ground rights in contingencies of this sort. Antony Duff reminds us of:

> "the familiar objection to any purely consequentialist theory, that it makes such protections for the individual contingent on the likely effects of particular policies in particular contexts and, thus, vulnerable to infringement when it would be useful to sacrifice the individual for some greater social good".[14]

I think this must be what Lyons has in mind when he appeals to the *moral force* of claims of right. The thought is that claims of right must be invulnerable to the

involuntary and were improperly admitted in evidence and that the convictions were erroneous. That would mean the Home Secretary would either have to recommend they be pardoned or he would have to remit the case to the Court of Appeal. This is such an appalling vista that every sensible person in the land would say: It cannot be right these actions should go any further": Lord Denning, quoted in C. Mullin, *Errors of Judgement* (Dublin, Poolbeg Press, revised edn. 1990), cited from J. Wolff, *An Introduction to Political Philosophy* (Oxford, Oxford University Press, 1996), at pp. 58–9.

[14] R. A. Duff, "Penal Communications: Recent Work in the Philosophy of Punishment", (1996) 20 *Crime and Justice* 1–97, at p. 22. This argument is amplified throughout ch. 6 of Duff's *Trials and Punishments* (Cambridge, Cambridge University Press, 1986). See particularly at pp. 160–1.

contingencies of time, place and occasion in a way that the utilitarian cannot guarantee.

This is a severe charge, but the utilitarian is not helpless. His first response, which I don't want to pursue here, is of the nature of *tu quoque*. Unless one is prepared to defend the view that rights, under an alternative derivation, are absolute[15]—not justifiably infringed in cases of prospective catastrophe, not susceptible to possible conflict with other, more stringent, rights claims—rights are ever vulnerable to contingent violation, infringement, abrogation, suspension: whatever vocabulary one uses makes little difference.[16] (Interestingly, under the utilitarian conception, if there is an "overwhelming public interest" defence incorporated into the content of the right, this right may be judged absolute!).

More directly to the point, the utilitarian must concede the charge of contingency, but he can emphasise that this does not characterise a flaw in his position. If it happens to be the case, contingently, but true nonetheless, that practices which outlaw the punishment of the innocent or protect rights maximise utility, the fact that it is logically possible that things could have been otherwise is not germane. If this is the truth of the matter, the utilitarian is not concerned one whit with the thought that rights are instrumental rather than intrinsic values. What we have here is a stand-off or a shouting match, dependent on the temperament of the protagonists. Wherever consequences are to be reckoned with, contingency enters the calculation and delivers the judgement of right.

If there is a difficulty hereabouts for the utilitarian, it is cognitive rather than formal. How can the utilitarian make good his claim that the practices of rights and punishment are optimal? But this is a question for another occasion.

6. Rights and Moral Status

John Locke claims for us (humans) the status of bearers of natural rights—those rights to life, health, liberty and possessions which are necessary for us to execute the trustee-ship of the purposes God has ordained for us. To these rights a further one is appended as required for their protection, the executive right of the law of nature whereby "every *Man hath a right to punish the Offender, and be Executioner of the Law of Nature*".[17] Locke does not address directly the problem that is raised by adding the executive right to the first cluster, since he makes it clear that our having the status of bearers of natural rights is

---

[15] A. Gewirth argues for this conclusion in "Are there any Absolute Rights?", (1981) 31 *Philosophical Quarterly* 1–16, reprinted in J. Waldron (ed.), *Theories of Rights* (Oxford, Oxford University Press, 1984) pp. 91–109.

[16] Judith Jarvis Thomson distinguishes between *infringement*, which may be justifiable, and *violation*, which is not: *The Realm of Rights* (Cambridge, Mass., Harvard University Press, 1990), at p. 122.

[17] J. Locke, *Second Treatise of Government*, (P. Laslett ed.) Cambridge, Cambridge University Press, 1960 at §8.

conditional on our behaviour, in particular on our respecting the rights of others. The criminal, through his offending act, renounces Reason as expressed by the Law of Nature. Such "a Man so far becomes degenerate, and declares himself to quit the Principles of Human Nature and to be a Noxious Creature".[18] In:

> "so revolting from his own kind to that of Beasts and by making Force which is theirs, to be his rule of right, he renders himself liable to be despised . . . as any other wild beast or noxious brute".[19]

The bestiary is detailed elsewhere: the criminal is to be treated as one would deal with a Wolf, a Lion or a Tyger, wild Savage Beasts each of them.

This is a very clear picture of the history of the criminal's moral standing. As a rational agent she is bound by the law of nature as well as protected by the rights she holds under it. These rights function as a moral shield; they establish what Nozick has described as the agent's moral boundaries.[20] Following the criminal's transgression, the moral shield falls away, the moral boundaries shift.

The central idea here is that the rights of the criminal, which would otherwise inhibit actions deemed to be boundary crossings, are *forfeit*. Alan H. Goldman makes this claim explicit:

> "If we are to justify punishment of particular wrongdoers or law breakers, that is, if we are to show why they cannot legitimately complain of injustice done to them by the imposition of punishment, we must argue that they have forfeited those rights of which we are depriving them . . . by violating the rights of others in their criminal activities, they have lost or forfeited their legitimate demands that others honour all their formerly held rights . . . If we are to justifiably ignore these rights, it could only be when they have been forfeited or alienated. And the only way in which this can be done involuntarily is by violation of the rights of others. Since having rights generally entails having duties to honour the same rights of others, it is plausible that when these duties are not fulfilled, the rights cease to exist".[21]

I quote Goldman at such length as an illustration of the philosophical rhetoric in which this point is couched, since there is no argument here, despite the whiff of *modus tollens* carried by the last sentence. Mischievously, taking Locke and Goldman together, we can see that these questions need to be settled: *Which*

---

[18] *Ibid.*, at § 10.
[19] *Ibid.*, at § 172.
[20] Robert Nozick sees the problem created by rights theorists who acknowledge a right to punish: "one might try to derive the right to punish from other moral considerations: from the right to protect, combined with the view that a moral wrong-doer's moral boundaries change. One might take a contract-like view of moral prohibitions and hold that those who themselves violate another's boundaries forfeit the right to have certain of their own boundaries respected. On this view, one is not morally prohibited from doing certain sorts of things to others who have violated certain prohibitions (and gone unpunished for this). Certain wrong-doing gives others a liberty to cross certain boundaries (an absence of a duty not to do it); the details might be those of some retributive view": R. Nozick, *Anarchy, State and Utopia* (Oxford, Blackwell, 1974), at pp. 137–8.
[21] A. H. Goldman, "The Paradox of Punishment", (1979) 9 *Philosophy and Public Affairs*, at p. 43.

rights are forfeit? Does the criminal, following the crime, have no rights, or some but not all, or some or all in a state of suspension? *How does the forfeiture work*? Does the criminal give up his rights, as I might if I don't turn up for a match in a competition? Or are they stripped from me by some external agency? Or both, perhaps?

I shan't tackle the first couple of questions since they impinge strongly on the crucial issue of the appropriate measure of punishment, which I've been studiously avoiding. As for our authors, Locke suggests that such rights are forfeit as "will suffice to make it an ill bargain for the Offender, give him cause to repent and terrifie others from doing the like".[22] Goldman, more fastidiously, would have the criminal forfeit just such rights as enable the punishing agency to exact an equivalent (proportionate) measure of punishment, whilst posing the dilemma that this may be insufficient to achieve a satisfactory level of social protection.

The second clutch of questions, enquiring about the mechanism of forfeiture, concerns us more directly. Ideally, at this point in our investigation, we should be able to refer to a paper, *circa* 1954, entitled "Gifts, Forfeits and Penalties", which would sort out analytically the implications of forfeiture, distinguishing it from other ways of losing (or granting) possession. Then we could cite authority for our analysis of the quality of transference of rights. Sadly, there is none available (to my knowledge!). I hope we can agree that talk of forfeiture is apt where two (or three) parties and one good are concerned. A standard pattern requires that some good be yielded (in the case of the third party; otherwise given up) upon failure to comply with a rule. Thus forfeiture can be effected voluntarily or upon the insistence of the regulative authority.

If this language is used to justify punishment, we can state the terms of the relation. The good may be specified as one's immunity to actions which violate rights—imprisonment and the like; otherwise, and negatively, one's liability to punishment. The parties comprise the possessor of the right, whose goods are forfeit, and the keeper of the rules, the authority. My hunch is that we speak of forfeiture as a consequence of one's failure to abide by the norms of a practice, her breaking the rules of a game, where the forfeit is exacted by the appropriate authority. In these circumstances, we may attach responsibility for the forfeiture either to the agent, who loses the good, (if punished, then legitimately, in view of her lack of immunity) or to the authority who establishes the status of rule-breaker (and who imposes the penalty).

When thinking about punishment it makes a difference who does the forfeiting. If she who breaks the rules is the one who forfeits the immunity to what would otherwise be rights-violations, we need an argument to establish that this is the correct description of her normative status. Why should she be thought of as giving up what she would otherwise protect? If, on the other hand, we think of forfeiture as a consequence exacted by an appropriate authority, the language

---

[22] J. Locke, n.17 above, at § 12.

of forfeiture cannot *justify* punishment, since it is simply an alternative description of what authorities characteristically do, i.e. punish offenders.[23] My conclusion is that talk of criminals forfeiting their rights makes no sense as a *justification* of punishment if forfeiture is identified with the agency of the punishing authority. If, by contrast, forfeiture is effected by the agency of the rule-breaker, we need to explain how this comes about. How can we view the agent as, in effect, changing her own moral boundaries, giving up her rights and assuming a liability to punishment?

7. Punishment and Consent

Perhaps the criminal consents to her own punishment. This is an odd claim, but it exhibits an impeccable logic, and has a classical pedigree. It has its sources in Hobbes's account of the subject's authorisation of the sovereign power, Beccaria's rejection of capital punishment, and Rousseau's doctrine that men may be forced to be free. It is one of the elements of Hegel's view that just punishment is willed by the criminal. Rousseau makes the point clearly when he argues that even:

> "the death penalty inflicted upon criminals may be looked on in much the same light [as conscription]: it is in order that we may not fall victims to an assassin that we consent to die if we ourselves turn assassins".[24]

The classical sources should be treated with very great caution when they employ arguments from consent. It is often hard to distinguish consent from contract, and each of these have actual and hypothetical variants. In my view, the structure of argument is very different in each case—and the differences need to made clear. I can't sort out these matters in this chapter. Instead, after a preliminary discussion of consent arguments, I shall focus directly on the consent theory of punishment developed in recent times by C.S. Nino.[25]

For most purposes, on most occasions, we cannot complain of things that are done to us if it is established that they are done with our consent. If our obedience to law is enforced by the threat of punishment, if punishment is inflicted on us as a consequence of our wrongdoing, this enforcement, this punishment

---

[23] Not quite: in forfeiting my rights, whether by first person avowal or third person ascription, I give up my immunity to punishment. The status of the punishing agency has changed, too. It now has no duty not to punish, i.e. a Hohfeldian liberty to punish. A separate argument is needed to establish that it has a duty to punish. It has been objected to Hegel's theory of punishment that, at most, his arguments grant the punishing agency a liberty to punish. See A. W. Wood, *Hegel's Ethical Thought* (Cambridge, Cambridge University Press, 1990), at p. 116. This difficulty evidently attends Nino's theory, which I discuss in what follows.

[24] J.-J. Rousseau, *The Social Contract and Discourses* (trans. and ed. G. D. H. Cole), London, Dent, 1973, Bk.II, ch.V.

[25] C. S. Nino, "A Consensual Theory of Punishment", (1983) 12 *Philosophy and Public Affairs* 289–306. This account is expanded, and defended against critics, in C. S. Nino, *The Ethics of Human Rights* (Oxford, Clarendon Press, 1991), ch.8.

would be legitimate if it were shown that we consented. More generally, if it could be shown that we consented to accept an authority, say the state or the University Court, as legitimate over a given area of decision-making, substantive decisions within this granted competence should be accepted as decisive for us. More generally still, if, with respect to a given subject matter, we have consented to the employment of specific principles as uniquely germane to the solution of problems raised within it, we cannot object to particular determinations which are effected through their application.

Just as soon as these truths are applied to the traditional concerns of political philosophy, their weakness becomes apparent; this, for a simple reason. Whereas the *acknowledgement* of consent is generally decisive, its attribution is often problematic; though not in any sense private, consent is always first-person and proxies are always suspect. Unless we can get someone to agree that she has consented, she hasn't. Her sincere disavowal is enough to refute the claims of observers. Hence it is an important result when individuals deny the imputation of consent either by claiming that they did not express the desire in question or by arguing that the expression was not voluntary. And, just as important, where consent is deemed to be tacit, complete ignorance as to the upshot of her behaviour on the agent's part forces us to retract our claim that she consented.

These facts would not be so important if real consent, either express or tacit, was a live element in our political culture. But if we believe that it isn't, they are important. And even if tacit consent is a more familiar reality than many philosophers would acknowledge, say because participation in democratic decision procedures can establish it, consent theorists still face the insuperable difficulty of witnessing consent where it is especially important that it be located—with the sceptical, bloody-minded, non-co-operative wrongdoer.

It may be that in the case of political duties consent theory can be profitably resuscitated, but I have my doubts. In the case of punishment, it is difficult to establish a parallel claim. Whilst some criminals may recognise a personal need for expiation and view punishment as the only way this may be achieved, I guess they will remain a small minority. The rest are not likely to be persuaded that conventional punitive practices will remedy a personal deficiency through treatment, further education or the opportunity to display appropriate remorse. So we may discount at the outset the possibility that all criminals will consent on the basis that their advantage is served by the punishments they undergo.

Nino is emphatic that a case for grounding punishment in the criminal's consent can be established without recourse to these ostensibly useful but, in fact, implausible premisses. It is, he says "as preposterous to think that criminals generally want to be punished as to think that volunteers want to die in battle".[26] Indeed, on this consensualist account, it is not punishment itself which is deemed to be the object of the criminal's consent. Rather it is a consent to

---

[26] "A Consensual Theory of Punishment", n. 25 above, at 297.

"assume a liability to punishment", "to forgo his immunity from punishment".[27] Consequently the punishing authorities are granted the right, in the sense of the liberty or privilege, of inflicting the harm which is otherwise prohibited.[28]

How can this be? Nino begins by claiming that:

> "the consent of the individual to some duty or responsibility is shown by the performance of *any* voluntary act with the knowledge that the act has as a necessary consequence the assumption of the duty or responsibility in question".[29]

Given that the act which we take to imply consent is fully voluntary and that the agent has full knowledge of the liabilities that arise in consequence of his performing it, we may conclude that he consents to these liabilities.

Nino is employing Hobbes's precept that "whoever voluntarily doth any action, accepteth all the known consequences of it", but he approaches it with the caution due to a Trojan horse. He does not want to say that it is the known or expected factual consequences to which the agent consents. Indeed an agent may not consent to possible consequences of which he is aware. Some may be beyond the phenomenological range of the possibility of consent. The soldier should not be imputed consent to his death, however alive he may be to that possibility. On this account, the agent is deemed to consent, rather, to the necessary *normative* consequences of his action, supposing he is aware of them. This applies to the particular legal consequences of an action and, derivatively, to the moral consequences of the consent which we can attribute in law. Thus:

> "the individual who, for instance, consents to undertake some legal obligation is, in principle, morally obliged to do the act which is the object of this obligation".[30]

Where the legal normative consequence of an action is the legal liability to suffer punishment we conclude that this, too, occurs with the consent of the agent.

This is a lovely argument. If the premisses are true, the conclusion follows. If the conclusion is true, we have dissolved the potential contradiction which threatens where rights-holders are imputed to have their rights violated by punishment. In consenting to punishment, the criminals have forfeited their rights. If no rights are held, none are violated, should punishment be exacted by the holders of the legal power. Unfortunately, I don't think the argument works.[31] My objections, in what follows, are motivated by the thought that arguments from actual consent, whether express or tacit, fail if a case can be made out that the subject need not accept the imputation of consent.

[27] *Ibid.*, at 298–9.
[28] See n.23 above.
[29] Nino, "A Consensual Theory of Punishment", n. 25 above, at 294.
[30] *Ibid.*, at 296.
[31] I'm not alone. Other critics include T. Honderich, *Punishment: The Supposed Justifications* (Harmondsworth, Penguin, revised edn. 1988), and L. Alexander, "Consent, Punishment and Proportionality", (1986) 15 *Philosophy and Public Affairs* [178–182]. Nino replies in *The Ethics of Human Rights*, n. 25 above. R. A. Duff, "Penal Communications", n.14 above, at 13–14, broaches some of the questions I address.

Suppose I am well aware of the law against making remarks derogatory to the Party Leadership, and understand that imprisonment is the penalty for conviction. The necessary (legal) normative consequence of guilt is that I lose my immunity to incarceration. Suppose I flout this law, am convicted, and consequently, jailed. The offence was voluntary, indeed carefully premeditated to have maximum impact on public opinion, and I anticipated, even welcomed, the authority's response. Do these facts amount to an assumption of consent on my part? Clearly not. If I don't accept the authority of the sovereign, either in general or with respect to the law in question or concerning the punishment attached to it, I can intelligibly disavow the normative consequences of my lawbreaking. Indeed, we are familiar with the strategy of public disobedience as a sign of dissent to the government and all its works.

Nino has an inkling that this objection is in the offing. In his fullest statement of his thesis, he prefaces his claim that the subject's consent justifies her liability to punishment with the conditionals:

"If the punishment is attached to a justifiable obligation, if the authorities involved are legitimate, if the punishment deprives the individual of goods he can alienate, and if it is a necessary and effective means of protecting the community against greater harms . . .".[32]

These conditions are evidently not met in the case I describe, so consent may not be imputed and the consequent liability can be denied.

It looks as though Nino is off the hook. But matters are not so straightforward. Where do these conditions come from? What is their relevance to the question at issue? They clearly disarm the objection, but they need to be better motivated than that. If I do accept the legitimacy of a normative authority and do accept the legitimacy of the duties to which punishment is attached and do accept that the measure of punishment is appropriate to the breach of obligation, why does one need to go any further and provide an argument which establishes my *consent* to the imposed liability? This is Hume's famous unnecessary circuit.[33]

Again, although the dialectic of his paper is difficult to follow hereabouts, Nino seems to see this objection coming, for he insists that his thesis:

"does not rely on an explicit or implicit acceptance by the citizens of the criminal laws imposing obligations or stipulating penalties for non-compliance . . . the grounds on which the obligations that the offender violates can be justified are irrelevant to this thesis."[34]

The claim must now be that the criminal's consent to the consequences of her law-breaking depends, in part, on conditions—that the authority, or the law, or the measure of punishment, be legitimate—conditions that may hold *whether or*

---

[32] Nino, "A Consensual Theory of Punishment", n. 25 above, at p. 299.
[33] D. Hume, "Of the Original Contract", in *Essays Moral, Political and Literary*, (Oxford, Oxford University Press, 1963), at p. 468.
[34] Nino, "A Consensual Theory of Punishment", n. 25 above, at p. 305.

not the criminal is aware of the necessity of their holding. If the conditions hold, she consents, (but presumably may not know this in the case where she mistakenly rejects their legitimacy). However much she screams dissent, she consents! As Carole Pateman reminds us,[35] we've heard this sort of thing before: this is Byron reporting Don Juan's seduction of Julia:

> "A little still she strove, and much repented,
> And whispering 'I will ne'er consent'—consented".
> Byron, *Don Juan*, Canto I, CXVII

Arguments from actual consent reach the point of *reductio* when those who sincerely dissent can be held to consent nonetheless. If pressed hard, such arguments may defeat complacency, deviousness and hypocrisy, but they cannot conquer innocent bloody-mindedness. To this end, we need the additional resources of the social contract tradition, specifically its hypothetical contract variant—to which we shall now turn.

8. A Hypothetical Contract Solution[36]

"A hypothetical contract is not simply a pale form of an actual contract; it is no contract all".[37] What is it, then? It is a structure of practical reason. Let me explain by discussing first the associated notion of hypothetical *consent*.

A doctor might justify an emergency operation on an unconscious patient by claiming that the patient consents hypothetically. The reality behind the metaphor is the doctor's belief that, counterfactually, had the patient been conscious, rational and in possession of the necessary facts, she would have consented. The doctor, we may presume, could outline the reasons which motivate this judgement. But don't these reasons, by themselves, justify the intervention? Why adduce an imaginary consent to support a case that is sound when advanced without it? Once again we encounter Hume's unnecessary circuit.

But there is a point in taking it. Doctors generally *ask for* the consent of the patient before an operation. That consent will only be meaningful if it is informed. When patients are in possession of the appropriate facts, they can decide whether or not to go ahead with the operation in the light of their ends. They may choose a very risky operation if it will grant them a minimally satisfactory quality of life they wouldn't otherwise attain. They may choose not to be operated on if the life that the treatment would prolong is of a poorer qual-

---

[35] C. Pateman, *The Sexual Contract* (Cambridge, Polity Press, 1988).

[36] To my knowledge, the first modern application of contract-style thinking to the problem of punishment is found in J. Murphy, "Marxism and Retribution", (1973) 2 *Philosophy and Public Affairs* 217–43. Murphy attributes the view he describes to Kant. My account of this theory is different in point of the reasoning imputed to the contractor.

[37] R. Dworkin, "The Original Position", in N. Daniels (ed.) *Reading Rawls* (Oxford, Blackwell, 1975), pp. 16–53, at p. 18.

ity than they could tolerate. And so on. When patients cannot deliberate in the fashion sketched, the doctor, assisted by relatives, friends and whoever else is pertinent to the facts that would counterfactually inform the patients, decides what to do, from the stance and for the reasons they hypothesise, the patient would adopt. The language of hypothetical consent alerts us to the role of the decision-maker in attempting to mimic the reasoning of agents who are unable to reason on their own behalf. It is metaphorical, but the metaphor is potent in reminding us of the appropriate perspective from which decisions should be taken.

Likewise, the hypothetical contract is a metaphor, an argumentative device. Paraphrasing Dworkin, we should not see the device as calling attention to just any arguments which might serve as independent grounding of the principles, rather we should ask 'What is it about the independent arguments that make the contract or consent an appropriate representational device?'.[38]

Let us see how this works in the case of punishment. We shall first of all present a contract argument, then unravel the metaphor to examine the cogency of the arguments that are signalled by its employment. The argument I shall examine derives from Rousseau; he uses contract reasoning both to state the general justifying aim of punishment and to defend an appropriate distribution of it.[39] Thus he claims that the contract (which, on my reading, *justifies* the obligations of the citizens) "includes the undertaking ... that whoever refuses to obey the general will shall be compelled to do so by the whole body".[40]

Rousseau's contractors share a bundle of ends. They wish to promote their lives and property consistently with their respect for principles of equality and liberty. We can orientate the discussion back towards the specific agenda of this paper by supposing that they wish to promote and protect their rights.[41] The argument then has the following structure.

(1) Individuals claim rights against each other and recognise that others claim equivalent rights against themselves.
(2) They see no prospect of others respecting their rights whilst they themselves are immune to the rights claims of others.
(3) They believe that others may attempt to become free-riders on the convention of respect for rights, since they understand the attractions of wrong-doing on their own part.
(4) They demand a guarantee of good faith in the principles of rights from those others who avow them, and they are willing to give such a guarantee on their own part.

---

[38] Ibid.
[39] I employ the terminology of H. L. A. Hart in "Prologomenon to the Principles of Punishment", in H.L.A. Hart, *Punishment and Responsibility* (Oxford, Oxford University Press, 1963), pp. 1–27.
[40] J.-J. Rousseau, n. 24 above.
[41] I don't defend this as a reading of Rousseau, but others have—plausibly too. See R. Derathé, *Jean-Jacques Rousseau et la science politique de son temps*, (Paris, Vrin, 1950).

(5) The guarantee which is universally offered and taken up is a recognition of the legitimacy of punishment exacted against criminals; themselves, of course, included, should they become criminals.
(6) They accept that punishment may take the form of actions which, in other contexts, would amount to a violation of their rights.
(7) Hence, those who wish their rights to be promoted and protected are willing to alienate their rights should they, themselves, violate the rights of others.

This is an argument which dissolves the paradox of punishment. Whether or not it is successful will depend on the plausibility of the contract model. Is it an apt device for displaying this reasoning? It calls attention to three features of the deliberations of the rational agent: First, she claims for herself the moral status of a rights-bearer, a *person* to use Hegel's specific terminology.[42] I don't justify this claim or this ascription. Nor, in a sense, does Hegel. It is just a feature of the modern world that individuals see themselves as (but importantly, on his account, not only as) discrete, bounded, atomic particulars—as persons. The normative vocabulary appropriate to this mode of universal self-ascription is that of rights. Others will seek to amplify this insight, perhaps building on Kantian foundations which emphasise autonomy, the importance of treating people as ends, not as means merely. I am inclined to think this is not necessary. I recognise the voice of Arthur Danto's man from the law-school who said:

"with the tried patience of someone required to explain what should be as plain as day, and in a tone of voice I can still hear: 'This is the way it is with rights. You want 'em, so you say you got 'em, and if nobody says you don't then you do' ".[43]

But note, for the purposes of this argument, the foundations (or lack of them!) of rights is irrelevant. Our prime concern is the alleged *inconsistency* between claims of right and the practice of punishment, so we may fairly assume what, on Hegel's and Danto's account, folks as a matter of fact claim.

Secondly, and this is a feature of the language of rights which is perhaps implicit in Hegel's metaphysics of the person, the rational contractor demands that "whatever it is to recognize as valid shall be seen by it as good".[44] The model contract argument advances with each party seeking some designated good(s). Hobbes's shopping list is familiar—the preservation of life and commodious living. In Locke and Rousseau, this sparse theory of the good is supplemented by more recognizably moral ends—natural rights to liberty (Locke

---

[42] G. W. F. Hegel, n. 2 above, at pp. 34–8.
[43] A. C. Danto, "Comment on Gewirth", in E. F. Paul, F. D. Miller, Jr., J. Paul (eds.) *Human Rights* (Oxford, Blackwell, 1984), at p. 30.
[44] Hegel, n.2 above, at p. 132. This is Hegel's "right of the subjective will". In the Remark to §132, he claims that "the right of giving recognition only to what my insight sees as rational is the highest right of the subject". This right is distinctive of the normative order of "Morality", which, together with Abstract Right elaborates the insights of ethical individualism. One crux of Hegel's interpretation is the judgement of how far this right, together with those of the person, are recognised, compromised or ignored in the institutions of ethical life, particularly the state.

and Rousseau) and equality (Rousseau alone?). Rawls's thin theory of the good, his list of primary goods as those things agents want, whatever else they want, is a descendant of these accounts. These ends will determine how far the contractors will accept the terms of any proffered contract. It is clear, though, that each contractor has the standing of an adjudicator, appraising prospective institutions and principles from the perspective of the (moral or non-moral) goods they seek. Jeremy Waldron has argued that this feature of contract theory:

> "expresses in clear and provocative form a view . . . most liberals do share: that the social order must be one that can be justified to the people who have to live under it".[45]

The particular feature of the social world this chapter examines is the institution of punishment. The contract argument addresses everyone who is liable to it, taking each of them to be bearers of rights. It concludes, in familiar terms, that not only are rights compatible with punishment, but that they require it.

It will still be objected that the contract is an inappropriate device for elucidating this structure of practical reasoning since the deliberations we have modelled could perfectly well have been conducted by a solitary individual.[46] Each person has the same ends and can deliberate about the most effective way of achieving them. The agreement modelled here is agreement in the thinnest sense of *congruence in deliberation*, the sort of agreement one might hypothesise amongst a maths class, each of whom gives the same answer to the same question. I think this objection is mistaken, and diagnosing the mistakes takes us on to the third feature of contract arguments.

Whilst it is true that the argument takes the stance of each contractor from their own point of view, the problem they seek to address is a social problem, that is, they have a clear view that the solution will have to be acceptable to all parties. They will somehow have to incorporate into their reasoning the requirement that their favoured solution be acceptable to each other. They will have to recognise that their schedule of preferences cannot dominate the dialectic. So they will, in thought, have to put themselves in the position of each of the other contractors to see if their solution is acceptable. It may look as if this procedure is straightforward, given the congruence of values amongst the parties. Whilst this may be true in respect of the values they endorse, the calculation may be harder if some of their ends (or goods) are prudential, including, for example, the preservation of life and commodious living. In other words, their solitary reflections will have to reach towards an anticipated compromise solution which will command universal agreement. Scanlon's version of contractarianism, ("contractualism" is his term) states this explicitly:

---

[45] J. Waldron, "Theoretical Foundations of Liberalism" (1987) 37 *Philosophical Quarterly*, 127–150, reprinted in Waldron, *Liberal Rights* (Cambridge, Cambridge University Press, 1993), 35–62, cited at pp. 57–8. Earlier at pp. 36–7 he claims that liberals are committed to "a requirement that all aspects of the social world should either be made acceptable or be capable of being made acceptable to every last individual".

[46] This objection is put to Rawls by Jean Hampton in "Contracts and Choices: does Rawls have a social contract theory?", (1980) 77 *Journal of Philosophy* 315–38.

"An act is wrong if its performance under the circumstances would be disallowed by any system of rules for the general regulation of behaviour which no one could reasonably reject as a basis for informed, unforced general agreement".[47]

Of course, the hypothesised agreement will have to be tested. And one useful, if not definitive, way of doing this will be to leave the armchair and canvass opinion. Still what makes reasoning of this sort resonant of contracts is the imaginative attempt to encompass the points of view of all other parties, according to each a power of veto if they deem the moral rule unreasonable in point of their interests and (I would say, but Scanlon cannot) their values.

There is yet one last feature of this reasoning which makes talk of a metaphorical contract appropriate—and this is particularly apt when the question of punishment is taken up. It is the thought that *we can't win 'em all*. The optimal principle will fix some losses as the price of agreement. You want the coal and I want the money. You can't have the coal without paying the money. I can't have the money without delivering the coal. Take this to be the model of a contract and it is evident that both parties have to give up something. In the case where one employs a contract argument to justify punishment, this loss is incurred as each party accepts a liability to suffer acts which would otherwise violate their rights as the cost of securing an agreement which will protect and promote their rights.

9. Conclusion

The rights theorist can breathe a sigh of relief. It looked initially as though one who claimed a traditional set of rights would have to forswear any institution of punishment which comprises coercive activities. I have argued that if we adopt a Millian (utilitarian) understanding of rights, punishment may still be justifiable on the grounds of the superior utility of a practice of rights which includes the provision for punishment in its articulation of the rights in question. This may be thought an advantage of the utilitarian account. But not for long, since I have also argued that non-consequentialist theories of rights (Kantian or Hegelian in spirit), if cast in the garb of an hypothetical contract theory, can also eliminate the threatened inconsistency. Either way, and this, to some, may be a miserable conclusion, proponents of punishment on each of these traditional grounds, may not fear the charge of self-contradiction. What would be really attractive would be a Humean synthesis of these radically different moral stances, a synthesis (of Kant and Hegel and Mill!) which theorises punishment as the outcome of conventions arrived at by individuals in histori-

---

[47] T. M. Scanlon "Contractualism and Utilitarianism", in A. Sen and B. Williams (eds.), *Utilitarianism and Beyond* (Cambridge, Cambridge University Press, 1982), pp. 103–28, at p. 110. In *Equality and Partiality* (Oxford, Oxford University Press, 1991), at pp. 36–8, Thomas Nagel points out how very close this principle comes to Kant's categorical imperative.

cal communities who have been, and still are, concerned to protect the rights which they claim, and which institutional development promotes general utility. As they say, investigation of this possibility is material for another essay (or two or twenty two!)—and, I guess, for most philosophers, the prospects look none too good.[48]

---

[48] Drafts of the paper on which this chapter is based, some unrecognisable to participants, no doubt, have been given to seminars in the Universities of Liverpool, Stirling, St.Andrews and Glasgow. Some suggestions I remember with thanks, others I forget (with apologies). I record that Ray Frey, Stephen Clark, and Gordon Graham pressed me hard! In York I had a difficult time. I learned from Matt Matravers, Sue Mendus, and Tom Sorrell, though they will rightly believe that the lessons are not apparent in this version. I must have learned something from the two hour inquisition I had from Antony Duff on the train home!

3
Punishment, Communication, and Community

R. A. DUFF

One theme in the "retributivist revival" of the last two decades has been that of punishment as a communicative practice. The central retributivist slogan is that punishment is justified as being *deserved* for the crime which is punished: the concept of desert is supposed to indicate the justificatory relationship between past crime and present punishment in virtue of which punishment is an intrinsically appropriate response to crime. For "negative" retributivists, who argue only that punishment must not be *un*deserved, criminal desert is supposed to provide a necessary, but not a sufficient, condition for punishment; for "positive" retributivists, who argue that punishment is justified just insofar as it is deserved, criminal desert is supposed to provide a sufficient condition for punishment.[1] For either kind of retributivist, however, the central task is to explain this idea of desert—this supposed justificatory relationship between past crime and present punishment: what does it mean to say that crime deserves punishment, or that the guilty deserve to suffer punishment; how does crime call for punishment, or make punishment appropriate?[2] One kind of answer to such questions has portrayed punishment as a communicative process: what crime deserves or makes appropriate is a response which punishment communicates to the criminal.

I want to explore two aspects of such a communicative conception of punishment: but I must first explain in a little more detail what it amounts to. This task will occupy section 1 of this chapter. Section 2 will discuss the role of penal "hard treatment" within a communicative conception of punishment: I will contrast two accounts of that role (von Hirsch's and mine), which appeal respectively to a liberal and to a communitarian view of the proper nature and function of the state. Finally, section 3 will raise (but will not try to answer)

---

[1] On "negative" and "positive" retributivisms, see D. Dolinko, "Some Thoughts about Retributivism", (1991) 101 *Ethics* 537–59.

[2] See P. Ardal, "Does Anyone Ever Deserve to Suffer?", (1984) 91–92 *Queens Quarterley* 241–57; D. Husak, "Why Punish the Deserving?", (1992) 26 *Nous* 447–64; T. Honderich, *Punishment: The Supposed Justifications* (Cambridge, Polity, revd. edn. 1989), ch. 2; Honderich, "Culpability and Mystery", in R. A. Duff and N. E. Simmonds (eds.), *Philosophy and the Criminal Law* (Franz Steiner, 1984), pp. 71–7.

some questions about the moral and political conditions which must be satisfied if criminal punishment is in practice to be justified in the way that, on a communicative conception, it should ideally be justified.

1. PUNISHMENT AS COMMUNICATION

The thought that punishment serves or should serve a communicative purpose is neither new, nor necessarily retributivist.

It is at least a close relative of the familiar thought that punishment serves an expressive function.[3] However, I think it matters that we should talk of "communication", rather than of "expression": for the idea of communication involves, as that of expression need not, the idea of a *reciprocal* and *rational* activity. Expression requires only one who expresses; if there is someone at whom it is directed, that person need figure only as its passive recipient; and if it aims (as it need not) to bring about any effect on its recipient, that intended effect could be entirely non-rational—it need not be mediated by the recipient's reason or understanding. By contrast, communication requires someone to, or with, whom we try to communicate; that person must (if the communication is to be successful) be an active participant in the process, who receives and responds to the communication; and that reception and response must (are intended to) be rational, in that communication appeals to the other's rational understanding, and seeks a response mediated by that understanding. That punishment should be a mode of rational communication (primarily with the offender) is, I believe, an implication of a more general conception of law, and of how a state should treat its citizens—of the view that it should treat and address its citizens as rational, responsible agents.[4]

Now non-retributive theories can, of course, talk of communication. Most obviously, a deterrent theory can portray punishment as a mode of rational communication, which offers potential criminals prudential reason to obey the law: what the punishment of actual offenders communicates—to others, but also to those offenders—is that the threat of punishment is to be taken seriously.[5] What is distinctive about a retributivist version of communication?

Two features distinguish it. First, whereas for a consequentialist (a deterrence theorist for instance) punishment may communicate with anyone who might be

---

[3] See, famously, J. Feinberg, "The Expressive Function of Punishment" (1965) 49 *The Monist* 397–408; also I. Primoratz, "Punishment as Language", (1989) 64 *Philosophy* 187–205. For critical discussion, see A. J. Skillen, "How to Say Things with Walls", (1980) 55 *Philosophy* 509–23; M. Davis, "Punishment as a Language: Misleading Analogy for Desert Theorists", (1991) 10 *Law and Philosophy* 310–22.

[4] See my *Trials and Punishments* (Cambridge, Cambridge University Press, 1986), especially chs. 3, 4, 9, 10.

[5] For other, more sophisticated, consequentialist accounts of punishment which give communication an important role, see N. Lacey, *State Punishment* (London, Routledge, 1988); J. Braithwaite and P. Pettit, *Not Just Deserts* (Oxford, Oxford University Press, 1990).

usefully affected by the communication, and in particular with the public at large or with those members of it who are tempted by crime, for retributivists the communication must be focused primarily (though not exclusively) on the offender who is being punished: if we are to avoid (as retributivists are keen to avoid) the Kantian accusation of using the offender "merely as a means", we must focus punishment on him, as response to him which is justified by his past offence. Secondly, for a consequentialist *what* is communicated by punishment may be any message which can be expected to assist the further aims that punishment should serve—for instance the message that crime is likely to be followed by sanctions which provides prudential reasons for obeying the law. For a retributivist, by contrast, the message which is communicated by punishment must be a message focused on, and justified by, the offender's past offence: it must be a message appropriate to that past offence.

What kind of message could that be? One obvious answer, on which I will focus here, is that what is communicated should be the censure or condemnation which the crime deserves. Whatever puzzles there might be about the general idea that crimes "deserve" punishment, puzzles of which some anti-retributivists make quite a meal,[6] there is surely nothing puzzling about the idea that wrongdoing deserves censure. An honest response to another's culpable wrongdoing—a response that respects and treats her as a responsible moral agent—is to criticise or censure that conduct; and if we think we have the moral standing to pass moral comment on her conduct (a matter to be discussed in section 3 below), we may indeed sometimes think that we *ought* to censure her—that we owe it to those she wronged, to the values she flouted, and also to her, to censure her. So too, a society which declares certain kinds of conduct to be wrong, as criminal, can and should then censure those who nonetheless engage in such conduct (subject to the qualification about moral standing). Censure addresses the wrongdoer as a responsible citizen; it is owed to him, as an honest response to his crime; to his victims (if there are any), as expressive of a concern for their wronged status; and to the whole society, whose values the law claims to embody.

Now censure can be communicated in various ways. In particular, in the context of the criminal law, it can be communicated by the formal conviction which follows proof of guilt in a criminal trial; or it could be communicated by a system of purely symbolic punishments—punishments which are burdensome or unwelcome *solely* in virtue of the censure which they communicate. It *can* also be communicated by the kind of "hard treatment" punishments that characterise our existing penal systems:[7] punishments—for example, imprisonment, fines, compulsory community service—which are (at least typically) burdensome or unwelcome independently of their condemnatory meaning. For given the appropriate kind of conventions, an appropriate institutional setting, an appropriate shared understanding between those who are punished and those

[6] See e.g. Honderich, "Culpability and Mystery", n. 2 above.
[7] On "hard treatment", see Feinberg, n. 3 above.

who punish (or in whose name punishment is imposed), hard treatment punishments can carry this kind of meaning (but I will have more to say later about the conditions under which they can be expected to be understood in this way).

However, to say that hard treatment punishment *can* carry such a meaning, that censure *can* be communicated in this way, is clearly a long way from saying that this is how censure *should* be formally communicated to those who break the law; or that a society or a state has the right to use this method of communicating censure. Thus the familiar task for those who offer any kind of communicative (or for that matter expressive) account of punishment is to explain and justify the role of hard treatment.

This leads me into the first of my two main topics. Various accounts could be offered of the proper role of hard treatment punishments within a roughly communicative, and roughly retributivist, account of punishment.[8] They differ primarily in whether they try to justify hard treatment in terms of the communicative purpose of punishment itself; or accept that it requires some other, separate kind of justification. For present purposes, I will focus on the contrast between the account I have argued for, which is of the first kind, and that which von Hirsch offers, which is of the second kind: this contrast will also lead us into aspects of the tension between communitarian and liberal political theories.

2. Penal Hard Treatment: Penance or Prudential Supplement?

On the account I have developed and defended elsewhere, the communicative purpose of criminal punishment runs all the way down, even to the justification (at, I should emphasise, the level of ideal theory) of particular kinds of hard treatment punishment. The aim of penal hard treatment should ideally be to bring the criminal to understand, and to repent, the wrong he has done: it tries to direct (to force) his attention onto his crime, aiming thereby to bring him to understand that crime's character and implications as a wrong, and to persuade him to accept as deserved the censure which punishment communicates—an acceptance which must involve repentance. Punishment also provides a vehicle through which he can strengthen or deepen that repentant understanding of his wrongdoing, and express it to others: a vehicle, that is, both for the attempt at self-correction and self-reform that sincere repentance involves, and for the communication to others (to those he has wronged, to his fellow citizens) of that sincere repentance. Finally, by undergoing such penitential punishment the wrongdoer can reconcile himself with his fellow citizens, and restore himself to full membership of the community from which his wrongdoing threatened to

---

[8] See, for instance, J. R. Lucas, *On Justice* (Oxford, Oxford University Press, 1980), pp. 132–6; M. M. Falls, "Retribution, Reciprocity and Respect for Persons", (1987) 6 *Law and Philosophy* 25–51; I. Primoratz, n. 3 above, J. Kleinig, "Punishment and Moral Seriousness", (1991) 25 *Israel Law Review* 401–21; J. Hampton, "Correcting Harms versus Righting Wrongs: The Goal of Retribution", (1992) 39 *UCLA Law Review* 201–44.

exclude him. Punishment is, in other words, a secular penance; and the particular modes of punishment should be suitable to such an enterprise of penitential communication.[9]

I should emphasise four initial points about this account. First, it is retributivist in that it justifies punishment as an intrinsically appropriate response to a past crime—a response that seeks to communicate to the offender, and to persuade her to understand and accept, the fact, nature, and implications of the wrong she has done. Unlike many more traditional retributivist accounts, it also looks to the future: punishment aims to induce a process of repentance, self-reform, and reconciliation. However, this is not to say that it seeks to combine retributivist and consequentialist elements in a "mixed" penal theory. Whereas on a consequentialist account the relationship between punishment and the ends which justify it is purely *contingent* (punishment is justified if it is a contingently efficient means of securing some independently identifiable end), on my account that relationship is *internal*: for the end to be achieved (the offender's repentant understanding of her crime) is such that punishment (the attempt to induce such an understanding by the communication of censure) is an intrinsically appropriate way to achieve it.

Secondly, this account is intended to provide, not a justification of punishment as it actually operates in our existing penal systems (which cannot in general be seen as administering such communicative, penitential punishments), but an account of what punishment should *ideally* be: an account against which we can measure, and no doubt find seriously wanting, our existing penal practices. I take this to be a general feature of normative theories of punishment: that they should aim to provide, not a comforting justification of the penal status quo, but a critical, ideal standard against which our penal actualities should be judged.[10]

Thirdly, this account does not warrant grossly oppressive kinds of punishment which seek to break or grind the offender down until he repents: for his punishment must, if it is to communicate the kind and degree of censure he deserves, be proportionate to his offence; and it must address and appeal to him as a rational moral agent, whose moral understanding it seeks to arouse but should not seek to coerce. This implies (as is anyway obvious enough) that punishment is necessarily fallible: it aims or aspires to induce repentance and self-reform but, like any attempt at moral persuasion, leaves the offender free to remain unpersuaded and unrepentant. Punishments which fail to persuade the offender are in one sense unsuccessful: but they can still be justified as attempts (even as attempts which we might reasonably believe are doomed to fail) to communicate with and to persuade a moral agent who is within the realm of our shared moral discourse; and they can succeed in communicating even if they fail to persuade.

---

[9] See my *Trials and Punishments*, n. 4 above; and "Penal Communications", (1996) 20 *Crime and Justice* 1–97.

[10] See J. G. Murphy, "Marxism and Retribution", (1973) 2 *Philosophy and Public Affairs* 217–43.

Fourthly, such communicative punishment is best exemplified, not by the kinds of long prison sentence which loom so large in penal discussion; nor by the fines which, though the penalty of choice for very many offenders, are usually ill-suited to this communicative purpose: but by such "punishments in the community" as community service orders and probation (as well as by "mediation" schemes whose aim is to bring the offender to recognise the nature and implications of what she has done, and thus to make material or symbolic reparation for it).

Now I think that punishments *can*, even in our own radically imperfect penal systems, serve such a communicative and penitential purpose.[11] Such an account nonetheless seems to many to be quite implausible as an account even of the ideal aims of a system of state punishment. I want to focus here on some of von Hirsch's objections, concerning the proper aims and purposes of the state—since these lead us into the issues in political theory that I want to discuss.[12]

Von Hirsch allows that in certain particular contexts punishment could have the kind of communicative and penitential character that I ascribe to criminal punishment: for instance, in the context of a monastic order. Three features of such a context might seem crucial. First, it involves a community membership of which is typically optional (or should be optional, if we are not to have serious doubts about its legitimacy): members are free to leave; and alternative modes of life are available which do not make such stringent or intrusive moral demands. Secondly, the community is structured and united by a rich set of shared spiritual values: to belong to the community is to be committed not just to behaving towards one's fellows in appropriate ways, but to orienting one's soul towards the proper values. Thirdly, it can then be plausible that breaches of the community's norms do threaten to separate the offender not just from others within the community, but from his own good—which, as he himself sees it (else he would not want to remain a member) consists in full membership of the community; and that penances imposed on him by the community or its proper authority can serve to bring him to a proper repentance (partly because they appeal to what he already believes and accepts), restoring him to full membership of the community—and thus to his own good. Monasteries do, by very their nature, have a proper interest in the spiritual condition and well-being of their members—an interest which those members accept in virtue of their membership; and that interest can properly be exercised in, *inter alia*, the application of penitential punishments.

However, matters are quite different in all three respects when we turn to the context of a modern state. First, membership of the state, and consequent

---

[11] For examples of such punishments, see my "Penal Communications", n. 9 above, at 52–3, 63–4; and my "Alternatives to Punishment—or Alternative Punishments?", in W. Cragg (ed.) *Retributivism and its Critics* (Franz Steiner, 1992), pp. 43–68.

[12] See his *Censure and Sanctions* (Oxford, Oxford University Press, 1993), especially chs. 2, 8; see also U. Narayan, "Appropriate Responses and Preventive Benefits: Justifying Censure and Hard Treatment in Legal Punishment" (1993) 13 *Oxford Journal of Legal Studies* 166–82.

subjection to its laws, are not optional: we are born into a state; and if we have any alternative at all, it is emigration to another state. Secondly, even if we can identify any shared values which help to structure the political community whose law it is (and there is certainly more scope here than there is in the case of a monastery for the identity and character of the "community" to be determined by institutional structures and power relationships, rather than by genuinely shared values), they are (and should be) far more modest and limited in their scope than are those which structure a monastic community: in particular, they do not and should not, as values of a political society, include spiritual values to do with the conditions of its members' souls. Thirdly, we therefore cannot see breaches of the law as separating the offender from her own good (we must recognise, if we also disapprove of, the fact that for many individuals and subgroups their good as they intelligibly understand it is not bound up with the values defined and protected by the law); nor can we see punishments imposed by the state as restoring the offender to membership of a community in which she herself finds her own good.

This kind of objection clearly appeals both to some obvious facts about modern political society, and to certain familiar, roughly liberal, values. Modern Western states of the kinds in which we live (excluding officially theocratic states) do not constitute the sorts of intimate spiritual community in which penance finds its natural home: nor *should* they do so, since that would be profoundly at odds with the liberal values of respect for individual freedom and autonomy, of pluralism and of privacy, and profoundly dangerous to individual good.

By contrast, my account might seem to embody a (to liberal ears) disturbingly intrusive and oppressive form of communitarianism. It locates the individual's identity and her good in her membership, not just of *some* community, but of the larger political community under whose laws she must live—in her relationship to the shared values by which that community is supposedly structured, and which its laws supposedly embody. It gives the state, as the institutional embodiment or structure of that political community, a proper interest not just in her (external) conduct towards her fellow citizens, but in her (internal) moral condition—an interest strong and extensive enough to justify it in trying to improve her moral condition by punitive coercion.

What then can a liberal critic like von Hirsch say about penal hard treatment—if he is still to justify it (as he wants to); if he is to preserve (as he wants to) the thought that punishment should serve primarily as a mode of moral communication which seeks to communicate to the offender the censure which his wrongdoing deserves; and if he is to avoid (as he wants to) the Hegelian objection that to use penal hard treatment *purely* as a mode of prudential deterrence is to treat the citizen (any potential criminal) "like a dog instead of with the freedom and respect due to him as a man"?[13] Von Hirsch's answer is that penal hard

---

[13] Hegel, *The Philosophy of Right,* trans. T. Knox (Oxford, Oxford University Press, 1942), at p. 246; see von Hirsch, n. 12 above, at pp. 12–14, and my *Trials and Punishments,* n. 4 above, at pp. 178–86.

treatment should serve as a prudential *supplement* to the law's normative voice. It serves as a deterrent, in that it aims to reduce crime by creating a prudential disincentive that might dissuade from crime at least some of those who are insufficiently motivated by the law's moral appeal. However, it should not replace or drown (as a system of purely deterrent hard treatment punishments replaces or drowns) the moral tones of censure: it offers an *additional*, prudential reason for obedience, as being suitable to moral agents like ourselves who are susceptible to moral censure but also susceptible to temptation—a reason which is not (or should not be) intended to be persuasive by itself (as the reasons offered by purely deterrent punishments are intended to be), but which can add additional persuasive force to the law's primarily moral appeal. It follows from this, of course, that hard treatment punishments must be strictly limited in their severity, if they are not to drown the law's moral voice: von Hirsch suggests that current levels of penal severity should be reduced towards a system that would allow no prison term of more than three years (or five years for homicide).[14]

One significant merit of such an account is that it portrays punishment as something we could plausibly impose on, and threaten against, *ourselves*. Purely deterrent justifications of punishment are liable to portray it as something that "we", the law-abiding and moral, must threaten against "them", the dangerously immoral or amoral, in order to coerce them into obeying "our" laws—laws for which they otherwise have no respect.[15] Von Hirsch's account, by contrast, aims to portray punishment as a system of prudentially supplemented censure that we could, as moral agents who recognise our own imperfections and inadequacies, plausibly impose on ourselves to help us to act as we know we ought to act (but fear we will not always act without such prudential incentives).

However, one objection to this solution to the problem of justifying penal hard treatment is that it is liable to be undermined by the tension between preserving the communication of censure to moral agents as the primary purpose of punishment, and using hard treatment as a prudential supplement which will have some additional crime-preventive efficacy. On the one hand, whilst the threat of a three-year prison term is certainly dramatically less coercive than are the maximum sentences currently provided (even in relatively liberal penal systems) for offences other than homicide, it still seems rather too severe to serve as a mere prudential supplement—as merely "an aid to carrying out what [the agent] himself recognizes as the proper course of conduct":[16] it seems more apt to replace, than to supplement, the moral voice of the law. On the other hand, if we seriously tried to reduce the severity of hard treatment punishments to a level at which they would provide no more than a subordinate prudential

---

[14] See *Censure and Sanctions*, n. 12 above, ch.5; for more detailed criticism of his account, see my "Penal Communications" n. 9 above, at 41–5.

[15] See further my "Inclusion and Exclusion: Citizens, Subjects and Outlaws" (1998) 51 *Current Legal Problems*.

[16] Von Hirsch, n. 12 above, at p. 13.

supplement to the law's moral voice, it is not at all clear that such punishments would have a preventive efficacy significantly greater than would flow from a system of purely symbolic punishments—an efficacy great enough to justify the creation and maintenance of the whole apparatus of penal hard treatment.

This account is perhaps most plausible in relation to relatively minor crimes, and the relatively light punishments they would attract. The fine I would receive for speeding or for dangerous driving might well not by itself, as a purely prudential disincentive (independently of its character as a punishment), suffice to dissuade me: but the prospect of it could provide a useful, modest supplement to the moral appeal of the law—an appeal to which I know I am sometimes liable to be insufficiently attentive. This is not too far removed from the kind of private punishment that someone might threaten against herself to encourage herself to do what she knows she ought to do. However, matters seem very different when we turn to much more serious kinds of crime. The prospect of three years' imprisonment might dissuade some potential murderers or rapists from committing such crimes: but if we ask how that prospect could figure in their deliberations or motivations, the only plausible answer is surely that it would replace, rather than supplement, the law's moral appeal to the wrongfulness of such conduct.

The problem about penal hard treatment, for communicative theorists, is that the obvious rationale to offer for communicating censure by hard treatment rather than by purely symbolic punishments is deterrence—recognising that too many potential criminals will be unmoved or insufficiently moved by the prospect of symbolically communicated censure, we create for them a prudentially persuasive reason to obey the law: but such a rationale is unacceptable to those who take seriously the Hegelian (and Kantian) objection that to secure obedience to the law by the threat of deterrent sanctions is to fail to respect the moral agency of those whom we threaten. Von Hirsch seeks to resolve this problem by transforming deterrence into a subordinate prudential supplement, of a kind that we might impose on ourselves: but I think his resolution fails.

Can my attempt to resolve this problem, by incorporating hard treatment *within* the aim of moral communication, fare any better? In particular, can it meet the liberal charge that it is inconsistent with the liberal values of respect for individual autonomy and privacy, and with a liberal conception of the proper role of the state—and of the limits that should be set on its exercise of its coercive punitive power?

My account is certainly and fundamentally inconsistent with some of the more strenuous and metaphysical versions of liberal individualism, which take their stand on the separate and distinct identity of each individual, allocating to the individual an extensive private sphere which includes her moral beliefs and attitudes; and which found political relationships and institutions on the model of a social contract. Social contracts are made between strangers, who wish to regulate their external dealings with each other; and whilst they may include clauses which require not just certain kinds of mutual non-interference, but also certain kinds of positive mutual assistance, they presuppose separateness and distance between the parties. They are of course likely to include penalty clauses, attaching agreed sanctions to breaches of the contract: but those provisions, when they do not aim to remedy the harm done by the breach,[17] can be most plausibly understood in deterrent terms—they provide prudential disincentives to breaches of the contract, and thus make the contract itself (and the parties' confidence in it) more secure.

The idea of punishment as secular penance would obviously be entirely alien to such an understanding of society and the state. So too, however, would be the idea of punishment as a mode of moral communication, for two reasons.

First, such moral communication—even if it aims only to communicate censure—must presuppose richer and closer relationships between the people concerned than this austere contractualist model provides. It presupposes a shared language of values (which itself requires some genuinely shared values) in which the communication can take place. It also presupposes that those involved have a proper interest in the moral character of each others' conduct, *and* a relationship with each other which gives them the moral standing to comment thus forcibly on that conduct. It presupposes, that is, a moral community, whose members see themselves as bound (or can at least intelligibly claim of each other that they *should* see themselves as bound) by certain shared values which inform their common life; a community whose members also have, in virtue of that common life, the standing to criticise each others' conduct in the light of those values.

Secondly, the purpose internal to censure as a communicative act is not just that the other should hear what is said, nor just that she should understand it, but that she should *accept* it: that she should come to see, if she does not already see, the censure as a justified response to the wrong she has done.[18] But to accept censure as justified is to recognise that I have done wrong; to recognise that I have done wrong should (if that recognition is sincere and whole-hearted) be to repent that wrong; and to repent my past conduct commits me to an attempt to reform my future conduct. The purpose internal to a practice of censure is thus not merely to transmit a message; nor merely to modify the external conduct of those who are censured: but to induce an appropriate moral change in their attitudes and dispositions—a purpose that can find no place within the austere contractualist model sketched above.

A conception of punishment as communicative is thus (in one of the many variegated senses of the term) "communitarian": it appeals to a linguistic and moral community whose members, in virtue of their shared language, values and form of life, can claim and have the moral standing to criticise each others'

---

[17] An idea which underpins one recent version of retributivism, according to which punishment serves to restore that fair balance of benefits and burdens which crime disturbs: see Murphy, n. 10 above.

[18] This is not to say that we can never properly criticise or censure someone who will, we are sure, remain unmoved and unpersuaded: of course we can, and we might think it important to do so. But our censure still has the character of an attempt (an attempt that we think is doomed to fail) to persuade him to recognise the wrong he has done.

conduct. It is important to notice, however, that such a community can be a *liberal* community, in that it can recognise as being of foundational importance some of the central values to which liberal theorists typically appeal. In particular, it can recognise individual autonomy (autonomy understood, of course, as autonomy *within* a shared form of life, which alone can give the notion any substantive sense) as a fundamental value—as something to be both promoted and respected; it can likewise recognise individual freedom and privacy—the preservation for each citizen of an extensive sphere within which they are free from coercion or intrusion by others and by the state—as essential values.

This kind of communitarianism thus rejects that metaphysical conception of the person, as an individual who can be identified (and treated as the basis of value) independently of their social context, which some forms of liberalism have taken to be foundational. To reject such a *metaphysical* conception, however, is not necessarily to reject the *normative* claims of liberalism, which can (suitably reinterpreted in line with a communitarian metaphysics) be detached from such dubious metaphysical foundations.

This account also rejects, or at least seeks to limit, some of the more extreme claims of normative liberalism. It insists that the community (and the state that should give institutional form to the central values and aims of the community) must respect the autonomy of its members or citizens: thus in the context of criminal law and punishment, the citizens must be addressed as moral agents whose obedience and allegiance are to be sought by modes of rational moral persuasion, but must not be coerced or manipulated. But it also allows the state to use the coercive apparatus of criminal punishment not just to provide prudential incentives for obedience, but to try to reach the offender's moral conscience and understanding—which many liberals would count as a dangerously intrusive, and potentially oppressive, use of the coercive power of the state. However, three points about this conception of punishment, about the nature of criminal law and of (communicative) punishment in a community which takes autonomy seriously, should do something to allay such concerns. None are inconsistent with the idea that hard treatment punishments can and should serve the aims of penitential communication: rather, they will help to structure a more precise articulation of that idea, which will show it to be fully consistent (at the level, I emphasise again, of ideal theory) with a proper regard for individual autonomy, freedom, and privacy.

First, a community which takes autonomy seriously (and the related values of individual freedom and privacy, and of a plurality of conceptions of the good life) will set strict limits on the scope of the criminal law: given the law's peremptory nature, and its demand that the individual citizen subject their own judgement to its authority, it should be used to prohibit only kinds of conduct which seriously threaten interests or values which are of central importance to the community and its members.[19] This is one difference between the criminal

---

[19] See e.g. Lacey, n. 5 above, ch.5.

law (as on this view it should be) and the laws of a monastic order: that the laws of a monastic order will be far more extensive (and far more intrusive) in scope than those of a liberal community.

Secondly, the criminal law, and the criminal justice system, do have a proper interest in the moral character (the moral attitudes and values) of the citizens: the law condemns, and seeks to persuade to self-reform, those whose criminal conduct manifests a serious disrespect for the legally protected rights and interests of others, and for the values which the law protects. But that interest is strictly limited to those aspects of the citizen's moral character which are fully displayed in (indeed constituted by) criminal conduct: it is only the offender's actualised criminal dispositions that properly concern the criminal law.[20] This is then another difference between the criminal law (as it should be) and the laws of a monastic order: a monastic order has a proper interest in every aspect of its members' spiritual and moral condition, whereas the criminal law has a very much more restricted proper interest in the moral condition of its citizens.

Thirdly, a respect for autonomy will preclude any attempt to *force* a citizen to change her moral attitudes, or to bring about such a change by any means other than those of rational moral persuasion—it precludes both the coercion and the manipulation of attitudes or beliefs. Thus although the aim of communicative punishment is to induce an appropriate change in the offender's attitudes and dispositions, that change must in the end be one that he himself brings about, because he sees it to be necessary (the aim, we could say, is not merely "reform" but *self*-reform); and although punishment is, obviously, coercive, what it should aim to force on the offender is not the desirable change in his attitudes, dispositions and future conduct, but the awareness that his community thinks such a change necessary. He is forced to hear the punitive message: but it must be up to him whether or not he accepts that message, and the opportunity for repentance and reconciliation which his punishment provides. (A further, and related, constraint is that an offender's punishment should not be continued until he (appears to) repent: partly because that would clearly constitute an attempt at coercive change; partly because if his punishment is to communicate an appropriate censure of his crime, it must be roughly proportionate to the seriousness of that crime.)

A penal system structured by such (liberal-communitarian) values and constraints could, in principle, use hard treatment punishments to serve the communicative and penitential aims which (on my account) punishment should serve—and to serve those aims in a way which respects the autonomy, the moral standing and the privacy of conscience of those who are punished (as of all citizens). It would differ quite significantly from our own penal system in its use of

---

[20] Thus I am not grounding criminal liability in "character" *rather than* in action or "choice" (which could open the way to extensive and intrusive inquiries into every aspect of offenders' characters): liability should rather be grounded in "character" (moral attitudes and dispositions) *as displayed in action*; see my "Choice, Character and Criminal Liability" (1993) 12 *Law and Philosophy* 345–83.

penal hard treatment: it would make much less use of imprisonment (which, as communicating the message that exclusion from the community is the only appropriate moral response to the offender's crime, must be reserved for the most serious community-destroying crimes); it would make less use of fines (which lack an appropriately meaningful relationship to many of the offences for which they are currently imposed); it would make far more use of a wide range of non-custodial punishments—including but not limited to community service orders and probation (which are better suited to the task of bringing offenders to understand the nature and implications of their crimes, and of constituting appropriate penances for those crimes). But its punishments would still involve penal hard treatment, in that they would be at least typically burdensome or unwelcome independently of their condemnatory meaning.

I have argued so far that a fully communicative account of punishment, which portrays penal hard treatment as an integral part of the communicative penal process, can be defended against von Hirsch's liberal criticisms: it is not fundamentally inconsistent with the values (or with a communitarian version of the values) of autonomy, freedom, and privacy on which his criticisms rest. However, such liberal worries have more, although now non-foundational,[21] force when we turn from the level of ideal theory at which I have so far been arguing, to that of practical actuality. Are we really to urge those who administer our penal system to see themselves as properly engaged in an enterprise of moral persuasion and reform: to allow and urge judges to find new and creative kinds of punishment which will be communicatively appropriate to the individual offender; to urge prison officers to seek to persuade their charges of the need for repentance and moral reform; to urge those who administer non-custodial punishments to see their task as that of administering secular penances? The dangers of any such programme (of distortion, of oppression, of manipulation) are all too obvious—though again this is more true if we look at our prisons, and less true if we look at the ways in which some programmes of non-custodial punishment are administered; and those dangers might throw a more attractive light on a less ambitious communicative account like von Hirsch's.

I will not, however, pursue this question here. It concerns the practical possibility (and the moral dangers) of seeking to actualise an ambitiously communicative conception of punishment in an existing penal system like our own, and focuses on the internal workings of that system: how far could we realistically expect, given the nature and structure of that system, that punishments would actually be administered or received in the way, in the spirit, with the restraint and respect, which this conception of punishment requires? But there are deeper worries than this about the applicability of this (or, I would argue, of any plausible) justifying account of punishment to our actual world; and it is to these that I now turn.

---

[21] By which I mean that they concern, not the basic principles and conceptions on which this communicative theory rests, but the dangers involved in trying to apply it in our actual world.

3. COMMUNICATION AND MORAL STANDING

The question raised (but left unanswered) at the end of the previous section concerned the internal operations of a would-be communicative practice of punishment: how far could we realistically expect that the actual administrations of punishment would satisfy the conditions for just and justified punishment specified by a communicative theory? The deeper worries to which I referred concern the conditions which must be satisfied if any such practice is to be legitimate, whatever its internal operations: conditions whose existence must be presupposed by any such practice, but whose existence is also, in our present situation, doubtful.[22] I think that worries of this kind should undermine our confidence in the applicability of any plausible justifying theory of criminal punishment which takes the demands of justice seriously:[23] but a communicative theory raises them in a particular, and perhaps illuminating, form.

I want to note two such conditions here: one concerns "moral standing"; the other what we might call the accent of penal communication—the voice in which it is administered and can be received. Both conditions reflect the fact that the possibility, and the legitimacy, of a communicative process depend on there existing an appropriate relationship between the parties concerned. They also remind us that the question of the justification of punishment is not just the question of whether, from some abstract point of view, criminals deserve to be punished, or of whether their punishment would achieve some good, but also and crucially the question of whether some particular person or body can justly and justifiably punish them.

If, as an individual, I criticise another's conduct on moral grounds, the justifiability of my action depends on two kinds of condition. First, did she actually (and culpably) commit the wrong for which I criticise and condemn her (a question which of course involves a host of subordinate questions about the facts, the proper interpretation, and the moral character of her conduct)? Secondly, and even if she did do such a culpable wrong, do I have the moral standing to criticise or condemn her for it? This second question is clearly crucial, but also (at least to a significant degree) independent of the first: the person I criticise could reject my criticism, not on the grounds that she did not do the wrong I accuse her of doing (she might admit *that*), but on the grounds that it is not for *me* to judge or to criticise her.

We can note two such grounds. She might argue, on the one hand, that I lack the appropriate relationship to her, or to the action in question, for that action to be any of my business: she is not answerable to me, though she may be

---

[22] The worries thus concern, we can say, the preconditions rather than the conditions of justified punishment: see my "Law, Language and Community: Some Preconditions of Criminal Liability" (1998) 18 *Oxford Journal of Legal Studies* 189–206.

[23] See e.g. Murphy, n. 10 above; also A. W. Norrie, *Law, Ideology and Punishment* (Dordrecht, Kluwer, 1991).

answerable to others, for what she has done; my criticism is not a piece of justified moral comment, but an unwarranted interference (just what kind of relationship is required for moral criticism to be legitimate depends crucially, of course, on the nature of the wrong I accuse her of doing). Or, alternatively, she might argue that though her conduct is indeed my business (for instance because it directly affected me), my previous dealings with her deprive me of the moral standing to criticise her: if I have unrepentantly betrayed her, or wrongfully deceived her, I am not now well placed to criticise her for betraying or deceiving me in a similar way. (Notice again that this is not to claim that my past conduct to her *justifies* or *excuses* her present conduct to me, rendering it non-culpable: it is to claim that *I* lack the moral standing to criticise her.)

Communicative punishments censure or criticise the conduct of those who are punished. They are formally imposed by the courts, and administered by officials of the penal system: but they are supposedly imposed and administered on behalf of, in the name of, the political community whose laws the offender has breached; the content of the communication is not "*I* (the judge, the prison officer, the probation officer) censure your conduct", but "*We* (the whole community, to which you belong, and by whose laws you are bound) censure your conduct". We therefore need to ask what is required to constitute an appropriate "we"; and whether "we" have the moral standing to criticise and censure this person's conduct.

The first of these questions concerns some of the conditions required for the existence of a political community—as a linguistic community which shares a normative language, and so also a set of substantive values,[24] rich enough to render mutually intelligible the normative demands that the law makes on all citizens, and the normative judgments it makes on their conduct. If the law is to be *their* law, as citizens of the political community (rather than being an alien imposition on them), it must express values that are widely shared; and those values, and the language in which they are expressed, must be at least accessible to all the citizens, as values which they *could* share—and which others can properly claim that they *should* share.

This requirement might not be *enormously* demanding, if the law is as modest in scope as I suggested it should be on a liberal-communitarian view. It is certainly consistent, on such a view, with wide differences in forms of life, in normative concepts, in values, within the same political community: perhaps what it requires is something more like a Rawlsian overlapping consensus than a Habermassian ideal speech community. But it is nonetheless a substantive requirement, as reflecting an important precondition of legal obligation (for I can be obligated only by laws that reflect values which are accessible to me, and which I could reasonably be expected to accept);[25] and we need to ask how far

---

[24] See L. Wittgenstein, *Philosophical Investigations*, trans. G. E. M. Anscombe (Oxford, Blackwell, 1963) para. 242: "If language is to be a means of communication, there must be agreement not only in definitions but also (queer as this may sound) in judgements".

[25] I realise that to talk of what a person "could reasonably be expected to accept" conceals a multitude of questions about what can make such (normative) expectations reasonable or unreasonable: but I cannot pursue those questions here.

it is satisfied by any actual legal system—including our own. Answers to this question are likely to be complicated and messy, rather than simple and straightforward: we might expect to find that some aspects of the law satisfy this requirement, whilst others do not, at least in relation to some groups. But insofar as this requirement is not fully satisfied, the law's claim to obligate all citizens (and thus to condemn and punish them legitimately for breaches of its demands) is weakened or undermined.

However, even if a satisfactory answer can be provided to the first question (about the existence of a linguistic and political community which constitutes an appropriate "we"), there remains the second question—about whether "we" also have the moral standing to condemn, through the courts, the conduct of this defendant. For just as my own previous and unrepented conduct towards the person I would now criticise can disqualify me from having the standing to criticise her, so can the (collective and institutional, rather than personal and informal) behaviour of a political community towards some of its members deprive it of the standing to condemn at least some of their conduct through the law. Someone who has been not merely unfortunately disadvantaged, but unjustly excluded from many of those opportunities and benefits that others enjoy, seeks by criminal means some modest improvement in her unjustly disadvantaged lot—for instance by committing a social security fraud: I think there is then a real question about whether "we"—the comfortably included—have the standing to condemn her, insofar as we either benefit from those political and economic structures which treat her thus unjustly, or are passively complicit in those injustices; in which case there is also a real question about whether the courts have the moral standing to condemn and punish her.

I should emphasise that to raise this question is not to suggest that the courts might lack moral standing to condemn *any* crime that such a person might commit: just as my previous deception of another person, whilst it might disqualify me from condemning her deception of me, need not disqualify me from condemning other kinds of wrong that she commits (an act of gratuitous cruelty, perhaps), so the courts could be morally disqualified from condemning some, but not all, kinds of crime committed by one who has been unjustly disadvantaged. Nor is it to suggest that her crime (her social security fraud) is either justified or excusable: it is rather to raise the issue of who has the standing to judge it at all. Nor, finally, is it to suggest that *no one* has the standing to judge, or indeed to condemn, her conduct: for instance, those whose situation is similar to hers might have that standing; and might indeed justly condemn her, on the grounds that hers is not an appropriate response to the injustices which she, and they, admittedly suffer.

We should also note, however, that the two questions I have so far raised in this section (about the existence of an appropriate political community, and about its moral standing to judge a defendant's conduct) are closely connected in at least the following way: that a radical enough failure to satisfy the conditions of moral standing (to have behaved towards this person in a way that entitles "us" to judge her) also undermines the conditions of community between her and "us"—between her and those for whom and in whose voice the law speaks. We can reasonably expect, if we are not overcome by a radical MacIntyrean scepticism about the contemporary existence or possibility of moral community,[26] to find that *some* political community of the appropriate sort exists, whose law the actual law can plausibly claim to be: a community whose members do indeed share the values which the law embodies. But this is not yet to say that that community includes as full members *all* those whom the law claims to bind and to have the standing to judge and punish—that every defendant who appears before the courts will be a member of the "we" in whose name he is judged; and those who suffer persistent, systematic, and serious injustice under an existing set of political, economic, and legal structures may indeed be excluded from that "we". In one sense they are members of the political community: since they live within it, they have a legitimate claim to be treated as full members of it, and suffer injustice in so far as they are not thus treated. In another sense, however, they may be excluded (or may reasonably exclude themselves) from the community: they are not accorded the respect, the concern, which is due to fellow citizens; in response to which they may no longer see themselves as bound by the laws or demands of a community which thus excludes them.

These points about the moral standing to punish can, I think, help us to understand the problem of "doing justice in an unjust society".[27] Sometimes the issue here is taken to be that of whether the law should recognise some special defence of acute (unjust) social disadvantage:[28] which implies that the unjustly disadvantaged defendant is indeed answerable before the law for her conduct, but should perhaps be able to plead some special justification or excuse. We must also ask, however (which is the force of the questions I have raised here) whether such a defendant *is* answerable before the courts for this conduct. This is to ask, in part, whether she was genuinely obligated to obey the law which she allegedly broke:[29] but it is also and relatedly to ask in part about the existence of an appropriate political community to which she belongs and whose law this is; and to ask whether the courts have the moral standing to judge her.

The questions I have raised so far in this section concern the moral standing of those who would punish offenders, or on whose behalf and in whose name offenders are to be punished. They are thus independent of, and prior to, the

---

[26] See A. MacIntyre, *After Virtue*, 2nd edn. (London, Duckworth, 1985).

[27] See, e.g., B. Hudson, *Penal Policy and Social Justice* (London, Macmillan, 1993), and von Hirsch, n. 12 above, at pp. 97–9, pp. 106–8; this is also a theme which underpins much of Alan Norrie's work—see *Crime, Reason and History* (Wiedenfeld and Nicolson, 1993). For more detailed discussion of some of the issues I raise here, see my "Principle and Contradiction in the Criminal Law", in Duff (ed.), *Philosophy and the Criminal Law: Principle and Critique* (Cambridge, Cambridge University Press, 1998), pp. 156–204.

[28] See e.g., B. Hudson, "Beyond Proportionate Punishment: Difficult Cases and the 1991 Criminal Justice Act", (1995) 22 *Crime, Law and Social Change* 59–78.

[29] See my "Principle and Contradiction in the Criminal Law", n. 27 above, at pp. 187–9.

question of whether the *content* of the penal communication is, from some abstract point of view, justified or appropriate—the question of whether this person did culpably commit the criminal wrong for which his punishment would censure him: they concern, as I have emphasised, not the issue of whether this person acted rightly or wrongly, justifiably or unjustifiably, excusably or inexcusably (from either a legal or a moral point of view), but the question of who has the appropriate standing to judge that issue. I want now, finally, to raise a further and related question, concerning not so much the moral standing of those who punish, but the accent or tones in which they speak the language of punishment, and in which they can be heard to speak by those who are punished.

There is a multitude of ways in which communications can be misunderstood; and whilst some misunderstandings reflect some fault or failing on the part of the listener, many others are, from her point of view, quite reasonable. Some such reasonable misunderstandings have to do with the content of the communication: the language, the concepts, the structures of thought, might be obscure, equivocal, or simply unfamiliar to the listener. Others, however, have rather to do with the accent or voice in which the speaker speaks—or is heard to speak. What is sincerely intended as an expression of sympathetic fellow feeling might be heard as an expression of patronising pity; what is intended as a polite and tentative request might be heard instead as a peremptory order; what a teacher intends to be a constructive but tentative suggestion in discussion with a student might be heard instead as a dogmatic instruction that that is what the student must write in her essay or her exam if she wants a good mark. Such misunderstandings depend, of course, on a variety of factors: on the expectations which the hearer brings to the particular situation; on the personal, social, or institutional context within which the interchange is set; on the speaker's (whether actual, or as perceived by the listener) position and attitudes in relation to the listener; on the past dealings between the speaker (or the institutional structures from within which she speaks) and the listener; and so on. All of these contextual factors help to determine just what it is that the listener hears.[30]

A sensitive speaker will of course be alert to the possibility of such misunderstandings, and might sometimes rightly feel that she should refrain from speaking at all: not because the content of what she said would (as she intends it) be wrong or inappropriate; nor because she lacks the standing to say it; but because she realises that it is likely to be misunderstood—that she is likely to be heard to speak in the (inappropriate) accent of condescending pity rather than in the (appropriate) accent of fellow feeling, or in the accent of peremptory instruction rather than in that of polite request. The prospective misunderstanding might

---

[30] Though for convenience I have spoken in this paragraph of "content" and "context" as if they were two quite separate elements in a communicative exercise, a more thorough (and Wittgensteinian) account would start to break down the distinction between "content" and "context": the content, the sense, of what is said cannot be divorced from the context in which it is said. See C. Travis, *The Uses of Sense* (Oxford, Oxford University Press, 1989).

not be one for which she (or the hearer) could be criticised, or one that she could avoid: this is particularly likely to be true in institutional contexts, when what the listener hears will be conditioned in crucial part by his perception of, and past dealings with, the institution from within which and with whose institutional voice she must speak. But if such misunderstanding is likely enough, and would be damaging enough to the aims of her communicative enterprise, it might be that she should not speak.

What has this to do with criminal punishment? Nothing, if we do not see punishment as a communicative enterprise: but a lot, if we do see it as communicative. For we must then ask, not just whether the content of the penal communication (either in the abstract, or as intended by those who punish) is appropriate to the wrongful conduct of the person to be punished; nor just whether those who would judge and punish him (or in whose name he is to be judged and punished) have the moral standing to do so: but also whether he can be reasonably expected to receive and to interpret the penal message with the meaning, in the accents, that it should have and is intended to have. The mere fact that an offender will, predictably, misinterpret his punishment does not of course render its imposition unjustified. We, or the court, might be confident that a career robber will interpret his latest conviction and prison sentence not as an expression of the condemnation which (in the eyes of the law and the community) his conduct deserves (for he has no interest in such moralising), but simply as one of the hazards of his chosen profession: but so long as we can properly attribute that interpretation to his wilful refusal to face up to the wrongful character of his conduct (a refusal which his punishment is intended, albeit perhaps with little hope of success, to persuade him to rethink), we can still hold that he is justly punished. Not all such predictable misunderstandings can, however, be thus blamed on the offender.

A penal practitioner (a probation officer, for instance, or a prison governor) might see her proper task as being to engage in the kind of communicative enterprise that I have sketched. But she might also recognise that, in a particular case or perhaps even in general, that task is not one that she can now perform: that in the context in which she must try to perform it (a context structured by the whole institutional apparatus of the criminal justice system, and by the offenders' histories of past dealings with various parts of that system), her communicative endeavours are almost bound to be misinterpreted by those towards whom they are directed; they will be interpreted (and, given those past histories, not unreasonably so) not as attempts at moral communication, but as the coercive—perhaps also hypocritical—impositions of an alien or oppressive institutional structure.

If this would happen only in a (relatively) few particular cases, it would create a problem within the penal system for the practitioners who must deal with those cases, but it would not threaten the legitimacy of the system as a whole. If, however, something like this would be a predictable general result of an attempt to transform our existing penal practices into the kind of communicative enterprise that I have suggested punishment ought (in ideal theory) to be; if what were intended to be (and would be justified only as being) the accents of moral communication would predictably and not unreasonably be heard in other quite inappropriate tones: then the problem—at least for an ambitiously communicative theory of punishment—is much more serious. We would have to conclude that such a conception of punishment cannot—at least at present—be actualised as the conception which structures our penal practices.

In this section, I have suggested various conditions which would need to be satisfied for punishment to serve, as I believe it should ideally serve, as a mode of moral communication that aims to induce repentance and self-reform in the offender: conditions which have to do, not so much with the internal workings of a penal system, but with the social and political context on which such a system depends. I have not tried to answer the question of whether or how far those conditions are satisfied in a society such as our own; nor am I at all sure what the answer (or rather, the answers, since we cannot suppose that any one unitary answer will be available) should be. It will not, we can be sure, be a very reassuring answer: but I find that I veer back and forth between, on the one hand, a wholly pessimistic view that under present—and foreseeable—conditions criminal punishment simply cannot be or become such a mode of moral communication; and the slightly more optimistic view that, once we grasp the fact that "the criminal justice system" is less a monolithic and unitary institution than a set of diverse and partly autonomous sub-systems and practices, we will also see that there may be room, in some contexts, for at least modest efforts at a communicative penality.

Some will no doubt think that an ideal account of punishment which raises such complex questions about its own practicability, which is as far removed from penal actuality as I admit that mine is, and which sets such demanding preconditions for the legitimacy of punishment, should simply be rejected as a philosopher's dream: a dream that might be interesting to those who enjoy the intellectual game of imagining ideal communities, but that has nothing to say to those who want to engage with the real world of crime and punishment. If we want to see punishment as a morally communicative process at all, we should abandon such ambitious communicative aims in favour of a more modest model like von Hirsch's, which does not aim to use penal hard treatment itself as part of the communicative process. Or, alternatively, we should abandon the idea of moral communication in the penal sphere altogether, in favour of some other justifying theory (some other version of retributivism; a suitably side-constrained deterrent theory; an account of punishment as "social defence"?) which has more chance of being practicably realisable.

However (and unsurprisingly), that does not seem to me to be the right way forward, for two reasons. First, *if* such an ambitious communicative theory is plausible, as part of an ideal account of how a state should deal with its citizens and how they should deal with each other, then the impracticability of that ideal does not render it irrelevant to practice: it should, at the very least, serve as a standard against which the radical imperfections of penal actuality can be assessed and highlighted. Secondly, I think that *any* justifying account of punishment (or any account which is to have any moral credibility) must face versions of the questions which I have posed for a communicative theory. Any such account faces a version of the question of moral standing—the question of who has the right or the standing to judge and to punish those who break the law. Furthermore, I take it to be a basic principle (a principle independent of any particular theory of punishment) for a state which is to treat its citizens as rational and autonomous agents that punishment, like any other application of the state's coercive power, must not only be justified, but must be justified *to* those on whom it is imposed. But if that is so, then a communicative endeavour (the justification of the punishment) must be involved in any infliction of punishment, under any acceptable theory of punishment; and if that is so, any acceptable theory of punishment must face some version of the questions I have raised about the preconditions of legitimate and effective communication.

4

Punishment, Penance, and the State

ANDREW VON HIRSCH

1. Introduction: Duff's and my Views Contrasted

Antony Duff and I share, as he points out in his chapter, a *communicative* perspective on the criminal sanction's general justification:[1] punishment, we both believe, should be conceptualised as a form of censure. Penal censure has important moral functions that are not reducible to crime prevention. A response to criminal wrongdoing that conveys blame gives the individual the opportunity to respond in ways that are typically those of an agent capable of moral deliberation: to recognise the wrongfulness of the action; feel remorse; make efforts to desist in future—or else, to try to give reasons why the conduct was not actually wrong. What a purely "neutral" sanction not embodying blame would deny, even if no less effective in preventing crime, is precisely this recognition of the person's status as a moral agent. A neutral sanction would treat offenders and potential offenders much as beasts in a circus, as creatures which must merely be conditioned, intimidated, or restrained.

Can the institution of punishment, however, be explained *purely* in terms of censure? Punishment conveys blame, but does so in a special way—through visitation of deprivation ("hard treatment") on the offender. That deprivation is the vehicle through which the blame is expressed. But why use *this* vehicle, rather than simply expressing blame in symbolic fashion? It is on this latter issue that Duff and I part company. Duff maintains that the hard treatment component of the penal sanction can itself be explained in reprobative terms; he treats the deprivations involved in punishment as providing a kind of secular penance—for reasons he explains in his chapter and in earlier writings.[2]

I take a different view: that the reason for having the hard treatment element in punishment has to do with helping to keep predatory behaviour within tolerable limits. Had the criminal sanction no usefulness in preventing crime, there

---

[1] "General justification" addresses the question "why punish at all?"; it concerns, that is, the reasons justifying the existence of the institution of legal punishment; see H. L. A. Hart, *Punishment and Responsibility* (Oxford, Oxford University Press, 1986), ch. 1. For the criteria for allocating quanta of punishment, see section 7 below.

[2] R. A. Duff, *Trials and Punishments* (Cambridge, Cambridge University Press, 1986), ch. 9; R. A. Duff, "Penal Communications", (1996) 20 *Crime and Justice: A Review of Research* 1–97.

should be no need to visit material deprivations on those who offend. True, one might still wish to devise another way of issuing authoritative judgements of blame, for such predatory behaviour as occurs. But those judgements, in the interest of keeping state-inflicted suffering to a minimum, would no longer be linked to purposive infliction of suffering.

If the institution of legal punishment thus serves to prevent crime as well as to censure, how is this consistent with treating offenders and potential offenders as moral agents? The hard treatment in punishment, I have argued, serves as a prudential reason for obedience to those insufficiently motivated by the penal censure's moral appeal. But this should *supplement* rather than replace the normative reasons for desisting from crime conveyed by penal censure—that is, provide an *additional* reason for compliance to those who are capable of recognising the law's moral demands, but who are also tempted to flout them.[3] The law thus addresses *ourselves*, not a distinct "criminal" class of those considered incapable of grasping moral appeals. And it addresses us neither as perfectly moral agents (we are not like angels), nor as beasts which only can be coerced through threats; but rather, as moral but fallible agents who need some prudential supplement to help us resist criminal temptation. However, this account calls for moderation in the overall severity in punishment levels. The harsher the penalty system is, the less plausible it becomes to see it as including a moral appeal rather than constituting a system of bare threats.[4]

Behind this disagreement about hard treatment lies different views of the function of the *state* in the area of criminal justice. In a previous discussion,[5] I have questioned whether administering penances is a proper role for a liberal state. Duff gives his response in the present volume, and sketches further some of his ideas concerning the state's role in punishment. My aim here is to comment on some of his arguments, and spell out my own views on punishment and the state.

2. Some Points of Clarification

Before proceeding, two points of clarification are in order. One concerns the role of crime-prevention under my view; the other, the function of penances under Duff's.

The question of sufficient deterrence

Duff suggests that my "prudential supplement" model may provide insufficient deterrence for a penal system (see Chapter 3, pp. 55–6). But I do not claim that

---

[3] A. von Hirsch, *Censure and Sanctions* (Oxford, Oxford University Press, 1993), ch. 2; see also U. Narayan, "Adequate Responses and Preventive Benefits: Justifying Censure and Hard Treatment in Legal Punishment", (1993) 13 *Oxford Journal of Legal Studies* 166–82.

[4] Von Hirsch, n. 3 above, at pp. 38–46.

[5] *Ibid.*, at pp. 72–7.

a penal system based on my theory would necessarily deliver as much crime prevention as, say, the tougher penal policies generally prevailing today (although that is difficult to judge, given the limited state of present knowledge concerning marginal deterrent effects).[6] I merely assert that my model would be capable to a degree of preventing crime, while nevertheless treating offenders as moral agents. If severer overall penalty levels are thought necessary to prevent crime more effectively, adopting those higher penalty levels would simply constitute a deviation from my model—and thus not fully justifiable in its terms. How problematic this would be would depend on how much more severe those overall penalty levels were. The theory nevertheless would remain useful as a heuristic model: to point toward a reduction of overall sentence levels, to the extent practicable.[7]

Duff's objection would be a disturbing one only if my theory were to fail to support any substantial sanctions at all. But it is not clear why that should be true. I have argued that if the penalty scale is inflated sufficiently, the resulting sanctions may become almost wholly coercive, and render largely meaningless the communicative content of the sanction.[8] This, however, would not seem to rule out moderate but still significant penalties. Inflating the penalty scale sufficiently could also undermine the penitential functions of which Duff speaks, for comparable reasons. But this, again, would not necessitate insubstantial criminal penalties.

Functions of penance

Duff claims that, on his penance perspective, punishment can be accounted for wholly in communicative terms. But what communicative functions are involved in the hard treatment aspects of punishment?

One function, of which Duff speaks, is that of *forcing the offender's attention*: the unpleasantness of the sanction may compel the actor to attend to the disapproval visited through the sanction (Chapter 3, p. 51). The moral logic of this function needs explanation, however. Ordinarily, when A censures B for

---

[6] For a survey of recent deterrence research, see A. von Hirsch, A. E. Bottoms *et al.*, *Criminal Deterrence and Sentence Severity* (forthcoming 1999). This survey concludes that while there is a modicum of evidence pointing to possible deterrent effects of varying the *certainty* of punishment (e. g., the likelihood of an offender's being apprehended and convicted), there is still little firm evidence concerning the marginal deterrent effects of altering *severity* levels.

[7] Duff's penance view actually would need to address this same issue of "sufficient" deterrence, even though his account does not explicitly invoke crime-preventative aims—for the sanction levels that would serve as penances might also be substantially lower than existing penalty levels. So to the extent Duff wishes to use his view as a support for a state punishment system, the same question arises: does it justify a practicably adequate level of sanctions? His answer, presumably, would be the same as mine: that it may or may not do so; and to the extent it does not, then practicably "needed" sanction levels could not wholly be justified on his terms. See Duff, n. 2 above, ch. 10.

[8] Von Hirsch, n. 3 above, at pp. 38–46.

some misdeed failing, it is up to B to decide whether or not to pay attention; A is not entitled to use force to get B to attend properly. Coercive attention-getting is warranted only when A holds a special position of moral authority over B. Perhaps, an abbot has such authority over the members of his monastery, in view of his special role as spiritual mentor, and in view of the fact that his charges have submitted themselves to his authority. Whether the *state* has that authority, however, is precisely the issue in dispute between Duff and myself. But at least, attention-getting *is* a communicative role, and thus can be part of a communicative theory of state punishment (provided that the state can be shown to have the requisite authority).

A second function for a penance may be that of *providing an appropriate psychological setting for feelings of shame and regret*. The material discomforts of the penance might be seen as a way of evoking the moral discomfort that the penitent offender should feel. This too, gives hard treatment a communicative character—of doing something to try to persuade the offender to think and feel in a certain way.

A third possible function of penances is that of *expiation*, but that is different. Expiation involves more that creating the right psychological setting; it involves the idea that undergoing certain discomforts is the *appropriate* manner through which repentance ought to be achieved. The deprivations of the punishment are not just ways of evoking regret for the deed; but are seen as required (that is, *morally* required) for the purging of guilt. This function does makes the link to hard treatment necessary rather than contingent: even the already-penitent offender needs to undergo some painful experience to "work through" his penance. The difficulty however, is that it is not clear why this is a communicative function. Moral communication involves conveying a normative judgement to someone; perhaps, trying to persuade him of the correctness of that judgement; and perhaps also, trying to get him to feel certain emotions that comport with that judgement. But if all of that could occur without invocation of hard treatment, it is far from clear what further *communicative* role necessitates offenders' actually having to undergo the pains of expiation.

Duff's explanation of expiation and its function do not illuminate. He asserts that the pains of punishment can "reconcile [the offender] with his fellow citizens, and restore himself to full membership in the community from which his wrongdoing threatened to exclude him" (Chapter 3, pp. 51–2). I find this puzzling for several reasons. First, Duff is relying here on a broad notion of community which refers to a group's having a shared set of behavioral norms; it is these shared norms that give members, and the institutions acting in their behalf, the basis for criticising the conduct of those who flout them. The state thus can act on behalf of a "community" of citizens in this sense, just as a university disciplinary committee can act on behalf of the university's community of scholars in taking action against a colleague who has committed a serious academic infraction. But what justifies an abbot in imposing expiatory penances is not merely that the monastery represents a community of shared values, but that it is one of a special kind, having very specific (and ambitious) moral purposes. Secondly, the connection between community and exclusion is unclear. If expiation is needed to restore the offender to "full membership", then the offender's wrongdoing must have removed him *pro tanto* from membership. But why should offending result in communal exclusion? The family, for example, represents a small community of a kind. Yet many parents feel strongly that misconduct by their children, while warranting criticism or even punishment, should *not* be grounds for actual or emotional loss of membership, even for brief periods; it is only the frigid parent that refuses to speak to his errant child. Thirdly, even if wrongdoing and separation from the community are linked, it is far from clear why *expiatory* penances are needed to restore the person's membership. If the offender comes to recognise and repent of his wrongdoing, for example, why should that not be enough to make him morally "one of us" again? Why is it also necessary for the penitent wrongdoer to undergo something nasty?

It is my suspicion that the expiatory function is not a communicative function at all. It seems, rather, to reflect the traditional retributive sense that suffering is needed to "wipe clean" the moral blemish of wrongdoing. Perhaps, I am mistaken; but if so, Duff needs to explain more clearly whether expiation is an essential element in his conception of penance; and if it is, how it might satisfactorily be explained in purely communicative terms.[9]

3. Standing to Impose Penances and the State Role

Duff (Chapter 3, pp. 61–8) mentions two dimensions of "moral standing", namely, (a) that the censurer has the requisite relationship to the actor to make the wrongfulness of the latter's conduct his proper business; and (b) "clean hands"—that the censurer is not disqualified through his own misconduct from standing in judgement on the actor. There is, however, a third dimension of standing that Duff does not address and that is crucial for present purposes: namely, that of how deeply the censurer may properly involve himself in seeking to bring about the morally appropriate response from the wrongdoer he censures. That may depend on his relationship to the wrongdoer.

---

[9] A possible account might be that the expiatory pains offer the offender the opportunity to communicate *back* his penitent understanding of the wrong. Indeed, Duff suggests this view in his Reponse (see pp. 83–4 below). If there is to be any communication back, however, it cannot be compulsory to have any meaning; and I am unconvinced how this communication can be located in the attitude of the offender to an imposed hard treatment. Treating the expiatory pains of punishment as a kind of enforced apology also raises the problem of compulsory attitudinising, which I have suggested may be a form of demeaning treatment; see von Hirsch, n. 3 above, at pp. 83–4.

What this leaves unexplained, moreover, is why expiatory hard treatment is *necessary* for communicating-back regret. Possibly, it might be a way of signalling such sentiments. But there are other ways: for example, the offender's simply expressing regret in a sincere fashion, or else, subjecting himself to deprivations voluntarily (e. g. deciding himself to put on the sackcloth and ash). Why then, should the offender be *made* to undergo the penalty for this purpose—especially when his acquiescence is needed anyway in order to convey true penitence?

Consider simple acts of censure: someone has acted inconsiderately toward me, and I respond in a reprobative manner. How far I may properly go in trying to elicit the morally appropriate response from him may depend on the character of our relationship. If a stranger negligently steps on my foot, I may give a simple blaming response (say, tell him he ought to be more careful), but it would be inappropriate of me to ask him why he acted in this inconsiderate manner, whether he feels regret, and so forth. A close friend, however, may have standing to make such further inquiries.

This dimension of standing also affects the appropriateness of imposing penances. There is no doubt the head of a monastic community has standing to visit a penance upon an erring monk. For a university disciplinary committee to undertake this role, however, would be more questionable. Yes, the committee is entitled to censure the faculty member, after the proper procedures have been undergone; and in appropriate cases that censure may properly embody some form of deprivation—say, a period of suspension. It might also be hoped that the penalty elicits sentiments of regret, etc. But if the committee characterises the sanction as a penance whose discomforts provide the vehicle for achieving a penitent understanding, one might well think they had overstepped their proper role.[10]

Duff concedes (Chapter 3, pp. 53–4) that the state operates differently from a monastic institution, in that membership is not optional; that the shared values underlying the criminal law are conduct-related and more restricted in scope, and that the state is not properly concerned with the person's own spiritual good *per se*. Notwithstanding these differences, however, he still wants to give the state the abbot-like function of imposing penances. My essential objection remains that (for reasons to be outlined below) this ascribes to the state a role beyond its proper standing (in the sense of that term just suggested), given its functions and its relationship to citizens.

Duff does attempt (Chapter 3, p. 52) to make his position more consistent with liberalism by imposing two kinds of side-constraints on penances: (a) a limitation of scope: penances may only be imposed for conduct threatening certain basic values of peaceable social coexistence, and (b) penances may not involve bringing about penitent attitudes through coercion. The second limitation is implict anyway in any proper notion of a penance: the abbot wants to bring forth the person's *own* penitent attitudes, not brainwash the person. The first limitation also seems insufficient, as it does not address the standing issue spoken of here: that even with respect to harmful conduct, the functions of which Duff speaks might go beyond the state's proper remit. I would scarcely be reassured if a university disciplinary committee sought to impose penances, but only for specified kinds of unprofessional conduct.

---

[10] In his Response (see pp. 84–5 below), Duff suggests departmental colleagues might seek to elicit penitential attitudes from an erring member. Perhaps, this might be appropriate for a small tightly-knit department—precisely in virtue of its character as such. But in larger institutional contexts (for example, that of a disciplinary committee acting on behalf of a large university) this seems a strange role.

4. PENANCE AND THE STATE'S ROLE: SOME HYPOTHETICALS

What more can be said on this issue of the state's penal role? Two hypotheticals might help to bring the differences between penances and state-administered punishments into sharper relief.

1. Suppose a penalty system, with quite moderate sanction levels, were instituted in State X; and that (given the relatively peaceable nature of the populace) it sufficed to help maintain low rates of offending. Suppose, however, that an in-depth survey of convicted offenders were to disclose that the sanctions had very little success in eliciting from them sentiments of shame, repentence, and the like; to the extent that such persons desisted from re-offending, that was mainly due to growing older, or to motives of wishing to avoid the unpleasantness or the stigma of further punishment. From my perspective, this scenario would represent a modest success. The sanctions do reflect and give public expression to a moral valuation of the conduct. Offenders are being treated as moral agents, by being given the *opportunity* of responding as such agents should. And the prudential disincentive embodied in the hard treatment has some apparent effect and yet is not so severe as to "drown out" the censuring message. While one might regret that actual offenders are so seldom penitent, this would not suffice to warrant a judgement of failure.

On Duff's view, however, this outcome of this scenario would seem to represent a failure—because the penalties, intended as penances, so seldom elicit the desired penitential response.[11] Now, if a comparable scenario occurred in a monastery, the abbot would quite rightly be concerned that he was failing: because his central concern is with the moral attitudes of his charges. But it would seem strange to carry over such a judgement to a liberal state, whose central mission seems so much less concerned with attitude than with conduct.

2. Consider a yet more peaceable society, in which punishment scarcely seems needed to prevent crime at all. Offending is relatively rare, being kept in check by people's moral inhibitions, plus fear of the social stigma associated with having been found to have offended. Not much difference in criminality could then be expected between instituting a system of state punishments and relying instead only on formal symbolic censure plus informal social controls. Suppose, however, that there was occasional offending in this society, and that something more than symbolic censure—some measure of hard treatment—was needed to help the few actual offenders achieve a penitent understanding of their misdeeds. Should one, then, insist on punishment with its attendant deprivations?

On my view, the answer would emphatically be no. The justification for the hard treatment would fall away, since it would not ordinarily be needed to help

---

[11] True, Duff points out that penances need not *always* succeed in eliciting penitence from the wrongdoers on whom they are imposed (Chapter 3, p. 52). But if the institutions of state-imposed penance almost *never* induced the desired response from offenders, one would have to query whether it was performing what he considers to be its desired function.

people overcome the temptations of offending.[12] On Duff's view, however, a system of punishments would seem to be called for—simply to provide penances for those few persons who do offend.

In the context of the monastic institution, this latter conclusion would make sense. Even if transgressions were rare in the institution, that would not suffice; if there are any infractions of monastic discipline, it would be the abbot's duty to attend to the consciences of those involved, and institute the purifying process of penance to help them achieve repentance. But for a liberal state, this would seem a strange conclusion. Duff does assert, as noted earlier, that the state should not be concerned with conscience or moral attitudes per se, but only with these as expressed through harmful conduct. But the present hypothetical should bring into relief why this concession is not enough. We *are* speaking of harmful conduct here, but the question remains what aspects of the conduct should be the state's main concern. In a situation where harm prevention is no longer significantly at issue, I cannot see why it is the business of the state to establish so coercive and burdensome an institution as punishment, merely to assist the consciences of some offenders.

5. Rehabilitation and Penance

Offender rehabilitation in the 1960s to 1980s tended to steer clear of attempts to moralise. The offender would be enlisted in a programme designed to improve his skills or resolve his psychological difficulties. The offence itself was seldom discussed. This reticence is now being questioned. Changing the offender's behaviour, current thinking about rehabilitation (or some of it) holds, requires one to talk to the offender about what he did, discuss the reasons why he did it, encourage the offender to consider other persons' interests, and try to get him to understand why his behaviour failed to do so.[13] Confronting the offender with his behaviour is again coming to seen as a legitimate part of rehabilitation.

In cruder versions, such strategies have been conceived in purely utilitarian terms: how much the offender is to be "shamed" would depend purely on what will work to prevent reoffending.[14] However, other penologists[15] see these strategies as constrained by strong proportionality limits: the duration and intensity of the sanction (including its treatment elements) should depend on the

---

[12] See more fully von Hirsch, n. 3 above, at p. 14.

[13] S. Rex, "A New Form of Rehabilitationaism?", in A. von Hirsch and A. Ashworth (eds.), *Principled Sentencing*, 2nd edn. (Oxford, Hart Publishing, 1998), pp. 34–41.

[14] See J. Braithwaite's view of "reintegrative shaming" in his *Crime, Shame and Reintegration* (Cambridge, Cambridge University Press, 1989); for a critique of Braithwaite, see A. von Hirsch and A. Ashworth, "Not Just Deserts: A Response to Braithwaite and Pettit" (1992) 13 *Oxford Journal of Legal Studies* 83–96, and also von Hirsch, n. 3 above, ch. 3.

[15] See Rex, n. 13 above, at pp. 38–9.

gravity of the offence. Thus restricted, these newer rehabilitation methods can be made consistent with a proportionality-oriented sentencing theory.[16]

But why is confronting the offender morally the legitimate business of the state? The seeming answer would be that this helps induce offenders to refrain from reoffending. It is thus a crime-prevention aim, and crime prevention (at least on my model) is a legitimate state function within appropriate desert limits. And while researchers are now less optimistic than they once were about the effectiveness of rehabilitative programmes, there seems to be reason to believe that certain programmes, carefully targeted to amenable offenders, might work to a modest extent to reduce recidivism.[17]

However, matters are not quite so simple, as becomes apparent when we consider recent research on another crime-prevention aim, incapacitation. That research has suggested that—even if imprisonment does "work" in the sense of preventing the imprisoned offender from reoffending while confined—it still may not succeed in reducing the public's net exposure to crime. Locking up the potential recidivist will not necessarily put others less at risk, if (for example) there are large numbers of other potential offenders not currently in prison or being sentenced who can replace his criminal activities. Incapacitation research is thus focusing increasingly on the issue of *net* effects on crime.[18] Were this question of net preventative impact asked of rehabilitation, the implications could be disturbing. If treatment works only for certain selected types of offenders carefully screened for amenability,[19] then the numbers of persons thus "reformed" might simply be too small to have a substantial impact on the incidence of crime. In that case, rehabilitation ceases to "work" as a conventional crime-prevention strategy, notwithstanding successes with particular individuals.

Perhaps, however, rehabilitation might have a somewhat different role, closer to the old notion of "reforming" offenders. The aim would not so much be to reduce overall rates of crime, as to induce some persons to live different lives. On this perspective, a predatory lifestyle is a bad way of living—bad not only in its destructive effects on victims, but in the values that it embodies. Inducing offenders to give up this kind of life and to treat others more decently might arguably (albeit controversially)[20] be seen as worthwhile, even if no net preventative impact ensues.

---

[16] For how treatment efforts can be made consistent with a model through observance of proportionality constraints, see also von Hirsch, n. 3 above, ch. 7. Certain limits on the modalities of treatment are also called for, designed to assure that they are not intrusive or demeaning—for example, a bar against forcing the offender to express attitudes or views to which he does not subscribe; see *ibid.*, at ch. 9.

[17] Rex, n. 13 above, at pp. 35–8.

[18] See von Hirsch and Ashworth (eds.), n. 13 above at pp. 113–27.

[19] Recent research indicates that successes tend to occur *selectively*, for treatment modalities targeted to particular sub-groups, selected for amenability, *ibid.*, at pp. 26–41.

[20] One might possibly argue that this is a species of moralistic paternalism, since the aim is in part to promote the moral well-being of the offender himself. However, the conduct with which the rehabilitative intervention is concerned is of the kind that is injurious to others.

Were we to go this far, would we have embraced Duff's position? We would be utilising a means of which he speaks: namely, using the vehicle of hard treatment to confront the offender, and bring about a recognition of wrongdoing and efforts to change. And the end seems close to his: namely, moral reform of the offender.

Nevertheless, we would still actually be a long way from Duff. Reform of the offender, in the scenario just mentioned, is not being offered as the basis the whole penal system, but merely as an incidence of a penal system which principally may derive its support from other grounds. The main reasons offered for punishing could still be those of my suggested kind—that the system conveys censure and provides a significant disincentive against criminal behaviour. The constraints applicable to punishments, namely, those of proportionality, derive from those aims.[21] If punishment fails or is not needed to promote these basic aims, then (as the hypotheticals in section 4 have indicated) it should not be retained, not even to "reform" some offenders. Offender reform, in the sense just described, is thus merely an additional permissible activity.[22]

6. THE CONSTITUTIVE GROUNDS FOR STATE PUNISHMENT

What view of the state is implicit in the arguments I have sketched in this paper? It is one that is far from the restricted contractualist liberalism to which Duff refers (Chapter 3, pp. 56–7). It admits that sentences may—so long as they observe proportionality constraints—seek a variety of objectives, including that of trying to induce an offender to desist from crime by fashioning a sanction designed to help him to recognise the wrongfulness of his conduct. But functions such as these presuppose the legitimacy of the criminal sanction, and that legitimacy should rest on more restricted claims.

The justification for the criminal sanction concerns its *constitutive* grounds: the reasons why such an institution should exist at all. What the foregoing illustrations (see section 4) are meant to suggest, is that those constitutive grounds should concern certain *public* functions: of expressing a valuation of certain kinds of (harmful) conduct,[23] and of providing a (modest) disincentive against it.

---

[21] von Hirsch, n. 3 above, ch. 2; von Hirsch and Ashworth, n. 18 above, at pp. 168–79.

[22] That is also why one would be entitled to retain the penal system even if few offenders could successfully be reformed; why one can legitimately take the risk of failure of treatment. With Duff's rationale, by contrast, systematic failure of offender-reform efforts would put the legitimacy of the whole system into question (see my first hypothetical in section 4 above).

[23] Holding that expressing a public valuation is a central role of punishment does not require one to accept German theorists' notion of "positive general prevention". According to that theory, the public message embodied in punishment, and its supposed resulting effect of reinforcing citizens' moral inhibitions, constitutes the chief justification of the criminal sanction. This theory cannot be correct, because it would be morally impermissable to censure or punish A *merely* to provide a moral message to B, C, and D. Essential to the case for penal censure, under both Duff's theory and my own, is that the actor has engaged in an act of wrongdoing, and the censure is the kind of response that treats the actor as a moral agent, by giving him the opportunity to respond in characteristically moral ways. For fuller discussion, see T. Hoernle and A. von Hirsch, "Positive Generalpraevention und Tadel" (1995) 142 *Goldtdammer's Archiv fuer Strafrecht* at 261–82.

These basic expressive and preventative functions are matters which concern the character of the minimum norms for peaceable co-existence,[24] and their enforcement. If the institution of the criminal sanction is incapable of carrying out these public functions (or if those functions can be performed without having to resort to the coercive and unpleasant features of punishment) then that institution would lose its *raison d'etre*. In that event, the pains of punishment cannot be sustained solely on the grounds that its pains help it function as a penance for certain wrongdoers.

My just-stated argument about constitutive grounds is designed to address only certain coercive state institutions. The assumption is that, in a free society, such institutions should exist only where necessary for certain fairly narrowly defined purposes, including those of the kind just described. Where sustainable on those grounds, these coercive institutions might also be given certain *supplemental* functions, perhaps concerned with the offender's moral well-being (see section 5). But the latter functions cannot alone support the existence of the criminal sanction. This perspective also should not restrict the availability of a plethora of state and communal institutions aimed at providing resources to citizens and encouraging co-operation among citizens. It is not the idea of a minimal state on which my arguments rest, but a certain minimalism concerning state *coercion*. My ultimate difficulty with Duff's view is that I do not grasp the conception of the state, and of "community" on which it rests.

7. What Difference Does It Make?
Criteria for Proportionality of Sentence

It is common ground between Duff and myself that the principle of proportionality of sentence is of central importance: punishments should be proportionate in their severity to the seriousness of the crime. On both our views, the principle derives from the censuring features of punishment: if punishment conveys blame, then the quantum of punishment should depend on the degree of blameworthiness (i. e. seriousness) of the offender's criminal conduct.

However, the criteria for proportionality appear to operate differently according to the two perspectives. My position calls for a rather demanding standard of proportionality: conduct of equal reprehensibleness should be punished with comparable severity, and penalties should also be ranked according to crime seriousness. With criminal prohibitions seen as public admonitions, and sanctions as public acts of censure, what counts is the degree of blameworthiness of the offence, and the degree of disapproval conveyed through the

---

[24] I am assuming, here, a theory of criminalisation which restricts the scope of criminal sanction primarily to conduct which does or risks immediate injury to others; see, e. g. N. Jareborg, "What Kind of Criminal Law Do We Want?" in A. Snare (ed.), *Beware of Punishment* (Oslo, Pax Forlag, 1995), at pp. 17–36.

severity of the sanction.[25] This conception, as mentioned in section 5, can still allow rehabilitative efforts that are designed to confront the offender personally, and to try to induce some awareness of wrongdoing in him. But given the preeminently public nature of the sanction, and the public character of its constitutive grounds (see section 6), the degree of seriousness of the offence should act as a strong constraint on how much the offender may be punished to achieve such reformative effects. The offender may not, for example, be held in a given penal regime for longer than someone having committed a similarly blameworthy offence, even were the extra time helpful in inducing "reform" on his part.

Duff also calls for proportionality in punishment, and thus opposes any tactic of confining the offender indefinitely until he repents (Chapter 3, p. 52). But his penance rationale does seem to dilute proportionality requirements. Suppose Offender A has a thicker skin than Offender B, and would require a tougher penance to help him achieve the desired penitential response. Since under Duff's view the imposition of penance is the *constitutive* aim of the criminal sanction, and not merely a permissible collateral aim of an institution resting on other constitutive grounds, it would seem difficult to resist punishing A more than B. This would not be seen as a limited (but possibly, permissible[26]) departure from proportionality requirements. Instead, imposing differential amounts of punishment on the two offenders—at least, when the differences are not great—would be seen as involving no moral cost at all.

In the context of a monastery, this latter conclusion could be acceptable. Suppose Brother A and Brother B commit sins of comparable gravity, and the abbot (in view of their differences in character and sensitivity) gives A a more onerous penance. Were A to have the temerity to complain that he has been unfairly treated, the abbot might rightly respond that penances are concerned with helping to promote a penitent response, and that the differences were designed to help bring such a response about. This type of argument seems misplaced, however, in the context of state-imposed punishment.

8. Punishment and Social Deprivation

Both Duff and I discuss the problem of social deprivation and punishment. I have suggested that social deprivation might possibly be a basis for ascribing reduced culpability to the offender, on grounds that such deprivation (if sufficiently serious) makes compliance with the law so much more difficult.[27] Duff,

---

[25] See von Hirsch, n. 3 above, at pp. 15–17. For the reasons why these proportionality requirements hold, even on a general justification for punishment (such as mine) that relies on crime prevention as well as censure, see *ibid*, at pp. 16–17.

[26] I have suggested elsewhere that it might be possible to see proportionality (in my strong sense) as a requirement of fairness, and yet permit *limited* departures from it, on grounds that these would involve no great degree of injustice (albeit concededly some), and permit pursuit of other aims seen as especially urgent. See my discussion of "hybrid models" in *ibid*., at pp. 54–6.

[27] See *ibid*., at pp. 106–8.

however, argues that social deprivation might undermine the state's moral authority to punish. The two claims are not necessarily exclusive; it might be possible to view social deprivation as a mitigating factor that reduces the offender's culpability; but also, in extreme cases, deny the state the standing to punish at all. Let me just make some brief comments on these differing perspectives and their implications.

1. On a culpability-reduction view, deprived offenders' claim to mitigation would depend on the extent of the social deprivation that exists: for it is that which (arguably) affects the offender's degree of blameworthiness. On Duff's moral standing view, however, the issue shifts to *how much at fault* the state or its more prosperous citizens are for the existence of such deprivation—indeed, Duff (Chapter 3, p. 63) speaks of complicity in social injustice. This means there is no direct link between social deprivation and exculpation; all would depend on the intermediate step of identifying governmental or class villainy or neglect. It will be far from easy to develop workable doctrines that enable one to judge when this kind of fault is present.[28] It also will mean that absent such fault, the state's standing to punish could not be called into question. Consider, for example, a country which is very poor but which nevertheless has a decent government making gallant efforts to alleviate poverty, efforts which, alas, are largely unavailing because of the country's limited economic resources. Since this government would have "clean hands", it would have standing to punish even the most deprived offenders.

2. On a culpability-reduction view, how much mitigation is granted would be a matter of degree, depending on the extent of the social deprivation involved and how it bears specifically on culpability. Only the most extreme conditions—for example, stealing to avoid starvation—would support complete exculpation.[29] On Duff's moral-standing perspective, however, the punishability of deprived persons would be an all-or-nothing matter: either the state is or it is not sufficiently at fault to lose standing to punish deprived offenders or certain classes of them.

3. At the end of his chapter, Duff raises the question of what should happen if it is concluded that the state lacks the standing to have a penance-based system of punishment. First, he suggests that a fallback position might be one such as mine, where state punishments are conceived of as conveying blame and providing some kind of disincentive. Then, however, he takes this concession back, on the grounds that such a fallback position would raise the same basic issue of the state's having insufficiently "clean hands" to censure deprived violators. But this may not be correct, for the criteria for "clean hands" standing may vary with how ambitious a communicative role is at issue. We rightly expect the head of a religious institution to lead an exemplary existence because his involvement in the moral lives of his charges is so deep. The less morally ambitious role

---

[28] In speaking of fault here, Duff seems to treat the state as something akin to a person, rather than a complex set of institutions, many with diverse and even conflicting policies.
[29] See von Hirsch, n. 3 above, at p. 108n.

presupposed by a penal theory such as mine could arguably permit less stringent "clean hands" requirements of moral standing.[30]

If matters are bad enough, of course, then the state may lose moral standing even to play the more modest role which my position would ascribe to it. In that event, however, there would appear to be no morally acceptable alternative basis for criminal sanctions. If an unjust state lacks the moral standing to censure lawbreakers, then it cannot avoid injustice merely by resorting to purely deterrent or incapacitative sanctions—for these are plainly objectionable on grounds of not treating offenders as moral agents at all. If the state is all that rotten, the appropriate response is revolution (or emigration, for those who can), and not finding alternate grounds for giving moral support to state sanctions.

---

[30] In that event, one might conclude that punishment remains justifiable on my censure-plus-disincentive rationale, but that rehabilitative interventions of the kind discussed in section 5 are no longer acceptable. While retaining the minimal moral standing needed to condemn the harmful conduct typical of law violations, the system may lack the standing to confront offenders personally with their wrongdoing. Indeed, some radical criminologists of the 1960s and 1970s objected to such efforts of "offender reform", precisely on such grounds.

Response to von Hirsch

R. A. DUFF

I'm grateful for the chance to respond briefly to some of the points that Andrew von Hirsch has raised. I must admit at once that much was left under-explained in my chapter (and will still be left under-explained here), in particular about the kind of communitarianism to which I appeal, and about the implications of the non-satisfaction of the preconditions of justified punishment which I discuss in section 3 of my chapter. However, whilst it is clear that the disagreement between von Hirsch and me depends in part on our different ideal conceptions of the state and of political community, I can indicate how I would hope to meet a few of his main criticisms and questions.

1. The Communicative Functions of Punishment

Von Hirsch rightly suggests (Chapter 4, pp. 71–3) that expiation is an important dimension of hard treatment punishments, and that its communicative significance lies, on my account, in what it enables the offender to communicate to others: a punishment which is (or becomes) *voluntarily* accepted and undergone communicates to the offender's fellow citizens his own repentant recognition of the wrong he has done. In this respect punishment is a kind of enforced apology. Like other modes of apology, whether informal or formal, it has two aspects: its public form, which conventionally bears a certain meaning (for instance, the words spoken in a formal apology); and its individual character and meaning as something undertaken or undergone by this particular wrongdoer (the terms in which *he* understands and undergoes it).

Now communicative punishment essentially involves the former aspect, and *aspires* to take on the latter aspect: the offender is required or forced to undergo the punishment, with its public meaning; and the hope is that he will come to accept it as an appropriate way to strengthen and to express his repentance. That acceptance, however, which would turn his punishment into a genuine expiation, cannot be coerced or compelled: by which I mean that whatever is coerced or compelled cannot count as genuine expiation, since it would not express the offender's own authentic understanding and repentance of his wrong; and that it would be wrong to try to coerce it, since that would be incompatible with a proper respect for the offender as a moral agent.

If the offender remains unrepentant, his punishment has thus failed in one of its aims: but it can still succeed as a communication with him. Furthermore, I think we owe it to the offender to treat him *as if* his punishment constituted a genuine expiation, just as we owe it to those non-intimate fellow citizens who may informally apologise to us to treat their apologies as (if they were) sincere: that is the proper meaning of the idea that the offender who has been punished has "paid his debt"; and it guards against the danger that offenders will effectively be coerced into inauthentic expressions of remorse by the prospect of some remission of punishment if they are seen to repent.

However, even if I can claim that punishment as (in part) expiation need not involve—at the level of ideal theory—an improper attempt to coerce or manipulate the offender's understanding and attitudes, this will no doubt do nothing to assuage von Hirsch's worries about the role that my account allows to the state.

2. STATES, MONASTERIES, AND DEPARTMENTS

The monastic example of penitential punishment is both useful and dangerous for my account. It is useful because this is a context in which punishment can clearly be seen to have the ambitiously communicative character of a penance; and I want to argue that criminal punishment should ideally share—to a *limited* extent—this character. But it is also dangerous, because it can be taken to imply that the criminal justice system and its penal officials should take the kind of intrusive and all-encompassing interest in the moral condition of the citizens that a monastery and its abbot properly take in the spiritual condition of its inhabitants. I tried in my chapter to indicate some of the stringent limits which should constrain a (liberal-communitarian) system of criminal law and punishment, and thus distinguish it from a monastery's rules and penances: limits both on the scope of the criminal law, and on the extent to which punishment should seek to address or impinge on the offender's moral character. Von Hirsch regards these limits as insufficient, even in the context of an ideal theory of punishment: whilst I cannot hope to persuade either him or a sceptical reader here, I can perhaps explain my account a little further by commenting on the case of punishment within an academic institution, and on the two hypothetical cases with which von Hirsch challenges me.

Von Hirsch would not want his "departmental chair . . . to impose penances", even if these were "only for specified kinds of unprofessional conduct" (Chapter 4, p. 74); and I agree that to talk in this context of "penance" is likely, given the religious connotations of the term, to grate on our ears. However, I think that a decent academic department, one whose members share a commitment both to the academic values which structure their activity and to each other as colleagues, would have a place for a secular, academic version of penance.

Note first that the department will have a proper interest only in strictly limited aspects of its members' conduct and attitudes, those which bear directly on their performance of their academic job. If I am doing my job badly, my colleagues (or the departmental chair acting in their name) have the standing to intervene—to comment, to criticise, to demand; but if I am misbehaving in my non-academic life, they have no such standing to intervene (this is not to say that some of them could not have such standing as my friends; but they do not have it as my colleagues). Furthermore, a liberal-minded department will tolerate, indeed encourage, a fair degree of diversity of professional attitudes and conduct, different approaches to teaching and to research, different ways of living and working as an academic. Nor will it seek, as a department, to delve into its members' deeper motivations or attitudes: its concern will be limited to their professional conduct and their attitudes directly manifested in that conduct.

Suppose then that a member of the department commits some serious academic wrong in her dealings with her colleagues or her students. Her colleagues will rightly criticise her (for it is their business; they have the standing to do so); they might *demand* that she listen to their criticism, explain herself to them, and apologise for what she has done; they might impose some appropriate academic sanction on her. The point of this whole process is not just (as von Hirsch would agree) to communicate to her the censure her wrongdoing deserves; nor such communication plus (as von Hirsch might add) the provision of a supplementary prudential disincentive against a repetition of the wrongdoing. It is rather, I suggest, to remind or persuade her of the nature and seriousness of that wrongdoing, and of the need to re-establish her standing within the department by assuring her colleagues and students that she is sorry for what she has done. Her colleagues' response is to her as someone who is, and who must remain (unless the wrong is so serious that expulsion is the only proper response), a colleague—someone whose relationship with the department and with the values which structure its academic life needs to be reinforced or re-established after the wrong she has done; and this is properly achieved by this process of criticism and punishment.

I am not suggesting that either an academic department or a monastery is an ideal model of society. What I do suggest is that, while a department should take a far less all-embracing, far less intrusive interest in its members' moral condition than a monastery takes in the spiritual condition of its members, we can see a proper place within it for a secular version of penance; and that this can help us to see the role that penitential punishment could play in other contexts, including that of the criminal law.

3. VON HIRSCH'S HYPOTHETICALS

What then of the two hypotheticals with which von Hirsch challenges me (Chapter 4, pp. 75–6)? One offers us a society in which hard treatment punishments (of only modest severity) serve as effective prudential supplements, but (almost) never secure the penitential response that should on my account be their aim; the other a society in which only very few offenders would need hard treatment punishment to elicit such a penitential response.

My initial (and I hope not merely evasive) response is that before we can discuss the role that punishment has or could have in such societies, we need to know a lot more about them—about the kinds of people who make them up, about the character of their social and moral relationships. For any normative account of punishment depends on a view not just of "human nature", but of human nature in some concrete social, context; it must locate punishment within the political, social and moral relationships and institutions which structure that context. The social context of von Hirsch's hypotheticals, however, is radically under-specified.

Thus in the first hypothetical, we are to imagine people who are in general susceptible to moral persuasion and censure, at least outside the context of the criminal justice system; and who are in principle open to moral persuasion through the kinds of punishment they suffer (else their punishments could not communicate censure to them, and give them "the opportunity of responding as [moral] agents should" (Chapter 4, p. 75)); but who are in fact (almost) never thus persuaded. But why is this? Is it because of the kinds of punishment which are imposed, or the manner and spirit in which they are imposed—in which case I need suggest only that their penal system needs reforming? Or is it because of some odd feature of their moral psychology—in which case we need to know more about that feature?

In the second hypothetical, we are to imagine people who for the most part do not need the apparatus of penitential hard treatment punishments, but a few of whom would occasionally need it, to "achieve a penitent understanding of their misdeeds" (Chapter 4, p. 75). But why is this? Does this have to do with the seriousness of those misdeeds, or with the nature of their relationships to their fellow citizens, or with some particular feature of their moral psychology? Again, we need a fuller account of the moral psychology of the offenders, and of their moral lives and relationships outside the context of punishment.

Depending on what that account turned out to be, I might suggest that in the first case there would indeed be no adequate justification for a system of hard treatment punishment; or that the character, manner, and institutional context of punishment should be reformed so that it might achieve its proper penitential aims. In the second, I might suggest that there would again, though on different grounds, be no adequate justification for a system of hard treatment punishments (because we should not create a large, complex, and dangerous penal institution for the sake of a few unusual offenders); or that it could still be justified, as still serving—for all offenders—the penitential ends that punishment should serve.

The point to emphasise here, however, is that any plausible justifying account of punishment will portray it as being necessary and justified, not *a priori* for any and every kind of (rational, human?) being, but for particular kinds of being (human beings like ourselves in relevant respects). If such an account is to be challenged, on the grounds that it has counter-intuitive or disturbing implications when applied to imagined beings radically different from ourselves, we need first to be clear whether and how it would apply to such beings—and we cannot guarantee in advance that it should so apply.

5

Justifying Punishment in Intercultural Contexts: Whose Norms? Which Values?

DUNCAN IVISON*

1. INTRODUCTION

There appears to be an important difference for a theory of punishment between underlying assumptions about liberal, communitarian, and republican accounts of state and community.[1] This seems especially true of attempts to justify punishment which focus on it as a mode of *communication* with offenders. For aside from the censure it is meant to deliver, punishment is—on the account we shall be examining below—meant to induce within the offender a process of self-interrogation and reform and to reconcile him with those he has wronged. Particular conceptions of the state and community turn out to be crucial components of a communicative theory of punishment.

What if we were to complicate slightly the underlying conception of community by substituting the usual liberal or communitarian version with what I shall call a "postcolonial" political community? I don't mean this as completely distinct from liberal or communitarian accounts. But I do think it is a context which raises interesting questions for theories of punishment generally, or so I hope to show. I mean to refer mainly to those countries such as Canada, Australia, New Zealand, and the USA where indigenous populations have been asserting their claims to traditional lands and, to varying degrees, rights to self-

---

* I am indebted for comments and help to John Braithwaite, Simon Caney, David Campbell, William Connolly, Antony Duff, Moira Gatens, Sidney Haring, Nicola Lacey, Matt Matravers, Susan Mendus, Alan Norrie, and Paul Patton. The chapter was written whilst I was a Visiting Fellow at the wonderful Humanities Research Centre at the Australian National University. My research was also generously supported by the Nuffield Foundation, for which I am extremely grateful.

[1] R. A. Duff, *Trials and Punishments* (Cambridge, Cambridge University Press, 1986); "Penal Communications: Recent Work in the Philosophy of Punishment", (1996) 20 *Crime and Justice: A Review of Research* 1-97; "Choice, Character and Criminal Liability", (1993) 12 *Law and Philosophy* 345-83; N. Lacey, *State Punishment: Political Principles and Community Values* (London, Routledge, 1988); J. Braithwaite and P. Pettit, *Not Just Deserts: A Republican Theory of Criminal Justice* (Cambridge, Cambridge University Press, 1990).

government. More specifically, I am referring to the apparent legal pluralism of such countries; "apparent" because it is a highly contested matter, especially with regard to the criminal law.

Is a communicative theory of punishment compatible with legal pluralism? The crucial issue is the relation between the conception of community and the role of communication. To what extent do the issues associated with Aboriginal claims about self-government affect the communicative function of the criminal law, and especially of punishment?

I shall admit now that much more needs to be said about the nature of a "postcolonial political community", and what makes it a distinct conception compared to liberal or communitarian ones. Some of this will, I hope, become clear below. But the bulk of this argument will have to be made elsewhere.[2] It is important to note that I am *not* arguing that countries such as Canada or Australia are, in fact, "postcolonial" states. Indigenous people continue to suffer from appalling deprivation and discrimination, much of it a direct legacy of colonialism. So colonialism is far from being perceived as something that has been overcome. To move beyond colonial to genuinely *post*colonial relations is thus an aspiration, not a description of the current state of relations between indigenous communities and the state.

The chapter is meant to prefigure larger claims about the historical and normative character of the relation between sovereignty and the public sphere. Very little will be said here to make this connection explicit. But crudely, if conceptions of the public sphere must, by definition, presuppose some kind of community and, not least, some kind of common language in which public deliberations take place—some common orientation in judgement (which is, of course, consistent with widespread disagreement between particular applications of judgement)—then what exactly is it that can be (or has been) shared?[3] My hunch is that conceptions of sovereignty and the public sphere are tightly intermeshed, and pursuing such connections sheds light on questions to do with the nature of late-modern political communities. For in contexts where the history of sovereignty is being rewritten (and thus the concept reshaped), and where it is as much the conditionality and negotiability of sovereignty that is at issue as it is its exercise, the nature of the public sphere must surely also be affected. Hence the focus on intercultural contexts. They present a palpable example of the preconditions for public communication under severe strain. Do "we" share, as a social, political, and legal community, a form of life within which diverse and overlapping sub-communities can find their place? Or are "we" instead merely a diverse collection of incompletely articulated

---

[2] For an initial attempt see D. Ivison, "Political Theory and Postcolonialism" in A. Vincent (ed.), *Political Theory: Tradition, Diversity and Ideology* (Cambridge, Cambridge University Press, 1997) pp. 154-71.

[3] The clearest analogy is to the nature of the common law. What are the preconditions for thinking about the law as "our" law, as one we understand as a source of legitimate obligations wherein those who judge and apply it possess the requisite standing—from our point of view—for doing so? I am grateful to Antony Duff for helpful discussion on this question.

communities between whom communication—when it occurs—is erratic, superficial and at worst, hostile?

The last claim is too swift—perhaps—if it suggests that the public sphere or the "common" law is literally inaccessible to certain individuals and groups, however much they feel themselves to be (or are) alienated from it. For it might be that under certain suitably stylised (i.e. hypothetical) conditions genuine communication *could* occur, and thus individuals or groups, given these conditions, might be said to be capable of belonging to a moral and political community whose normative rules and laws legitimately apply to them. I remain agnostic (for now) as to the ultimate success of this Rawlsian move. But the particularities of the intercultural context I examine below present an acute challenge for such thought-experiments.

The structure of the chapter is as follows. In section 2 I lay out an initial (and very cursory) distinction between liberal and communitarian accounts of the state, citizenship, and the criminal law. In section 3 I present my intercultural example. In section 4, I provide a sketch of a communicative theory of punishment, relying mainly on the work of R.A. Duff, who is particularly sensitive to underlying theories of state and community when thinking about punishment. I shall not be defending the "communicative theory of punishment" as a mode of punishment *per se*. Instead, I shall assume that it is at least a plausible account of punishment and indeed, one worth taking seriously (as I do). In section 5 I return to the intercultural example and try to draw out the challenges it presents for a communicative theory of punishment, and hopefully, how it prefigures a distinctive approach to thinking about the public sphere in these fractious times.

2. Liberal and Communitarian Accounts of the State Distinguished

On the communitarian view, citizens are bound together by "shared concerns, affections, projects and values".[4] Ideally, social interaction is structured by shared values and mutual concerns, and the criminal law is focused on not only protecting individuals from obvious and general wrongs (such as murder or theft), but from conduct that "strikes at [the community's] most central values, or its members most important interests".[5] Since a person can only find her well-being in some sort of community, which is structured by certain shared values and norms, a criminal is someone who flouts the laws of her community and thus the shared values therein. She "damages or destroys her relationships with other members of the community, and separates herself from them".[6] In breaching important community norms, the offender deserves censure, and it is the role of the criminal law not only to define and proscribe such public wrongdoing, but

---

[4] Duff, "Choice, Character and Criminal Liability", n. 1 above, at 381.

[5] Duff, "Penal Communications", n. 1 above, at 79; Lacey, n. 1 above, at p. 176 on upholding the "framework of values" of a community.

[6] Duff, "A Reply to Bickenback", (1988) 18 *Canadian Journal of Philosophy* 787–93.

also contribute to rectifying the damage done to the community and to the *offender herself*. Thus the distinction between public and private becomes more fluid, as some "private" dimensions of an offender's conduct might become relevant, given a communitarian account of the importance of the social framework within which she acts. Furthermore, it suggests that punishment plays a part in promoting and contributing to certain communal values and goods which are intrinsically related to our individual well-being, given a view of the person in which our relations with others (and social institutions) is central to our self-understanding.

On the liberal view (admittedly, close to caricature) social interaction is framed in contractual terms. Thus "discrete individuals" pursue their own conception of the good subject to constraints which allow others to do the same. Liberal citizens work out a way of living "next to each other" rather than "truly together".[7] The criminal law is meant to be focused mainly on breaches of the social contract; on those forms of conduct which harm or threaten interests that need to be protected if social life (conceived in contractual terms) is to be possible.[8] The law is "our" law insofar as it refers to a contractual "we" determined with reference to the terms of the social contract—with what we agreed or *would have* agreed to under certain hypothetical conditions.[9] Even if, from a liberal perspective, the communitarian conception of society is an attractive one, it doesn't follow that the state should be given the scope to promote such values through the coercive means of the criminal law (especially given the danger of our communitarian urges becoming nastily distorted).[10] Liberal theories, at least in relation to the criminal law and punishment, are said to be committed less to the promotion of public virtues or communal goods than they are to the enforcement of a basic framework of individual rights.[11]

3. AN INTERCULTURAL EXAMPLE

The most distinctive aspect of the postcolonial example for our purposes is the relation between legal pluralism and conceptions of political community. What are the consequences of legal pluralism for conceptions of political community? If more than one source of law is said to exist within a polity, then to what extent are we still considering a *single* political community? To what extent are we still able to talk about collective goods or public norms as being *shared* between citizens? Are different sets of norms applicable to different spheres of

---

[7] Duff, "Penal Communications", n. 1 above, at 85.
[8] Duff, "Choice, Character and Criminal Liability", n. 1 above, at 383.
[9] Duff, "The Common Law", unpublished paper.
[10] See R. Hardin, *One for All: The Logic of Group Conflict* (Princeton, Princeton University Press, 1995).
[11] See Lacey. n. 1 above, at pp. 164-5, at 181; but cf. D. Ivison, *The Self at Liberty: Political Argument and the Arts of Government* (Ithaca and London, Cornell University Press, 1997) on the promotion of liberal conduct.

the community? If so, how can the communicative function of the criminal law—and thus of punishment—be served? How can we speak of the offender violating our common norms and values. Whose norms? Which values?

I want to try and flesh out this intercultural example with reference to some recent political and legal developments in Australia. In 1992, the High Court of Australia declared that the common law recognised that Aboriginal customary law could provide a basis for title to land. Thus, "native title" survived the imposition of British sovereignty where there had been no legal extinguishment of this title, and where Aboriginal people had maintained some kind of connection to their "country". The basic formula for recognition in the decision was this:

> "Native title has its origin in and is given its content by the traditional laws acknowledged by and the traditional customs observed by the indigenous inhabitants of a territory. The nature and incidents of native title must be ascertained as a matter of fact by reference to those laws and customs".[12]

As a result, "Aboriginal law and custom is now a source of law in [Australia]".[13]

The majority judges were careful in limiting the implications of the decision with regard to further claims of sovereignty. Unlike countries such as Canada, the USA and New Zealand, where some form of legal and/or constitutional recognition of sovereignty had been accepted (if only in theory), no such precedent existed in Australia.[14] However it has not taken long for the logic of *Mabo* to be stretched to promote claims about self-government, if not by the court then by others. If native title arises out of Aboriginal law and custom, then that law and custom will direct other forms of conduct on the land. And if inherent rights to land exist, then why not inherent rights of self-government?[15] Granted, the settlement of land claims is logically distinct from the settlement of self-government claims.[16] But as land claims are negotiated and settled in a range of different ways, territorial security will give rise to further jurisdictional claims.

If Aboriginal people retain some form of sovereignty (the precise forms of which might vary according to the different peoples, regions, and historical contexts), then what is it that they are sovereign over?[17] The criminal law is a bitterly contested domain in this regard. In the USA, for example, where a limited "Domestic Dependent Nations" doctrine of Aboriginal sovereignty has been

---

[12] *Mabo v. State of Queensland* (No. 2) (1992) 66 ALJR 429.

[13] N. Pearson, "From Remnant Title to Social Justice", in M. Goot and T. Rowse (eds.), *Make us an Offer: The Politics of Mabo* (Sydney, Pluto Press, 1994), at pp. 180-1.

[14] But see H. Reynolds, *The Law of the Land* (Melbourne, Penguin, 1992).

[15] For a comprehensive discussion in relation to the USA and Canada, see P. Macklem, "Distributing Sovereignty: Indian Nations and Equality of Peoples" (1993) 45 *Stanford LR* 9 1311-67.

[16] There might also be strategic reasons for focusing on land rights rather than sovereignty issues, as least in the short term. See N. Pearson, "To be or not to be—separate aboriginal nationhood or aboriginal self-determination and self-government within the Australian nation?" (1993) 3 *Aboriginal Law Bulletin* 16.

[17] See D. Ivison, "Decolonising the rule of law; Mabo's case and postcolonial constitutionalism", (1997) 17 *Oxford Journal of Legal Studies* 253-79.

operative since the nineteenth century, control over the criminal law has been the site of intense conflict between federal, state and tribal governments. For American Indians, the extension of federal and state criminal statutes to Indian lands was (and still is) perceived to be a major tool of assimilation (thus destruction)—as in fact it was.[18] It remains the case today that state and federal criminal law has only limited application in most Native American political communities. The situation in Australia is very different (and different again in Canada and New Zealand). In many ways, it brings to the fore much more clearly the issues of concern in this chapter—namely, the justification of punishment in multinational and multicultural communities. This is because in Australia the lines between Aboriginal and non-Aboriginal legal and political spheres are much less clearly drawn. Thus the justificatory challenge—on both sides—is more acute and complex.

The matter cannot be resolved away, I believe, by straightforward declarations of "national" sovereignty (as is often implied in legal literature originating from the USA). That is, if Aboriginal people possess national sovereignty, then it follows they possess the right to declare and enforce laws, including the criminal law. End of story. What better represents both the right and the capacity to exercise sovereignty then the ability to enforce the criminal law? However, the question of Aboriginal sovereignty is a complex one. It is important not to leap to the conclusion that claims for sovereignty are reducible to claims for separate nationhood (despite the fact that the *language* of nationhood is often invoked in this regard, indeed, by Aboriginal people themselves). Aboriginal sovereignty is not reducible to the sovereignty of nation states. Claims for self-government are not simply rehashed claims of romantic nationalism. They are best understood, I think, as demands for the rethinking of the nature and shape of dominant understandings of political community. Hence the challenge to any account of the criminal law (and theory of punishment) in which the purpose is to contribute to the "maintenance, stability, and continuing development" of the community.[19] The point is not that the criminal law lacks authority because it lacks sovereignty given a conflicting (Aboriginal) source of "absolute" sovereignty, but that the sovereignty it claims misrepresents—by not recognising—the plural and overlapping nature of sovereignty in intercultural contexts.[20] Relations between the different forms of sovereignty need not take the shape of *either* mutually

---

[18] See R. Clinton, "Criminal Jurisdiction over Indian Lands: A Journey Through a Jurisdictional Maze", (1975) 18 *Arizona Law Review* 508; R. Williams, "The Algebra of Indian Law: The Hard Trail of Decolonizing and Americanizing the White Man's Indian Jurisprudence" (1986) *Wisconsin Law Review* 219; and S. Haring, *Crow Dog's Case: American Indian Sovereignty, Tribal Law, and the United States Law in the Nineteenth Century* (New York, Cambridge University Press, 1994).

[19] Lacey, n. 1 above, at p. 172.

[20] This is true even in the USA, where there is a tight connection between Indian sovereignty and jurisdiction over the criminal law given the legacy of the Marshall decisions. Even the strongest defenders of Indian sovereignty often talk of the blending and co-ordination of legal traditions— where such blending involves positive recognition and respect rather than assimilation and imposition; see for example Williams, n. 18 above, at 219. Treaties (as in Canada, the USA and New Zealand) represent a tangible example of the layered nature of the sovereignty in these countries.

exclusive (thus inherently conflicting) domains, *or* the assimilation of one to the other. Insofar as a system of criminal law, and thus the conception of political community underpinning it, misrecognises Aboriginal law in this way, its legitimacy becomes problematic in two ways: (i) the values of the community it represents will not be those that Aboriginal people could possibly share or belong to, and thus (ii) its authority over Aboriginal people will be contestable in that it becomes an "alien imposition" rather than a legitimate source of obligation.

Note then that communicative theories which justify punishment, in part, as a means to reintegrate the offender into the moral community whose values he has offended against must be clear about the nature of the community to which the offender is being reconciled. I shall return to this point below. It is striking that historically, and in their day-to-day experience, many Aboriginal people have come to see the criminal law as simply a means to impose an alien and hostile conception of community over them, justified usually in terms of being for their own good. The fact that indigenous people in Australia, Canada, and the USA are amongst the most arrested and jailed people *in the world*, lends (depressingly) ample support to the acuity of such a perception.[21]

The initial sketch of a postcolonial context is still rather vague. Let me try to flesh it out a bit more with reference to some specific cases, again from Australia. Consider a recent case concerning the jurisdiction of Aboriginal law. In *Denis Walker* v. *State of NSW*, Mason CJ (as he then was) stated that:

> "there is nothing in *Mabo* [No. 2] to suggest that the parliaments of the Commonwealth and [New South Wales] lack legislative competence to regulate or affect the rights of Aboriginals or that these laws are subject to their acceptance, adoption, request or consent . . . English Criminal law did not, and Australian Criminal law does not, accommodate an alternative body of law operating alongside it".[22]

Walker had sought a declaration that the laws of New South Wales were inapplicable to him given that the offence for which he was charged occurred on Aboriginal land where customary laws and practices were still valid, and whose people had not consented to the imposition of British common law. Walker's counsel argued that the lack of consent undermined the assumed validity of colonial criminal law, and, moreover, that customary law was recognisable by the common law, as shown in *Mabo*. Mason CJ rejected this. If criminal statutes did not apply to Aboriginal people "it would offend the basic principle that all people should stand equal before the law". Different criminal sanctions applying to different persons for the same conduct, claimed Mason, "offends [against this] basic principle".[23] Furthermore, even if "customary criminal law" survived

---

[21] See for example the *Royal Commission into Aboriginal Deaths in Custody* (Canberra, 1991); Haring, n. 18 above, at p. 24; *Aboriginal Peoples and the Justice System* (Ottawa, Ministry of Supply and Services Canada, 1993).

[22] (1994) 26 ALR 321 at 322-3. A summary discussion of the case can be found in (1995) 3 *Aboriginal Law Bulletin* at 39-41. See also Mason CJ in *Coe* v. *Commonwealth* (1993) 118 ALR 193 at 200. In this paragraph I am drawing on Ivison, n. 17 above.

[23] (1994) 126 ALR 321, at 323.

settlement, it had been extinguished by the passage of general criminal statutes. There can be no "alternative body of law" operating alongside Australian criminal law. So it must either be unrecognisable by the court or have been extinguished.

Leaving aside some of the broader philosophical issues to do with Mason's conception of equality (he makes a strong assumption about equal treatment consisting in *identical* treatment), consider the reasoning about the imposition of the criminal law. It is far from obvious that the criminal codes of different states extinguished Aboriginal law on these matters.[24] The Australian Law Reform Commission certainly did not presume this in an exhaustive and quite extraordinary report on the possible recognition of Aboriginal law.[25] *Mabo* certainly did not suppose that the Crown's radical title to land extinguished native title, which is defined relative to Aboriginal law. So Mason must assume that Aboriginal customary law, *except to do with land title and management*, is incompatible with Australian law. But this is a rather arbitrarily drawn distinction. As one Aboriginal commentator has put it, it is "absurd [if] our title to land is recognized but the laws and customs which give meaning to that title are treated as if they do not exist".[26]

The conflict here is between two bodies of law in one political community, and between two different conceptions of the criminal law. The conflict might be even more acute then consideration of *Walker* suggests. Consider another case to do with alternative conceptions of punishment. In *R v. Minor*,[27] the Crown appealed against a sentence handed down to an Aboriginal defendant who pleaded guilty to counts of manslaughter, causing grievous bodily harm, and aggravated assault. He was sentenced to a total of ten years imprisonment. The sentencing judge directed that he be released upon entering into a bond (set at three years) after serving four years of his sentence. The crucial thing to note is that the sentencing judge took into account evidence concerning the punishment the defendant would be subject to under Aboriginal law—the "payback" (as it is referred to) that was to be delivered by his community (and which the defendant understood and apparently consented to undergo).[28] The Crown

---

[24] See K. E. Mulqueeny, "Folk-Law or Folklore: When a Law is Not a Law. Or is it?" in Stephenson and Ratnapala (eds.) *Mabo: A Judicial Revolution?* (St. Lucia, University of Queensland University Press, 1993), p. 177.
[25] *The Recognition of Aboriginal Customary Laws* (Canberra, 1986).
[26] M. Dodson, "From 'Lore' to 'Law': Indigenous Rights and Australian Legal Systems," (1995) 20 *Aboriginal Law Bulletin* 2.
[27] (1991/2) 2 NTR 183; cf. *R v. Warren, Coombs & Tucker* reported in (1996) 1 *Australian Indigenous Law Reporter,* at 622-6.
[28] Something needs to be said about Aboriginal conceptions of punishment generally, though the detail cannot be examined here. The important point is that disputes arise and are resolved with reference to the general moral framework of Aboriginal law, the goal of which is to rebalance relations upset by the offence or dispute. Punishments range from "spearing" to duelling, shaming, compensation, and banishment. (Note that the form of "payback" at issue in *Minor* was spearing in the thigh; see *Minor* at 195-6. I return to this case below.) Failing to carry out such punishments can mean a dispute not being "closed off", and thus perpetuate the conflict and sense of injustice felt by the victim, the families involved, and the community as a whole. Many of these practices, and

argued, on appeal, that the sentence was in error for (among other reasons) taking into consideration the relevance of Aboriginal law in calculating the respondent's release date. Furthermore, there was some question as to whether "payback" itself could even be considered lawful activity.

Now there are two important issues at stake in *Minor* (at least for our purposes); (a) that the release date was fixed with reference to the interests of the wrong community (i.e. the defendant's rather than the "community at large"),[29] and (b) that the form of punishment—"payback"—involved the court in sanctioning *unlawful* activity. So again, the conflict is between two bodies of law in one political community, and we can see further how this can involve competing, or at least very different, conceptions of punishment.

---

certainly the beliefs underpinning them, continue to be relevant in a number of Aboriginal communities today. Perhaps the most controversial of these has been spearing. This involves the offender being speared in the thigh or leg, though in a non-lethal, and more often than not, symbolic fashion. It has been made even more controversial given the fact that customary law does not always recognise that it is only the offender who should be punished, but sometimes the various kin relations as well. Thus blame and responsibility are distributed differently than in European systems. Some of these elements appear to violate the principles and spirit of the general criminal law, as well as aspects of the United Nations Declaration of Human Rights. Spearing might also simply be considered a form of torture, and thus condemnable whatever the cultural circumstances. I cannot consider this fully here. However, spearing is a form of punishment and not, strictly speaking, part of an initiation rite or ceremony required of all community members, or applicable exclusively to one sex (as in the case of cliterodectomy, for example). Nor is it meant to disable the offender permanently or cause grievous harm. The circumstances of it occurring are, rather, regulated and mediated by communal processes which include both the victim and the offender—the latter, admittedly, usually in light of social opinion and pressure. It is also striking the extent to which "traditional" punishments are subject to negotiation and modification given the specific circumstances. Spearing (and other modes of punishment, such as banishment) is justified as being a more appropriate punishment (in some but not all circumstances) compared to the "European" alternatives, namely imprisonment. This seems a reasonable given the importance Aboriginal people place upon the socialising and (re)integrative effects of clan and/or kin networks, and the vast over-representation of Aboriginal people in Australian prisons. The *explicit* toleration (or recognition) of non-lethal spearing is, however, a perplexing issue from a non-Aboriginal perspective. According to the common law, consent does not make deliberate woundings or beatings lawful, and indeed was rejected as a defence in one case concerning such a payback (see *Mamarika* v. *The Queen* (1982) 42 ALR 94). And yet the practice of Australian police and prosecution services has been to take into consideration the voluntary nature of these punishments when deciding whether prosecution is warranted—which has, in fact, been extremely rare. On Aboriginal conceptions of punishment generally, see D. Bird Rose, *Dingo Makes us Human* (Melbourne: Cambridge University Press, 1992), at pp. 153-64; *The Recognition of Aboriginal Customary Law*, 2 vols (Australian Law Reform Commission, 1986), at pp. 287, 364-8, 372-3, with detailed case studies at 351-9; K. Maddock, "Two Laws in One Community" in R. M. Berndt (ed.), *Aborigines and Change* (Canberra, AIAS, 1977); N. Williams, *Two Laws: managing disputes in a contemporary Aboriginal community* (Canberra, 1987); *Royal Commission into Deaths in Custody: Three Years On* (Canberra, 1995), at pp. 148-78; see the interviews with Aboriginal Legal Aid lawyers in J. Faine, *Lawyers in the Alice: Aboriginals and Whitefellas' Law* (Sydney, Federation Press, 1993). See *Minor* at 193-5. On the over-representation of Aboriginal people in prisons, and their relationship to the criminal law generally, see *Royal Commission into Aboriginal Deaths in Custody*, 5 vols (Canberra, 1991).

[29] *Minor*, n. 27 above, at 191.

4. A COMMUNICATIVE THEORY OF PUNISHMENT

How does a political theory of punishment that aspires to meet the justificatory demands of transparent communication cope with such deep diversity? Before we can tackle this question, we need to examine the basic framework of a communicative theory of punishment.

A communicative theory of punishment appears to combine two distinctive and yet usually opposed values.

1. A strong *Kantian* commitment to respect for individuals as rational moral agents. Thus it is invoked against consequentialist theories which allow for the utility or instrumental value of punishing individuals for the sake of promoting some overarching good. According to the communicative theory, individuals must be treated as agents to whom reasons must be given and from whom assent should be sought. Law is not a set of rules simply imposed on a community, but instead "addressed" to it on the basis of values held in common.[30]

2. A *communitarian* thesis about the content of individual citizens' conceptions of the good. Individuals are perceived as being constituted, in part, by their relations with others and various social institutions and practices. That is, these social relationships help constitute the moral identity of an individual and his conception of the good. Individual goods depend on this social framework, and thus on certain communal goods generally which enable and help maintain these social relations. Note that insofar as individuals realise the importance of such a common framework and thus have good reason to foster and help maintain it, they might seek (through political and social action) to shape and change it. Of course this too is often a collective enterprise.

It follows that those norms and values which are central to the framework of the community will occupy a key position in the justification of the domain and scope of the criminal law. Aside from the protection of important individual interests, it will include consideration of the social impact of various forms of conduct; the harm done to fellow citizens, to the values of the community, and (given the communitarian thesis) to the agent's *own good*. Crime involves a breach of these different relationships. The criminal separates himself from the community, his fellow citizens, and thus an important source of his own self-understanding and good.

If punishment can be justified, then it must be justified in terms acceptable to a rational moral agent who is a member of a community which partly constitutes his moral identity and self-understanding. Furthermore, the purpose of punishment will be to repair and restore what the crime has damaged, and not to deliver the criminal's "just deserts", express revenge, or be a means of promoting some other socially worthwhile end. Instead, given the conjunction between a Kantian respect for autonomy and a communitarian thesis about the

---

[30] R. Cotterrell, *Law's Community* (Oxford, Oxford University Press, 1995).

source of citizens' self-understanding, punishment becomes a *mode of communication* with a responsible moral agent who has—for various reasons—fallen astray of his community, his fellow citizens, and himself.

In what sense can punishment be conceived of as communicative? Mainly, it seems, in terms of its purpose. The purpose of punishment is to repair or restore what the crime has damaged.[31] Duff writes of the aim of punishment being to reconcile the moral breach opened up between the criminal, his community, and his own good. Punishment communicates insofar as it brings the offender to understand and repent the wrong he has done. It directs attention to the moral wrongness of the act.[32] Punishment censures, but it doesn't merely *express* censure; it (should, ideally) constitute a penance,[33] focusing attention on the wrongdoing and thus inducing and reinforcing a *re*pentant understanding of the act.

Punishment is necessary, and still merits being delivered in certain cases as "hard treatment", for two reasons: first, because of the kind of beings we are; "unwilling to face up to our wrong-doings, even when we are ourselves committed . . . to the values which we have flouted". A self-imposed penance, or that imposed by others, helps check the "powerful temptation to evade the issue by self-deceptive excuses or justifications".[34] Secondly, because if we take the common values and norms of our community seriously, then we must be prepared to criticise, condemn, and censure breaches of them. Such censure, communicated through hard treatment, is justified because its purpose is reparation, reconciliation, and rehabilitation. These communicative aims are best pursued through communicative punishments.[35] Of course, this suggests the theory will favour certain kinds of punishments (such as community orders, mediation schemes and the like) over others (such as incarceration; though imprisonment

[31] Duff, "Penal Communications", n. 1 above, at 48.

[32] *Ibid.*, at 52.

[33] The language is Duff's; a penance is defined as: "a painful imposition which expresses and symbolizes the painful remorse which the wrong-doer does or should feel"; see Duff, n. 6 above, at 788.

[34] *Ibid.*, at 787–8.

[35] I remain wary of this aspect of the theory; is hard treatment really compatible with an essentially communicative justification of punishment? If hard treatment is ineffective at deterring criminals, and if a consequentialist justification of hard treatment fails because it justifies treating individuals (sometimes) as less than rational moral agents, then why should we believe hard treatment will be any better as a mode of communication? And if communication is our goal, then why bother with punishment at all? Why not redescribe the issue as one of "solving communication conflicts" or "social problems". Duff addresses these challenges directly, arguing that a community must uphold certain basic values and thus recognise and censure breaches of those values, especially ones involving "serious victimising wrongs" ("Penal Communications", n. 1 above, at 74–87). Taking moral wrongs against the community seriously, even when we have reparation, reconciliation, and rehabilitation as our goals, does not mean abandoning punitive measures but adopting "communicative punishments". Inflicting hard treatment is thus compatible with the goals of communicative punishment (see especially *ibid.*, at 82-3). Duff argues that the issue is really one of reconceptualising—rather than abandoning—our understanding of punishment. I wonder about the extent to which such a reconceptualisation doesn't become, in fact, a demand for a different concept altogether. I am grateful to John Braithwaite for pushing me on this issue, and for his patience in discussing his own important work in this area.

is not ruled out by communicative theorists). It is meant as a critical ideal *against* which the (generally abominable) way in which offenders are treated today is meant to be judged, and not a justification of those practices.

So much for a rough sketch of the communicative theory. There are two key elements we need to be clear about: first, *the critical role of the communitarian thesis*. Individuals find their good in the context of a community. Communities are, in part, defined by a set of shared norms and values which need to be promoted and protected—as public goods—in order to enhance the social framework within which individuals develop and revise their own conceptions of the good. Citizens are members of a moral community, and insofar as this context is crucial for the development of their own identity and good, they have a duty to uphold this social and co-operative framework, for example, by obeying laws whose purpose is (genuinely) to promote and enhance fundamental collective and individual interests.[36] Punishment then, will be justified only when it involves censuring conduct which offends against these basic values, and where this process of censuring is essentially communicative, that is, where its purpose is to persuade the offender to get to grips with the wrongness of his action and to reintegrate himself into the community from which he has been separated.

The second key element is *the internal connection between community, communication, and punishment*. Given the Kantian insistence on treating individuals as rational moral beings, and thus as individuals who should come to understand and accept conceptions of the right and the good as autonomously as possible (where autonomy is a matter of degree, given the communitarian thesis), political modes of communication will have to be *transparent*. Punishment, understood as a mode of communication, is no different. It should bring the offender to understand and repent the wrong he has done, and thus rehabilitate and reconcile him to the community from which he has separated himself. In other words, punishment should be non-manipulative (but not necessarily non-coercive), and in keeping with treating the individual as a rational moral agent. What is being communicated? That the offender's conduct is inconsistent with certain fundamental values and norms of the community of which he is a member. The crucial connection is between the transparency of the communication and its content; i.e. the common values and norms which are

---

[36] If we are morally obliged to obey the laws of the political community of which we are a member, it doesn't mean that such obligations are rationally inescapable; no theory of obligation seems able to offer such an account, and there are good reasons to think none ever could. Political obligation follows from the communitarian thesis above, it seems, because we are obeying laws (including the criminal law) whose purpose is to maintain and enhance a social framework indispensable to important individual and communal goods. The obligation is thus owed to our fellow citizens and, it follows, to the institutions we establish in the name of upholding and maintaining such a community. Of course, it doesn't follow that a community couldn't pass unjust laws (i.e. ones which do not serve the "proper" ends—in this case, the communicative ends—of the criminal law) or that individual non-conformists wouldn't be justified in rejecting the dictates of a law or set of laws with which they disagreed. (Conversely, the mere existence of disagreement with a law or set of laws doesn't automatically undermine the obligatoriness of that law.)

said to bind individuals together such that the offence can be identified, the censure delivered, and thus the penance induced.[37]

At this point, however, the combination of communitarian and Kantian values becomes problematic.[38] On the one hand, a thoroughly communitarian communicative account of punishment might hold that the accused deserves to be offered appropriate reasons because he is entitled to such treatment as a member of that community. The appropriate reasons, in other words, would be relative to his standing in that community. According to a more Kantian account of punishment, on the other hand, the status of the accused is tied strictly to him deserving equal respect as a rational moral being, rather than to membership of a particular community. These Kantian and communitarian demands need not conflict, but they can. For them not to, the norms and values of a particular community of which one is a member must be consistent with the Kantian demand that everyone is deserving of equal respect. But there are diverse ways in which the demand for equal respect can be met. What counts as reasonable will depend, in part, on social practice and the particular circumstances of a political community. Can a balance be struck, in these instances, between the particular practices of a community and the universal demand for treating others with equal respect?

5. Communicative Theory and the Challenge of the Intercultural Context

Let us return to the intercultural context outlined in section 3. Remember there I identified the challenge I thought it might present to any communitarian theory: namely, if more than one source of law is said to exist within a polity, then to what extent are we still considering a single political community? In what sense are we still able to talk about fundamental values and norms as being *shared* between citizens? This is crucial for the communicative theory of punishment, for if we cannot show that a community of citizens share a set of fundamental norms and values, then it is not clear exactly what is being communicated to the offender via the "communicative punishments" carried out in the name of the community. This affects the claim about transparency, since individuals must understand (or come to understand) why it is they are being punished in order to be capable of sincere repentance and thus reconciliation and rehabilitation. If the norms and values in the name of which the (communicative) punishments are carried out are not norms or values the offender

---

[37] Duff distinguishes between "coercion by good and relevant reasons" and "the kind of coercion which aims simply to induce assent by whatever means may be effective". Note, however, that just because the justification for punishment is transparent, it doesn't follow that the offender will necessarily think it appropriate or just. I might be perfectly clear as to why you are punishing me but still think those reasons to be completely inappropriate, or indeed failing to "communicate" with me.

[38] I am grateful to discussions with Matt Matravers and Simon Caney on this point.

shares, or cannot be shown to be ones he *should* share, then communication becomes, if not blocked, then at the very least, scrambled.

The basic challenge is that given (what I have called) a Kantian insistence on treating persons as rational and autonomous moral beings, and a communitarian thesis about the source of people's self-understanding and conceptions of value, can the theory do with anything less than a very "thick" communitarian theory of shared beliefs and values? If it cannot, then the theory—despite all of its promise and appeal—is the worse for it, since contemporary political communities are becoming more diverse, not less. If it can, then just how "thin" can the communitarian thesis become before the communicative element is fatally undermined?

Note that the intercultural example is not meant as analogous to the philosophical problem of generating moral norms from scratch, or to the challenge presented by principled moral (and immoral) non-conformists. These examples assume that the problem is to generate some set of moral norms, and thus moral obligations, *ex nihilo*, usually by appeal to a story of rational bootstrapping (*a là* Hobbes or Hume). Our example is very different. The former is the problem of the relative absence of rationally inescapable principles of morality, the latter with the relative abundance of modes of moral understanding and commitment. Hence the problem of the nature of the community (and its norms and values) to which citizens are said to belong. Aboriginal people don't lack the concept of a moral community—or indeed of punishment—rather they have different conceptions of them. Assimilation, for example, was often justified precisely in terms of reintegrating and "rehabilitating" Aboriginal people into a proper moral and political community. From an Aboriginal perspective, the imposition of the common law and English legal norms in the Americas and Australasia was seen as the imposition of an alien system of legal norms meant to coerce them (if hardly induce, via rational persuasion) into membership of a literally foreign political community.[39]

These points are meant to press against the underlying conceptions of community in communicative theories of punishment. Now obviously the communitarian thesis, teamed as it is with a Kantian respect for individual autonomy,

---

[39] *A fortiori* it undermined the social basis of self-respect constituted by membership in a community, a good the communicative theory is particularly keen to recognise and protect. Assimilation, of course, is not a good example of the kind of reintegration sought by communicative modes of punishment. But it is part of the historical context which any justification of legal doctrine (or theory of punishment) runs up against in the intercultural contexts I have mentioned. I leave undeveloped the complex relation between historical context and philosophical justification. For an excellent discussion of the competing conceptions of historical time between indigenous and "settler" populations see P. McHugh "Crown-Tribe Relation: Contractualism and Co-existence in an Inter-cultural Context", in G. Davis *et al.* (eds.), *The New Contractualism?* (Melbourne, MacMillan, 1997), pp. 198-216; J. G. A. Pocock, "Tangata Whenua and Enlightenment Anthropology", (1992) 26 *New Zealand Journal of History* 28-53; Joseph Carens, "Complex Justice, Cultural Difference, and Political Community" in D. Miller and M. Walzer (eds.), *Pluralism, Justice and Equality* (Oxford, Clarendon Press, 1995), pp. 45-66; cf. J. Waldron, "Superseding Historic Injustice", (1992) 103 *Ethics* 4-28.

can tolerate some slack, some level of dissent and disagreement about values; for example, about:

> "fundamental or structural features of a community's life (as between capitalist and socialist ideals) . . . the precise meaning and implications of values . . . about values which are more fundamentally controversial [e.g. the institution of private property] . . . about how much the law should demand of us, and what its scope should be . . . about the proper aims of criminal punishment. In all these ways a citizen might find himself at odds with the laws of his community; and he may see moral reason to break those laws, either because they are themselves . . . immoral, or because their breach is, he thinks, a legitimate tactic of dissent or resistance; we cannot, I think, show that such disobedience is always irrational".[40]

Furthermore, a premium is placed on individuals coming to understand for *themselves* whatever values do structure a community—on "an autonomous and authentic allegiance" to these values. So there is no question of simply imposing some conception of the good or right, since "manipulative modes of persuasion or coercion" produce assent which is neither authentic or autonomous.[41] However this seems to be about identifying the plausible limits of community—of "principled non-conformism"—and about the need to allow as much scope as possible for disobedience (for example, by limiting the scope of the criminal law), rather than about the values actually constitutive of a particular community. And it is precisely this which is at issue in the intercultural case.

As I have tried to show, the two basic claims at the heart of the communicative theory are a Kantian principle of respect for individual autonomy, and a communitarian thesis about the sources of the self. These form the crucial background to the conception of community at work. But we need to know more. Turning to our example, would a political community constituted by different conceptions of law, and thus of punishment, be compatible with the goals of a communicative theory of punishment? It depends on the values constituting that community. If, for example, Aboriginal law was recognised as a genuine source of law, then one manifestation of a community's commitment to respecting individual autonomy and a communitarian thesis about the sources of individuals' self-understanding, might entail granting a significant degree of jurisdiction to that body of law. This commitment might also entail granting that conceptions (and modes) of punishment within this domain will not necessarily mirror those in other domains. Thus when someone is said to have offended against the fundamental interests or values of the community (triggering the need for censure and thus communicative modes of punishment), a prior question would have to be answered; against which community? And members of the different communities would have to be willing to accept the diversity of modes of justification and punishment as representative of different, but equal

---

[40] Duff, n. 6 above, at 790.
[41] *Ibid.*

and legitimate, expressions of membership to the same deeply diverse polity. A genuinely "postcolonial" community would be one in which such conceptions were not ruled out *a priori* as falling outside some predetermined set of common norms and values. This prefigures a very different conception of sovereignty and the state; one of different but co-ordinate internal sovereignties,[42] or as Patton has put it, a state which is "no longer a unique locus of sovereign power, but a space of negotiation and accommodation between two or more bodies of law".[43]

But if the values are sufficiently rich and diverse enough to accommodate Aboriginal claims, don't they present problems for the communicative force of the justification of punishment? To a certain extent, this is what Mason CJ and the Northern Territory court were struggling with in the cases discussed above. Remember that Mason talked about the impossibility of there being two bodies of law applicable in one territory because they might impose conflicting demands on an individual, as well as violate the principle of equality before the law. This is not only a claim about the nature of equality, but about a particular conception of moral and political community. For there obviously can be two bodies of law in a single territory as long as there is some agreed rule or procedure to determine what happens in the event of a conflict (as occurs, in fact, in federal and confederal systems). But Mason's point is an important one in the context of a communicative theory of punishment. Is the "violence" that might be sanctioned by a court in allowing Aboriginal "payback" an offence against the fundamental values of a political community aligned with the principles of Anglo-Australian law? In *Minor*, was the fixing of a release date with reference to the Aboriginal community to which the respondent belonged misplaced, insofar as it ignored the interests of the "community at large"?[44] We might see

---

[42] See Ivison, n. 17 above. Pocock writes of a partnership between distinct "layers of sovereignty" as constituting a fundamental rethinking of nation states such as New Zealand, Canada, and Australia; see "A discourse of sovereignty", in N. Philippson and Q. Skinner (eds.), *Political discourse in early modern Britain* (Cambridge, Cambridge University Press, 1993), p. 420.

[43] Paul Patton, "Aboriginal or Indigenous Sovereignty", unpublished paper, at p. 12. Another way to consider the pluralism of contemporary political communities might be to emphasise the democratic possibilities at hand. Thus, the fundamental values and interests of a community might be judged according to their democratic pedigree—whether arrived at and percolated through a robust democratic filter, and hence contestable and subject to revision. This raises interesting and complex issues in relation to intercultural contexts. Aboriginal people have only received the right to vote in the last 20 years. Some of the most abhorrent and destructive policies concerning land rights, education, and social welfare have been carried out with apparently strong "democratic" backing. This has occurred partly because of the under-representation of Aboriginal voices in policy-making forums, a situation often made worse by the majoritarian tendencies of many Western democracies. Of course, more positive and progressive democratic possibilities also exist. The vision of a democratic community outlined by Lacey is an attractive one (n. 1 above, at p. 176). The pursuit of a "common, if diffused social good, which all citizens have reasons to uphold and to the formation of which all citizens have a real chance to contribute" (*ibid.*, at p. 177) restates the challenge of identifying what constitutes *common* yet at the same time *diffused* social good(s) which all citizens—in a multinational and multicultural political community—can identify with and have equal opportunity to contribute to. See also I. Shapiro, *Democracy's Place* (Ithaca and London, Cornell University Press, 1996).

[44] *Minor*, n. 27 above, at 191.

each as representing a dilemma of communication; the offender in each instance receiving mixed signals from different communities, and thus the mode of punishment (either as sought in *Walker*, or as proposed in *Minor*) failing the communicative test. In other words, that the persuasive force of the mode of punishment is anything but transparent, and in danger of slipping from persuasion to coercion by means other than "good and relevant reasons".[45]

There might be resources, however, within the communicative approach which are useful in such complex intercultural circumstances. Duff mentions the importance of the "context of communication"; that is, the "appropriate communication with the particular offender".[46] This is crucial not only for communicating the censure the crime deserves, but to help bring the offender to understand and accept the wrongness of his action. Could this be extended in the direction of the deeply diverse ways in which citizens might understand their membership in a "postcolonial" political community? Could non-Aboriginal citizens accept an often radically different "context of communication" in recognising Aboriginal law as a relevant source of law? Could Aboriginal people accept the limits to their "law ways" which come not only with the rapidly changing nature of the world in which their laws now exist, but with trying to co-ordinate their varying forms of self-government with others in a social and political space of "accommodation and negotiation"?

It is instructive, I think, to turn back briefly to the discussion of Aboriginal punishment by Mildren J in *Minor*. This is a sensitive and extremely interesting judgment in light of the discussion above. He identifies very clearly that this is a case in which reference is being made to two distinct bodies of law in one territory, though obviously from the perspective of a judge charged under one body of law to pass judgment on the other. But Mildren argues:

> "[t]his was no occasion for blindly following an unthinking conservative path; it required, as this Court often has in the past been called upon to do when dealing with the approach to Aboriginals and the criminal law, to find a solution by means which ensured that justice was done, even if the means adopted were unusual or novel. I reject, therefore, the submission that the release date was fixed by reference to an extraneous circumstance, or for that matter, that undue emphasis was given to the interests of the Hermannsburg community [i.e. the Aboriginal community]".[47]

The matter, of course, was decided in an "Australian" court according to "Australian" criminal law, and thus might seem to render the question of any effective alternative body of law (or "coordinate sovereignty") moot. But this is much too simplistic an analysis of the competing conceptions of community (and sovereignty) at play, for it suggests that the question is either/or; *either* separate communities (based on separate sovereignties and separate laws), *or* one subsumed under (or assimilated to) the other. This not only misdescribes

---

[45] Duff, n. 6 above, at 792.
[46] Duff, "Penal Communications", n. 1 above, at 61.
[47] *Minor*, n. 27 above, at 197.

the complex overlapping nature of the history of relations between Aboriginal and non-Aboriginal people and systems (who have, after all, interacted for centuries), but overlooks the possibilities of alternative arrangements based on different conceptions of sovereignty and community.[48] Note that liberal political theorists worry that granting self-government rights might entail tolerating non-liberal norms and practices. Thus, self-government is acceptable, but only if compatible with generally liberal norms. This is a difficult issue which deserves more attention than I can give it here. But I shall make three points. First, a banal but important point; self-government does not *necessarily* entail the violation of civil and political rights, as if the analogy is with that of the "absolute" sovereignty of a nation state.[49] That view of sovereignty is dubious anyway, whether applied to Aboriginal or any other political community. The political forms of Aboriginal self-determination will emerge in relation to the diverse traditions and practices of Aboriginal people who, though obviously not insulated from Western conceptions and practices of government, are distinct from them. Secondly, the goods which are promoted and served by liberal rights are themselves realised in a myriad of ways within the liberal tradition itself. So it does not follow from a concern with individual rights that Aboriginal self-government should be presumptively suspect. A concern for civic participation, freedom of speech, or gender equity generates constraints on both non-Aboriginal and Aboriginal governments. But the manner in which these constraints are instantiated will vary with relation to Aboriginal institutions, just as they vary with regard to non-Aboriginal institutions (as for example between different provinces in Canada, or between Scotland and England in the United Kingdom). The evolving international law of indigenous peoples—in which Aboriginal people themselves are playing a large part—constitutes another source of constraint. Furthermore, some Aboriginal communities might in fact *choose* to be ruled by, for example, Canadian or Australian law in certain domains, and Aboriginal law in others. (Equally, non-Aboriginal people might choose to be ruled by Aboriginal norms or laws in certain domains.) Thirdly, the issue cannot be summarised as a straight-forward clash between collective and individual rights. As we have seen, a significant strand of liberal political theory accepts the importance of communal and collective goods as being intrinsically related to individual well-being. This is often reflected in the way basic rights are situated in particular constitutional contexts which allow for a variety of interpretations and expressions (as in the case of Canada's Charter of

---

[48] See the nuanced discussion in J. Tully, *Strange Multiplicity: constitutionalism in an age of diversity* (Cambridge, Cambridge University Press, 1995). For an interesting discussion of the different ways in which self-government arrangements might emerge, and the constraints and limits they might be subject to, see *Aboriginal Peoples and the Justice System* (Ottawa, Ministry of Supply and Services Canada, 1993).

[49] For a helpful discussion from an aboriginal perspective see M. Boldt and J. A. Long, "Tribal Traditions and European-Western Political Ideologies: The Dilemma of Canada's Native Indians", in M. Boldt and J. A. Lond (eds.), *The Quest for Justice: Aboriginal Peoples and Aboriginal Rights* (Toronto, University of Toronto Press, 1985), pp. 333-46.

Rights and Freedoms, to a certain extent). Now there are important senses in which some Aboriginal interests *are* best understood in communal rather than individualistic terms (for example, given the distinctive relation to land or "country"). And this might require some form of recognition or protection in terms of a collective right. But not every interest or good sought by Aboriginal communities will take this form.[50] There are important issues here to do with different conceptions of equality, but these are not reducible in every instance to a *conflict* between individual and collective rights.[51] A collective right to land, for example, is justified often in terms of not only protecting the particular relationship indigenous people have to their land, but also in terms of contributing to the capacity for individuals to lead meaningful lives.

But I cannot conclude an essay on punishment sounding so sanguine. When confronted with the possibility that the communicative purpose of punishment might escape the offender—that he might remain unpersuaded as to the need to repent and modify his conduct (other than for instrumental or prudential reasons)—Duff writes:

> "I must still aim, however despairingly, to transparently persuade you rather than to manipulate you. And, second, the fact that you might treat my forcible criticisms simply as providing a prudential reason for modifying your future conduct does not mean that in pressing them on you I am manipulating you; how you respond to my criticism is up to you; so long as my criticism is both in intention and in character aimed at and apt for transparent persuasion it accords you the respect which is your due".[52]

On one level, this is an admirable claim. No matter how much we might despair of the unconvinced (and thus unrepentant) criminal—whether principled, pathological, or amoral—we still owe it to them, as rational and moral beings, to accord them the respect of justifying their punishment in communicative terms. But on another level, it disconcerts. For it suggests that we can insulate ourselves from the moral discomfort of punishment, by fulfilling certain justificatory conditions so as to locate ourselves somehow beyond moral reproach. But the etiology of human will and desire is such a dense network of competing and contrasting influences and contexts, that to think a singular theory could extract us from the murky ambiguities of punishment might be thought of as a kind of conceptual violence itself. Communication and punishment just do not sit comfortably together. The latter is always in danger of being corrupted by the intrusion of desires for revenge or resentment, often fueled and borne by cultural and social markers of race, gender, and class, and by historical contexts

---

[50] Of course there will be conflicts; see M. E. Turpel, "Home/land", (1996) 10 *Canadian Journal of Family Law* 17-40; and R. Ross, *Returning to the Teachings: Exploring Aboriginal Justice* (London, Penguin, 1996).

[51] For example, does equality before the law require a *prima facie* rejection of all race-conscious distinctions (save for "temporary special measures"), or might a more contextualised understanding allow for concepts such as "native title" to be taken as compatible with a commitment to substantive equality?

[52] Duff, n. 6 above, at 792.

difficult to contain and transcend. The way in which the history of relations between Aboriginal and "settler" communities continues to condition and affect Aboriginal and non-Aboriginal attitudes towards criminal responsibility and punishment is a palpable example of this. The fact that it is so difficult to insulate the demand for punishment from such contexts is not, however, simply a counsel for despair. Rather, it provides an additional source of constraint on our modes of punishing; the constraint that comes from recognising the inherently ambiguous nature of our desire to punish. It should check our justificatory self-satisfaction at having punished someone (we reassure ourselves) for the sake of their own good. It should keep pushing the argument about punishment to go on, long after we think everything has been said and done.

6

"What to say?": The Communicative Element in Punishment and Moral Theory

MATT MATRAVERS

"The criminal law and the criminal trial are, like moral criticism, communicative enterprises which seek the assent and the participation of those whom they address: the law seeks the allegiance of the citizen as a rational moral agent, by appealing to the relevant moral reasons which justify its demands; the trial seeks to engage the defendant in a rational dialogue about the justice of the charge which she faces, and to persuade her—if that charge is proved against her—to accept and make her own the condemnation which the conviction expresses."[1]

"Judges are subject to the . . . debilitating psychological consequences of skepticism no less than the rest of us. The institutional role may even intensify these effects, for judges not only make value judgements, but also must impose them on other people. If one's daily task is to impose values on others, to think that these are only one's own personal values doubtlessly makes the job hard to perform at all."[2]

1. INTRODUCTION

A premise of this chapter is that punishment (in response to criminal wrongdoing) has some communicative element. That is not to endorse an account of punishment as having the transmission of censure or of any other communication as its general justifying aim. It is just to assume that the criminal justice system—the system of having laws, trials, and punishments—has as one of its central functions the task of expressing to the accused that (if he is found to be guilty) he is guilty of some wrongdoing and that that wrongdoing is of the type that deserves, and is appropriately responded to by, censure.[3] Accepting this

---

[1] R. A. Duff, *Trials and Punishments* (Cambridge, Cambridge University Press, 1986), at p. 233.
[2] M. Moore, "Moral Reality", (1982) *Wisconsin Law Review* 1061–1156 at 1064.
[3] The idea that punishment has an expressive element is most famously presented in J. Feinberg, "The Expressive Function of Punishment", (1965) 49 *The Monist* 397–423. The contemporary penal philosopher most closely associated with a "censure" view of punishment is Antony Duff (see n. 1 above and his chapter in this volume). Herbert Hart in *Punishment and Responsibility* (Oxford,

raises two questions. First, what is it that is said to the offender? Secondly, what kind of failure on the part of the offender is the appropriate subject of the communication?

The first of these questions is straightforward to understand, but difficult to answer. If punishment is to communicate something then there needs to be an account of what is to be said. Amongst those who make use of the idea of punishment as some form of communication,[4] those of the expressive and denunciatory schools tend to emphasise its role in giving voice to the abhorrence of the community. More genuine communicative (as against expressivist) theorists focus on the idea that something, some form of argument, is offered to the offender to explain that she has done *wrong* and to challenge her to answer that claim. The consensus on what is to be said is that the defendant should be condemned (if found guilty) for doing wrong and offered reasons that explain the wrongness of her conduct.

However, this is problematic for, as the quotation from Michael Moore offered at the beginning of the chapter indicates, there has been a loss of confidence (at least amongst some people) about what is wrong, and about the *status* of judgements of right and wrong. Part of this loss of confidence can be explained by what is sometimes called the argument from diversity. People differ both in their views of what kinds of things are right and what wrong, and in what they believe to be the status of moral judgements. This problem becomes particularly acute when such judgements are made by one person (or one group of persons) and applied to another (or another group) with different beliefs. Even if there are no normative or meta-ethical conclusions to be drawn from this fact of diversity, the mere existence of different moral understandings raises a *prima facie* problem for the communicative account. For it is important that the judge and the law speaks for a community (that is, they give voice to values that are *shared*) and that their language is at best that of the offender, at worst comprehensible to him. It is important that the offender can "hear" what is being said.

Although this is a significant problem it is not the primary concern of this chapter.[5] Rather, the central focus is on those who establish the laws and in whose name punishment is carried out. For this group punishment is ordinarily taken to be problematic because it involves the deliberate infliction of suffering; typically the doing to someone of things that if done to them in other circumstances would violate their most significant rights. Conceiving of punishment as having a communicative purpose adds a different problem. This is because it

---

Clarendon Press, 1968) at pp. 169–70 finds historical antecedents of the communicative view in the denunciatory theory of James Fitzjames Stephen.

[4] I shall refer to theories of punishment that include an essential communicative element as "theories of communicative punishment", although it should be remembered that this group is not limited to those theories in which the communicative element is the basis for the general justifying aim of punishment.

[5] It is discussed in Duncan Ivison's chapter in this volume, see Chapter 5 above.

emphasises the condemning of what the offender did as wrong. It is this feature of punishment to which Moore draws attention in the quotation at the beginning of this chapter. What we think about communicating a judgement through punishment is likely to be profoundly affected by what we believe to be the status of the judgement that we are making. Included, then, in the question, "What is to be said?" is consideration of both the *content* of morality and of its *status*. Of course, this problem only affects those who lack confidence in their moral judgements. Clerical courts that hand down punishments on the basis of the revealed word of some God are unlikely to be troubled by having to condemn offenders for wrongdoing. However, it may be that they should be so troubled, for it may be that their ethical beliefs are false.

The second question—what kind of failure on the part of the offender is the appropriate subject of the communication?—is apparently less straightforward. The point is this: on a communicative account the offender is offered reasons not merely for the conduct she performed being wrong, but for why it is that she should not have acted that way (for why its being wrong should matter to her). After all, the reaction from the offender, "Ah, so it is wrong to do what I did. Gee, it's bad that some wrong thing happened" is hardly satisfactory. Moreover, moral propositions are thought not merely to connect to motivation, but to do so with imperatival force. For many people it is an essential characteristic of moral reasons that in all but exceptional circumstances they trump prudential ones.[6] So, the response, "I agree that it is wrong to do what I did, but if it is in my interests and I could get away with it then its being wrong wouldn't really matter to me" is also unsatisfactory. What is desired (on the part of those doing the punishing) is that the offender should appreciate that she did something wrong and that this is some kind of failure on her part. A model offender should reflect on her conduct in the light of what is said to her. What the second question draws attention to is the way in which the penal communication should seek to direct such self-reflection.

These two questions recognisably overlap with ethical and meta-ethical questions concerning the content and status of morality and moral motivation. This chapter is an unambitious one. It tries to pose two questions and to offer only tentative answers to both. The first concerns whether in order to defend a plausible theory of punishment that includes a substantive communicative element—that can answer the two questions posed above—one needs first to address basic ethical and meta-ethical questions concerning the nature, content, and scope of justified moral beliefs. In sections 2 and 3 arguments for a negative answer to this question are considered and rejected. If the answer to this question is "yes", it raises a second. This second question concerns how different answers to basic ethical and meta-ethical questions affect the communicative account of punishment. This is addressed briefly in section 4.

---

[6] In saying this I mean to leave open whether morality provides reasons for action—whether it connects to motivation—in the absence of a connected desire. Such a question is, of course, very important to resolving what kind of failure immoral action is (see section 4).

In brief the underlying theme is this: it would seem that punishment must condemn certain actions as wrong and give reasons for that judgement if it is to have a communicative element. Yet our confidence in our beliefs about right and wrong, and in the status of those beliefs (in the kind of reasons we could offer), has been undermined. This need not worry us if the content of penal communications can be isolated from the moral sphere that is the locus of disenchantment and loss of confidence. If it cannot be so isolated then theorists of communicative punishment must address the loss of confidence directly. How they go about this will have a profound impact on their accounts of punishment. Thus the chapter is neither a defence of theories of communicative punishment nor of any particular meta-ethical position, but is an investigation of the relationship between penal and moral theory.

It is alleged above that a theory of communicative punishment must provide answers to two questions that concern (a) what is to be said and (b) to what those who do the speaking wish to direct the offender's attention. It might be thought that these (or, anyway, similar) questions apply to the whole "penality system".[7] Insofar as laws address citizens and direct, or attempt to direct, the behaviour of citizens we could pose these questions with reference to laws as well as to punishment (and the same will hold for other parts of the penality system). This is surely right. It would be odd if the way in which we condemned an offender did not relate to what we thought to be the message contained in the law that the offender contravened. However, when we look at the penality system as a whole there are many factors that might distort our vision. One advantage of separating out punishment for consideration, then, is simply that if punishment contains a communicative element this presumably concentrates the message and thus allows for closer scrutiny. The requirement to voice to the offender exactly what it is that he has done wrong forces a degree of analysis that reflection on the whole system might not demand so urgently.

However, noting that the two questions posed could be directed to the whole system and not just to the account of punishment suggests a reason for thinking that answering these questions does not require addressing substantive ethical and meta-ethical questions. This is because one might think of the penality system as autonomous, or quasi-autonomous, in the sense that there are reasons internal to the system that can be applied without substantive recourse to other spheres. In this way any disenchantment or uncertainty in ethics could be kept separate from what is needed to develop a successful theory of communicative punishment. One such account might emanate from a version of legal positivism. Another might be pragmatic: punishment should communicate to the offender whatever will work to achieve certain socially desirable goals,

---

[7] I borrow this phrase from David Garland *Punishment in Modern Society: A Study in Social Theory* (Oxford, Clarendon Press, 1990), at p. 10. Garland describes it as "a generic term which usefully describes the whole process of criminalizing and penalizing ... the complex of laws, processes, discourses, and institutions which are involved in this sphere".

specifically the reduction of crime. Finally, it might be thought that all that is needed is the best interpretation of the practices that constitute the law and punishment.

1. Saying What's Lawful, and Saying What Works

As it is undeniable that a convicted offender is condemned for having done something illegal, it would seem that the positivist[8] has strong grounds on which to claim that this is what needs to be communicated and that in answer to the question of motivation what needs to be considered is the offender's obligation to obey the law and *its* place in accounts of motivation. At its crudest such a theory could posit that all that needs to be communicated to the offender is that there are rules; that the rules stipulate that those found guilty of breaking them should suffer some penalty; that the offender has been found guilty of breaking a particular rule; therefore that the offender should suffer the penalty. However, this is surely a *reductio* of positivism. In any case, it hardly meets the requirements that the offender be condemned for doing wrong and that he be given reasons that explain this condemnation. Even on this narrow account one would need some account of the wrongfulness of breaking the law.

Such an account could develop in the way proposed by so-called "fair play" theorists. The suggestion of this school is that the rule of law brings great benefits to those who live within it, but does so only if those who gain from it restrain their behaviour in accordance with its demands. To do otherwise while still enjoying the benefits is to free ride, not to play fair. The details, and the faults, of this account are well known.[9] The essential problems from the perspective of the questions at hand are twofold. First, it is not clear why (even voluntarily) enjoying the benefits of some common scheme imposes a moral duty on one to contribute to that scheme (for this reason fair play theories are often run together with contractualist accounts). So it is not clear that the punishment could communicate to the offender that he has reason to obey the law, or that he has failed in his duty in not doing so. Secondly, and perhaps more significantly, it seems to "distort the essential character of crime"[10] in that in condemning the offender for free-riding it leaves out something significant. When an offender is condemned for murder what is to be said is not that he has free-

---

[8] I am using "positivist" in a very loose sense to cover the attempt to isolate legal from moral reasoning.

[9] For details see (amongst others), H. Morris, "Persons and Punishment", (1968) 52 *The Monist* 475–501; J. G. Murphy, "Marxism and Retribution", (1973) 2 *Philosophy and Public Affairs* 217–43; A. von Hirsch, *Doing Justice: The Choice of Punishments* (New York, Hill and Wang, 1976); W. Sadurski, "Distributive Justice and the Theory of Punishment", (1985) 5 *Oxford Journal of Legal Studies* 47–59; R. Dagger, "Playing Fair With Punishment" (1993) 103 *Ethics* 726–52. For a summary of faults see (again, among others) Duff, *Trials and Punishments*, n. 1 above, ch. 8.

[10] Duff, "Penal Communications: Recent Work in the Philosophy of Punishment", (1996) 20 *Crime and Justice: A Review of Research* 1–97, at 27.

ridden—that he has not done "his part" in sustaining the rule of law through which he and others benefit—but that he has committed murder and that *this*, not free-riding, *is wrong*.

What is wrong with the positivist response, and the fair play variant on it, is that whilst the offender has done something contrary to law he has also, and more importantly, performed an act that is contrary to a particular law; for example, contrary to the law of murder. In prosecuting and passing judgement on the offender what is communicated must include reference to the particular instance of illegality and this surely extends beyond its being a mere token of a general type. It is not that the offender has committed murder, that this is contrary to the law, and that therefore what is to be condemned is the offender's general unlawfulness; rather, the condemnation is for having committed the act of murder (as well as for having disobeyed the law) and if the offender were to ask why committing murder was a bad thing the answer, "because murder is contrary to the law (and doing things contrary to the law is a bad thing)" would not be sufficient. What is needed is an account of *why* murder is prohibited and this would seem to press towards an account of the wrongfulness of murder.

An alternative understanding of the communicative element in punishment looks for a justification for what is said not in the content of the communication, but in its effect. The question of what to say to the offender is answered by asking what will "work"; what will decrease the chances of the punished individual re-offending and deter others from committing offences. Similarly, in addressing the question of motivation the consequentially motivated theorist of communicative punishment looks to the particular individual (or, more likely given the numbers involved, the type of individual or offence) to determine what kind of communication is likely to result in reforming the offender. On such an account, for example, young petty offenders might be dealt with by local tribunals at which they are confronted with their parents, peers, their victims, and so on, so as to "shame" them without alienating them from the community in which they will continue to live.[11]

Although such an account has marked similarities to the picture of communicative accounts of punishment painted in the introduction—the offender is offered a chance of understanding his offence, of seeing the effects of what he has done, of reflecting on his wrongdoing, and so on—the difference is that on this account the ultimate justification for what is said is that it works. If the offender could not, or would not, hear what is said then there would be no point in saying it. The fact of diversity and the loss of confidence in the basis of moral judgements should not, then, affect this theory. Those who impose the judgement of wrongdoing, and who point to some moral failure on the part of the offender, do so in the name of manipulating the offender into a different life, not in the name of the truth or validity of what is being said.

---

[11] I am borrowing from, but not fairly representing, J. Braithwaite, *Crime, Shame and Reintegration* (Cambridge, Cambridge University Press, 1989).

Such an account of the communicative element in punishment is a plausible one and is increasingly fashionable with those who implement the criminal justice system. It also successfully avoids questions of the grounds of moral judgements (at least with respect to punishment theory narrowly conceived). However, it does so at some cost to the understanding of the communicative element in punishment. The consequentialist understanding reduces the role of communication significantly in response to certain kinds of offences. Although the empirical data is still incomplete, preliminary findings suggest that penal communication of this kind works only with particular kinds of offenders and offences.[12] More importantly, this use of the communicative element in punishment is in tension with what it is that drives non-consequentialist communicative theorists. For the latter, what is important in penal communications is that they treat the offender as a being of moral value. Rather than simply impose some hard treatment on the offender he is offered *reasons* for why his conduct is wrongful and the chance to respond to this condemnation. Condemnation is what the offender is *owed* (of course, the condemnation of the wrong might also be something to which the victim and the community at large have claims). This chapter is an investigation of how our different understandings of what those reasons might be affect our understanding of punishment. For the consequentialist this question is beside the point. What matters is whether giving voice to these reasons as opposed to some others works in rehabilitating this offender. Far from being a sign of the respect the offender is owed as a (potentially) moral being, the reasons the offender is offered are simply means of manipulating him, little more than ways of getting him to change his behaviour by making him feel bad.

Finally, it is worth noting that in this account the communicative element in punishment is no different from any other element. For some offenders the best way of reducing the likelihood of their re-offending is to make them suffer imprisonment, for others it is to talk to them in front of their parents. However, in making the communication just another punishment technique the consequentialist ultimately fails to isolate penal from moral theory. Although the consequentialist successfully avoids the need to resolve certain ethical and meta-ethical questions in asking what to say, she merely moves that need to the theory as a whole.

3. The Interpretivist Project

The positivist and consequentialist accounts avoid the questions that are posed at the beginning of this chapter for the proponent of a communicative element

---

[12] See Braithwaite, "Restorative Justice: Assessing an Immodest Theory and a Pessimistic Theory", (forthcoming) *Crime and Justice: A Review of Research*. Of course, this failure will affect all communicative theories. But it is only the consequentialist theory which is measured by success in this respect.

in, or understanding of, punishment, but only by draining from that element its significance as a communication between the offender and the community whose rules he has transgressed. However, this does not yet show that if punishment is to have a communicative function then this will be parasitic on resolving, or offering a particular account of, certain fundamental meta-ethical questions. In part this is because in the face of the diversity mentioned above, the argument might be offered that whilst the law expresses the wrongness of certain acts it does so (or ought to do so) only as a reflection of widespread agreement that those acts are wrong. The important point is that the law reflects and thus communicates a shared moral *conclusion* not a justified account of wrong or of the status of moral judgements. In this way the autonomy of the penality system is sacrificed, but it is still isolated from that part of the ethical most likely to have been affected by disenchantment.

To illustrate this position consider again the example of murder. As noted above, the crude positivist appears committed to the argument that all that is to be communicated to the murderer is that murder is an instance of unlawful behaviour and that unlawful behaviour is wrong. In contrast, someone committed to a particular substantive ethical theory may hold that what is to be communicated is both the fact that the action was wrong and the reasons for its being wrong. The position of the law "shadowing" shared moral conclusions falls between these two. The offender is condemned for the particular wrong, but no further account of the wrongness of the act is offered beyond that it is a widely shared conclusion of moral argument. Each person (or group) has reasons to believe that murder is wrong, but the reasons for different people (or groups) will be different. The existence of these reasons is important and is what makes it proper for the wrongness of the act to be referred to in penal communications, but the content of any or all of these particular reasons is not part of the communication.

Such an account is in one sense a good description of current practice in the diverse contemporary societies under discussion and in another not. The accuracy of the description lies in the claim that there is a diversity of views; an absence of a single compelling moral account of wrong. There is no agreement as to why murder is wrong—some people think it wrong because it is contrary to the word of (their) God; others that it possesses some mind-independent property of wrongness; others that it is a matter of convention; and so on—nor is there agreement on a moral theory of the criminal law. Where the account fails as a description of current practice is in the assumption that there is widespread agreement *in sufficient detail* to allow the law the claim that it shadows shared conclusions of moral debate. There is such agreement on the wrongness of intentional and premeditated killing, but not on what constitutes "intention", "premeditation" and even "killing".[13]

---

[13] I am grateful to Antony Duff for this point. The disagreement over killing may arise because if killing is "causing death" then there is scope for debate about what constitutes both causing and death.

Taken by itself the shadow argument, even in circumstances of detailed agreement, does not seem sufficiently rich to provide answers of the right kind to the questions of what to say and to what failure on the part of the offender to draw attention when engaged in penal communication. In condemning the offender it seems that all that might be said is that his action was wrong and that this is a matter of agreement in the society, although quite why it was wrong or what wrongness means is not something on which there is consensus. As for the motivation question it would seem that the most that could be said is that there is general agreement that something being wrong means that there is (at least *prima facie*) a reason not to do it.

These problems—that even in the most likely cases for consensus there will be insufficiently detailed agreement given the precision with which it is necessary to formulate laws, and that the shadow argument seems too shallow to act as the foundation for an account of penal communications—might be addressed by invoking an "interpretive" argument to supplement the "shadow" argument offered above. "Interpretive" refers to a methodology.[14] The idea is to make "best sense" of our intuitions, convictions and practices. In so doing it may be that certain convictions, or ways of doing things will be found to be inconsistent with others and in such cases the interpretivist must recommend how best to achieve consistency (that is, which convictions or practices to change and which to leave alone in the light of the whole). By examining the ideas, and use, of terms such as intention, responsibility, killing, and so on, the interpretivist might offer an account of, say, murder that is sufficiently detailed to differentiate it from manslaughter and that does least violence to the (more general) intuitions, convictions, and beliefs of the population. Whether such an interpretive procedure can sufficiently enrich the shadow argument so as to make it a plausible basis from which to answer the questions of what to say and what aspect of motivation to appeal to is examined below.

Although interpretivism is compatible with a number of meta-ethical positions its use here would be in avoiding meta-ethics. Recall, the questions that need to be answered if punishment is to have a communicative function are, "what can be said?" (and this question incorporates the question of the status of what is said) and "what failure on the part of the offender ought punishment draw to the offender's attention?". The strategy of this chapter is to claim that if these questions can be answered it is only through addressing and resolving certain meta-ethical questions. The interpretivist disputes this claim. Interpretivism offers an account of what might be called the surface of moral argument. The question is whether the surface is rich enough to provide the communicative theorist with what is needed.

A proponent of the "shadow argument" offers nothing but an account of where there is agreement in a society. Utilitarians, humanists, Christians, and

---

[14] The interpretative method is perhaps most closely associated with the work of Ronald Dworkin (see especially *Law's Empire* (London, Fontana Press, 1986)). That is not to say that what follows is in any way an explication of Dworkin's work or thought.

Muslims (to take some examples) all agree that in most circumstances at least some forms of killing are seriously wrong. In communicating with an offender who has performed such a killing what can be said is that "we all agree that (this kind of) killing is a serious wrong". The agreement provides both the content of the moral judgement and its status (which is nothing more than that this is a matter on which there is agreement). Very little could be said about the way in which the offender has failed in acting wrongly as each group has a different account of motivation. In contrast, the interpretivist is not primarily concerned with the points of agreement between different substantive conceptions of the good. The contrast is important because the interpretivist holds that the matters under consideration in this chapter are matters of first-order substantive moral argument and denies that there is the need for—perhaps denies the possibility of—second-order meta-ethical argument. What the interpretivist needs to provide is an account of the subject matter of the first-order debate.

Determining the subject matter of the interpretive project is more problematic than it might at first appear because if the debate is between, for example, holders of rival theocratic views then the scope for an interpretive resolution is limited. Faced with a discussion between someone who holds that killing apostates is wrong because the Bible places strict restrictions on when it is permissible to violate the sanctity of life and another person who holds that the teaching of Mohammed tells us that apostasy is punishable by death there is little that could be achieved through first-order moral discussion. However, the interpretivist is not committed to regarding all forms of substantive ethical debate as contributing to the interpretive project. Rather, as the name implies, interpretivism concerns itself with differences of account within some given boundary. Two questions then arise: What defines the relevant boundary? And, is an interpretive account of the surface of moral argument within the bounded community sufficiently rich to sustain the communicative element in punishment? The answer to the first question—within what boundary is the relevant interpretive project undertaken?—cannot be too broad, it would seem, for the interpretive project requires more than a kernel of agreement between those who otherwise differ on moral questions. There must be some agreement on what it is that is to be interpreted and how that process is to be undertaken. The interpretivist, as already noted, is not in the business of constructing from nothing but, rather, applies her technique when "members of particular communities who share practices and traditions make and dispute claims about the best interpretation of these".[15] This suggests a narrow and weak reading of the interpretivist project. Narrow, because on such an understanding the boundary is a community that is defined and constituted by certain practices and "social meanings".[16] Weak, because the role of interpretivism is only to assist in making these coherent and to resolve disputes about what is demanded in certain actual situations.

[15] *Ibid.*, at p. 46.
[16] To borrow a phrase from Michael Walzer (see Walzer, *Spheres of Justice* (Oxford, Blackwell, 1983)).

On such an account when communicating with an offender what is said is that the offender's conduct was wrongful according to the best understanding of the standards of the community, and this, too, provides the status of what is said. In addressing the question of motivation, the weak interpretivist is likely to call attention to what it means to be a member of the community. Just as the community is constituted by its traditions and practices so its members are those people who embrace these as in part constitutive of their identity. The precise motivational story, the details of the kind of failure on the part of the offender that is manifested in his offending conduct, will depend on the kind of community under consideration (and the kind of beliefs that constitute it), but the general form may be that the offender has failed in his duty as an X (an Athenian, Maori, etc.). Whether this in fact has any motivational force for the offender will depend on the degree to which membership is important to, or constitutive of, his identity. The weak interpretive argument generates sufficiently rich conclusions for the penal philosopher only if the community whose practices and understandings are being interpreted is itself a rich ethical, relatively homogenous, community.

This weak version of interpretivism is commonly criticised for being something more akin to an anthropological exercise rather than an attempt at moral justification.[17] *Within* particular practices—including that of punishment—it can of course offer justifications for certain acts. So, for example, if punishment is understood by a community as a form of reparation then when punishing a particular offender the judge or community can appeal to this understanding in defending both the distribution of punishment and the quantum of penalty imposed; just as a different community that understands punishment as necessary to placate the Gods might defend a different set of practices in the light of their understanding. It follows that the weak interpretivist can also criticise: as when in a society in which punishment is understood as a response to guilt what actually happens is that it is the poor rather than the guilty who are punished.[18] The difficulty is that the weak interpretivist is dependent on there being a rich, relatively harmonious and homogenous, set of practices in order to generate conclusions that are sufficiently substantial to sustain the communicative element in punishment. What the weak interpretivist can supply is the best account of what is wrong according to the "way things are done round here", and this will matter to the offender only if being from "'round here" is an essential constitutive part of his identity. Weak interpretivism is silent in answer to a question of why things should be done that way.

For many the implicit relativism in weak interpretivism is unacceptable. Even if the interpretivist can find general moral principles and even if these speak to the members of the community through their self-understandings, the weak

---

[17] B. Barry, "Spherical Justice and Global Injustice" in D. Miller and M. Walzer (eds.), *Pluralism, Justice, and Equality* (Oxford, Oxford University Press, 1995) pp. 67–80.

[18] Such criticism is the role of what Walzer calls the "social critic". See Walzer, *The Company of Critics* (New York, Basic Books, 1988).

interpretivist seems committed to the impossibility of intercommunal criticism. What is said in a penal communication might find internal justification in the practices of punishment in a given community, but there is no external standpoint from which the practice itself can be evaluated. Weak interpretivism isolates the sphere of the penality system (as it isolates all spheres), but at the cost of genuine critical engagement.

The point of this and the previous section was to examine whether a theory of communicative punishment could be sustained without having to engage with fundamental ethical and meta-ethical questions. A communicative theory needs to be able to provide satisfactory answers to the questions of what is to be said and of how the communication ought to direct the offender's critical self-evaluation (of why the reasons offered for his conduct being wrong should matter to him). Three positions—no doubt there are more—were examined each of which holds that these questions can be answered in relative isolation from broader ethical questions. This claim cannot be sustained. In what is said above it is suggested that this matters because of the lack of moral confidence that characterises the secular, post-modern, West. In fact, even if one believes that the death of such confidence has been greatly exaggerated the above conclusion still matters. This is because it follows from the above that the full development of any communicative theory will have to offer an account of the content, status, and motivational force of what it seeks to communicate. One purpose of the next, concluding section, is to show that how the communicative theorist does this will have a significant effect on how she understands the nature of the communicative enterprise.

4. THE CONSEQUENCES OF INTERDEPENDENCE

Before going on to consider the consequences of the interdependence of theories of communicative punishment and moral theory it is worth pausing to complete the examination of interpretivism. As noted above, the interpretivist would seem to be committed to the restricted role of making best sense out of some set of given practices and for many this entails an unacceptable relativism. Yet, also as noted above, a self-confessed objectivist in ethics, Ronald Dworkin, is famously associated with the interpretive method.[19] The difference between Dworkin's strong (and broad) interpretivism and the weak version is that Dworkin argues that the interpretivist can include in her considerations general moral principles (thus making it broad) and that this changes the status of what is delivered from the interpretive procedure.[20] Thus, when accused by Michael

---

[19] See Dworkin, n. 14 above. For Dworkin's objectivism see "Objectivity and Truth: You'd Better Believe It", (1996) 25 *Philosophy and Public Affairs* 87–139.

[20] Dworkin's interpretivism thus shares much in common with Rawls's account of (wide) reflective equilibrium. A possible difference is that Rawls includes some general moral commitments (such as to freedom and equality) in the procedure whereas Dworkin conceives of abstract justice as outside of interpretivism (its function is to select from a variety of interpretive outcomes). See

Walzer of providing a model for the latter's weak interpretive reasoning in the figure of Dworkin's ideal judge, "Hercules",[21] Dworkin replies that this is entirely wrong and that his model of legal reasoning could not be adopted by Walzer "without undermining his [Walzer's] entire case".[22] This is because Hercules' task is not merely to decide which interpretations of the law fit past precedents and make best sense of our practices, but also which are in accordance with the demands of "abstract justice".[23]

Including reference to such things as "abstract justice" could unproblematically be seen as altering the whole nature of the interpretive exercise. Imagine, for example, that Hercules correctly believes that there are certain principles of morality—of abstract justice—that are given by God and that we know what they are. Nevertheless these principles require interpretation in order to be useful in the contemporary world. The addition of such principles clearly changes the nature of the interpretive enterprise. The status of what emerges is given by the status of the fixed principles, in this case that they are the word of God.

This position is structurally similar to that of weak interpretivism. The difference is that the fixed points for the weak interpretivist are the social meanings that obtain in a given society rather than the declarations of God. This difference is, of course, significant for the two questions posed to the theorist of communicative punishments. In the case of the word of God the status of what is said to the offender is clear. What the offender has done is something that is wrong and we know that it is because God—or the best interpretation of God's will—commands that it is so. In addition, assuming that there is some story of how human beings share some essential nature with God whose commands thus link to our motivations, there is a clear failure on the part of the offender to which his attention can be drawn through penal communication.

Dworkin is not a theist. Yet it would seem that the importing of the demands of abstract justice into (strong) interpretivism preclude it from forming the basis of some "half way house" between the isolationist, but unsatisfactory, weak interpretive position and the need for a full-blown account of the nature of wrong and of moral motivation. This is because the extra status that is brought to the interpretive procedure by the inclusion of reference to abstract justice would seem to require that there is underlying the account some more developed meta-ethical theory. Dworkin denies this. Instead he claims that our commitment to abstract justice is just another first-order moral commitment. Nevertheless, Dworkin continues to deny that this weakens his position. Morality, Dworkin argues, needs no (non-moral or external) foundations and

J. Rawls, *A Theory of Justice* (Cambridge Mass., Harvard University Press, 1971); "The Independence of Moral Theory", (1974) 47 *Proceedings and Addresses of the American Philosophical Association* 5–22; N. Daniels, *Justice and Justification* (Cambridge, Cambridge University Press, 1996).

[21] See Dworkin, n. 14 above, chs. 7–11.

[22] See the exchange between Dworkin and Walzer in *The New York Review of Books*, 21 July 1983, pp. 43–47.

[23] *Ibid*.

thus should be untroubled by the claims of those who try to undermine it, or our confidence in employing moral propositions and judgements, by casting doubts on the possibility of finding foundations.[24] His position, which is similar to Simon Blackburn's quasi-realism, is thus of interest because it is an attempt not to isolate the penal from the ethical, but rather the ethical from the meta-ethical.

Dworkin's argument is hard to follow. The first part of his thesis is that sentences such as "X is wrong", "it is true that X is wrong", "it is objectively true that X is wrong" are all of the same kind. They are all first-order moral propositions. The difference between them is one of emphasis. As such the argument is one that concerns what kind of thing we are doing when we utter certain kinds of sentences. Whereas for Blackburn, though, this argument is part of an attempt to rescue our moral language given the truth of a broadly Humean metaphysics, Dworkin seems to hold it as a substantive moral position, one that has normative implications. Quite why Dworkin thinks this is unclear. Of course, our moral judgements must be consistent not only with one another but also with other things that we know, for example about psychology, economics, and cosmology,[25] but unless Dworkin believes that there is only one set of such consistent moral judgements his thesis about the kinds of things moral propositions are cannot be used to generate substantive moral conclusions. *This* argument cannot tell us what to say, what is wrong.

Nevertheless, Dworkin's argument might yet prove useful. If interpretivism can generate the best account of our practices, including those of punishment, and Dworkin can provide an argument to rescue the status of what is said then in combination these would provide an answer to the first question posed for the theorists of a communicative element in punishment. The difficulty with interpretivism, after all, is primarily one of the status of its conclusions. However, Dworkin's account of the nature of the "objectivity" of moral propositions is not clear-cut. On the one hand he argues that on his account "there really are objective and normative properties or facts in the universe" and that when we use such to make moral judgements we should do so in a way that is "old-fashioned, full-blooded, [and] shameless".[26] On the other hand he holds that in the face of moral disagreement:

> "we should be less judgmental, more modest, more aware of the possibility that in the future we will be thought as insensitive as we now think others [with whom we disagree] were".[27]

The point is that Dworkin's position characterises words like "objectivity" as merely emphasis giving, as without "metaphysical resonance",[28] so when we are

---

[24] Dworkin, "Objectivity and Truth: You'd Better Believe It", n. 19 above.
[25] See *ibid.*, at 128.
[26] *Ibid.*, at 127.
[27] *Ibid.*
[28] *Ibid.*, 128.

advised to use such terms in a full-blooded or shameless way all Dworkin can be suggesting is that we say what it is that we wish to say with conviction (or perhaps just more loudly). This may be, if we take a fairly robust Humean view of the way the world is, the only way to rescue words such as objectivity, but as Simon Blackburn comments:

> "Who knows whether the people, depressed and unconfident [because of moral scepticism] are likely to be grateful for this ceremonial return of words like 'objectivity' and 'truth'? They might think that with the resonances gone, they have been offered only a mocking corpse".[29]

Dworkin's argument is, then, unhelpful. Nothing can follow from it for the content of what is to be said to the offender, that must be left to the interpretation of current practices. Dworkin would seem to bolster such interpretive results, but in the end it is unclear whether the voice of condemnation should be robust and "full-blooded" or "modest" and non-judgemental. Finally, the question of motivation is left open.

The purpose of this section was primarily to argue that the account of the content, status, and motivational force of what is to be communicated by punishment will have a significant effect on how the communicative enterprise is understood and the above digression may seem to have taken the argument some distance away from this. However, some of the easiest arguments to that effect have been made in passing. Most basically, knowing what to say, what to condemn as wrongful, will depend on what moral account we endorse. Equally basic: whereas for a conventionalist or weak interpretivist all that could be offered is an appeal to the standards implicit in the community and the importance to the offender of membership of that community, for the theist the situation is different, as it would be for a comprehensive utilitarian. Similarly, the kind of justification (if any) that we have for punishing those whose moral beliefs are different from our own will depend on what account of the nature and scope of moral norms we are justified in endorsing. These are hardly surprising observations. However, the interdependence of moral and penal theory may also have more profound, or at least less obvious, consequences.

Clearly in the space available it is not possible to illustrate this by describing every conceivable meta-ethical position and its consequences for a given theory of communicative punishment. Fortunately this is not necessary. Rather, focus on one question within meta-ethics: whether (or how) morality is linked to motivation. Consider three answers: that recognising something as morally good provides a reason to do it; that recognising something as morally good must be combined with a desire to do what is good in order to be a reason to do it; that recognising something as morally good in itself creates an accompanying desire and thus provides a reason to do it.

---

[29] S. Blackburn, "Review of R Dworkin, 'Objectivity and Truth: You'd Better Believe It'", J. Dreier and D. Estlund (eds.), *Brown Electronic Review Service*, WWW (http://www.brown.edu/Departments/Philosophy/bears/homepage.html). Posted 11/11/96.

How we answer this question and thus how we relate prudential and moral reasons may significantly alter the understanding that we have of how to address the offender in penal communication. For example, communicative theorists have traditionally been perplexed by how to integrate hard treatment into their accounts. For expressivists this problem is primarily one of knowing why the language in which the society condemns should be one of hard treatment rather than "saying it with flowers". For censure-based theorists the problem is more fundamental. The censure account is based on treating people as moral agents, as worthy of being given reasons for why their conduct was wrong. To threaten them with sanctions is taken to undermine this status. It does not give them reasons of the right kind for altering their behaviour or for expressing remorse. Yet this position suggests a strict separation of moral and prudential reasons—a claim that moral agency involves acting *only* from moral reasons. This is a strong claim and one that might be undermined (or at the very least illuminated) by serious meta-ethical reflection.

The final argument of this chapter is necessarily speculative. The purpose of the earlier sections is to establish that communicative theories of punishment cannot stand in isolation from substantive ethical and meta-ethical questions. The purpose of the final section is simply to indicate why this may be important and why communicative theorists, and punishment theorists more generally, might consider being more explicit about the accounts of value, of personal identity, practical rationality (and so on) that they assume or develop.[30]

---

[30] I have attempted a full statement of this argument and a theory of punishment located within a broad ethical theory in my *Justice and Punishment: The Rationale of Coercion* (Oxford, Oxford University Press, forthcoming).

7
Punishment, Communication, and Resentment

THOMAS BALDWIN

Antony Duff has argued that it is only by conceiving punishment as a "communicative enterprise" that we are able to see how, in principle, the practice of punishment can be legitimate.[1] Other conceptions of punishment, he argues, fail to respect the autonomy of those who are punished and, for this reason, fail to provide a basis for the justification of punishment. It is, on the face of it, odd to think of punishment as basically a form of communication—for how can communications be harsh or lenient, deserved or undeserved? But the idea is nonetheless worth exploring. I shall argue, however, that Duff's detailed account of the role of communication in punishment is unsatisfactory before exploring two alternative ways of conceiving of punishment as essentially communicative. It turns out, I think, that the communication of resentment is indeed an important feature of a justifiable practice of punishment, but that, so conceived, communication does not have quite the fundamental role in the justification of the practice that protagonists of a communicative conception of punishment might like it to have.

1. Duff's Communicative Theory of Punishment

I start from Duff's account of the matter. His parenthetical comments in the following passage provide a summary of his position:

> "[We need] to ask more carefully about both the content and the purpose of the communicative enterprise which punishment is meant to be. We need a richer and more subtle account of what punishment is meant to communicate to the criminal (a better understanding of the nature and implications of his crime); of why it is so important to communicate this (because we hope that this will bring the criminal to repent his crime and thus enable him to restore those relationships which his crime threatened to injure or destroy); and of the part which hard treatment can properly play in this com-

[1] R. A. Duff, *Trials and Punishments* (Cambridge, Cambridge University Press, 1986).

municative and reformative endeavour (it serves as a penance which the criminal should ideally come to will for himself)".[2]

A tension in Duff's position is immediately apparent here: what was initially described as a "communicative enterprise" has become, by the end, a "communicative and reformative endeavour". How, we may ask, are these communicative and reformative aspects related? When one looks at Duff's explanation here of the importance of communication it appears that the fundamental purpose of punishment is reform of the criminal through repentance, and the role of communication is that it helps to bring the criminal to repentance through his understanding of "the nature and implications of his crime". But if this is the case, then communication is secondary to the reformative purpose of punishment. We can agree that, where reform is to be through repentance, the criminal needs to understand his crime properly and that some "communication" is normally required to bring about this understanding. But this gives communication only an instrumental role in the process, and such a role is scarcely sufficient to fulfil Duff's intention of providing "an ideal account of criminal punishment as a communicative enterprise in which we engage with the criminal".[3] Indeed it is not clear that communication is essential at all. For it may be that the criminal's understanding of his crime is not achieved through communication with others at all, perhaps because he is the only person who fully understands his crime. Dostoevsky's account of Rashkolnikov in *Crime and Punishment* is a case in point.

Duff's difficulty arises from his account of the content of the communication which he takes to be the essential feature of punishment: as we have seen, it is to be a form of communication which brings the criminal to "a better understanding of the nature and implications of his crime". Taken at face value, this suggests a denunciation of the crime by the judge, together with an informal introduction to social, political, and legal theory in order to explain what is wrong about the crime from other participants in the penal process (probation officers, prison visitors, social workers etc.). As Duff well recognises, however, communications of this kind do not suffice by themselves for punishment: for they have no essential connection with the element of "hard treatment" which expressive theorists from Feinberg onwards have recognised as characteristic of punishment.[4] It is precisely in order to provide a role for some such "hard treatment" that Duff introduces his further thought that punishment has a reformative purpose. For he holds that reform of the criminal is to be accomplished by imposing some hard treatment in the hope that the criminal may come to regard this as a penance for his crime. Yet once this further thought is introduced it threatens to displace the supposed primary role of communication within punishment.

[2] *Ibid.*, at p. 245.
[3] *Ibid.*, at p. 267.
[4] J. Feinberg, "The Expressive Function of Punishment" in *Doing and Deserving* (Princeton, Princeton University Press, 1970), p. 98.

Duff will respond that this complaint fails to do justice to the way in which the reformative and communicative aspects of punishment are supposed to be integrated in his position. For he is well aware of the familiar objection that reformative conceptions of punishment encourage invasive forms of psychological manipulation which violate the criminal's autonomy, and he maintains that it is precisely because he locates the aim of reform within a communicative enterprise that his position is not vulnerable to this objection. And it does indeed seem right that if reform is to be achieved through a process which involves communicative dialogue then gross forms of psychological manipulation are ruled out. But it also has to be admitted that there are many forms of communication, admittedly less than ideal, which are quite compatible with psychological manipulation, as in propaganda, incitement, insinuation, and the like. So it is not communication per se which is incompatible with the wrong kind of reform, but only one kind of communication—communication which engages sincerely and openly with its audience as rational thinkers. Yet the more this is stressed, the weaker the connection with "hard treatment" becomes: for now punishment is conceived as a process which seeks to reform criminals through rational discussion with them. Equally, the other familiar objection to reformative conceptions of punishment remains unanswered, that it implies that punishment should take as long as it takes for the criminal to reform—which may in some cases seem much too brief a period of punishment and in other cases far too long.

Duff's way of accommodating these issues is to suggest that the reform in question is to be achieved through the criminal's repentance of his crime, which is supposed to involve his acceptance of some appropriate hard treatment as a penance for his crime. While I do not deny that there is merit in stressing the penitential aspect of punishment, it cannot provide the missing link which Duff needs to hold his position together. First, because repentance is essentially voluntary, it cannot be a fundamental purpose of a just system of punishment that it should aim to secure repentance. For where a criminal fails to repent after a process that we would intuitively regard as a sufficient punishment for his crime, are we to continue the punishment? If not, then reform through repentance arrived at after suitably respectful and rational communication cannot be the dominant purpose of punishment. Duff models his discussions of punishment on religious conceptions of sin, penance, expiation, and repentance, and the model is often enlightening. But it carries an implication that should be worrying to Duff: repentance, like religious faith, is deeply voluntary. Hence just as Locke's primary argument for religious toleration was that even true faith cannot be coerced, and therefore ought not to be demanded of citizens through the institutions of the state,[5] it seems quite wrong to hold that the institution of punishment exists primarily in order to bring criminals to perform a similarly deeply voluntary act of repentance. Furthermore, despite Duff's legitimate insis-

---

[5] J. Locke, *A Letter concerning Toleration* (Indianapolis, Bobbs-Merrill, 1955), at pp. 34–5.

tence that he is only concerned with an "ideal" system of punishment and not with our actual system, Nietzsche's acid scepticism concerning the attempt to enforce penitential behaviour is a warning to anyone seriously attracted by the prospect of converting prisons into literal "penitentiaries":

> "It is precisely among criminals and convicts that the sting of conscience is extremely rare; prisons and penitentiaries are *not* the kind of hotbed in which this species of gnawing worm is likely to flourish: all conscientious observers are agreed on that, in many cases unwillingly enough and contrary to their own inclinations. Generally speaking, punishment makes men hard and cold; it concentrates; it sharpens the feeling of alienation; it strengthens the power of resistance. If it happens that punishment destroys the vital energy and brings about a miserable prostration and self-abasement, such a result is even less pleasant than the usual effects of punishment—characterised by dry and gloomy seriousness".[6]

The second reason why it is unsatisfactory for Duff to invoke the role of penance in order to elucidate the need for punishment to involve hard treatment is that much the same questions can be asked about the relationship between penance and repentance as arise concerning the relationship between hard treatment and reform. Why, the sinner may ask, is it necessary for him to undergo some penance in order to expiate his sin of which he already repents? God's justice may well require it, but it is precisely the rationale of this kind of retributive justice which an account of punishment is supposed to provide, and it is not provided by simply pointing to its role in religious as well as in secular life. Finally, the question about the need for communication is particularly pressing once the penitential model of punishment is urged. For it may well be that communication with others has a minimal role in leading the sinner, or criminal, to repentance: Rashkolnikov is again a case in point.

One way to summarise these difficulties which, I think, undermine Duff's account is to apply J. L. Austin's theory of speech acts to his conception of punishment as a fundamentally "communicative enterprise".[7] If the communicative acts are conceived as basically "locutionary" (saying that so-and-so) and "illocutionary" (criticising, denouncing, encouraging etc.), then there is no necessary connection with hard treatment or penance. For it is of the essence of such acts that they are accomplished when they are properly understood, and no further act by speaker or audience is required. If the communicative act is conceived of as "perlocutionary", on the model of persuasion, then, since the act is described by reference to an effect it has helped to bring about (a change of mind by the audience), it may well be that further activity by the speaker was also involved. But although this does now permit a role for hard treatment within the general conception of punishment as a perlocutionary communicative act it remains wholly unacceptable as a model for just punishment. For now, if the requisite

---

[6] F. Nietzsche, *The Genealogy of Morals*, trans. Kaufmann (New York, Vintage, 1969), at pp. 81–2.
[7] J. Austin, *How to do Things with Words* (Oxford, Clarendon Press, 1960).

effect is (as Duff's account requires) the criminal's reform, then there has been no punishment until the criminal has actually reformed, just as there has been no persuasion until the audience has been actually persuaded. So whether the communication be conceived as illocutionary or perlocutionary it cannot provide the basis for a reformative account of punishment of the kind to which Duff aspires.

2. Alternative Views of Punishment as Communication

I think that if there is to be any chance of giving communication a central place within an account of punishment it is necessary to alter radically the specification of that which is communicated. For Duff, that which was communicated to the criminal was "a better understanding of the nature and implications of his crime". But if one looks back to expressive theorists such as Feinberg, the suggestion is that it is the expression of the *feelings* of members of the community concerning the crime, such as their resentment of it,[8] which is an essential characteristic of punishment. This suggests a very different approach to the matter, though I prefer to explore it by considering punishment as the communication of such a feeling, rather than simply its expression, since this carries the implication that the criminal understands the feeling which, supposedly, informs the process of punishment to which he is being subjected.

The importance of taking it that it is the communication of feelings that is the fundamental element in a communicative account of punishment is that it offers the prospect of providing a foundation for the thought that punishment characteristically requires some form of hard treatment. Putting the matter very simply: if punishment is a way of communicating to the criminal the community's resentment of his criminal conduct, then it is only to be expected that it is liable to include some hard treatment, since resentment typically includes a determination to impose a penalty on those who have done wrong. This is too simple, and may well appear question-begging. But one can get some initial grasp of the merit of reference to the communication of feelings if one considers the communication of positive feelings, such as love. If the lover is to communicate his love to the beloved, it is not enough for him just to say, or write, the appropriate words: he must also do the things with and for his beloved which show his love—above all he must spend enough time with the beloved to vindicate his claim that he cares more about being with her than about anything else. There is nothing puzzling here: for the feeling being communicated is such that, if sincere, it will motivate the lover to seek out opportunities for being with his beloved; further, since the beloved will know this she will expect to receive such attentions, and since her lover will know that he has given her reason to have

---

[8] Feinberg, n.4 above, at p. 101.

such expectations, he will be all the more concerned to ensure that his deeds conform to his words.

In this simple case, then, the communication of a positive feeling brings with it a mutual expectation of appropriate action. The hope that informs the communicative theorist must then be that one can provide a similar account of the actions appropriate to the communication of the negative feelings aroused by wrongdoing and thereby provide an account of punishment which connects hard treatment with its communicative aspect. But the matter is not straightforward. If one considers the communication of anger at some wrong done to oneself, it may well be the case that this anger includes a desire for retaliation, which, being communicated to the wrongdoer, leads him either to expect such retaliation or to seek to make some recompense in order to avoid it. Similarly, it may be that the communication of indignation at a wrong done to others leads the criminal to expect that this indignation will lead to an attempt at more impersonal retaliation or recompense. But to suppose that we can obtain in this way a satisfactory way of thinking about punishment is to suppose that, in the end, the bare existence of a desire for retaliation, personal or impersonal, provides the ultimate justification for the element of hard treatment in punishment, and thus that Stephen was right when he famously remarked that "The criminal law stands to the passion of revenge in much the same relation as marriage to the sexual appetite".[9]

Yet this is not acceptable. For the bare existence of a desire for retaliation cannot by itself justify its fulfilment where it causes harm to others. Just punishment needs to be more than a legally permitted form of collective retaliation. The difference between "sexual appetite" and "the passion of revenge" is that mutual exercise of the former between consenting partners does no harm to either, indeed provides them with the opportunity for the most intimate form of shared happiness, whereas exercise of the latter involves the prospect of suffering or loss that stands in need of a justification which points beyond the existence of the passion itself. The obvious thought is that the justification is to be found by looking to its cause, to the wrong done which has prompted the passion for revenge. But once the justification looks in this way beyond the feeling to its cause it is not clear what role there is for the feeling itself, or its communication, in an account of punishment.

The way forward here is to see that what is inadequate about the conception of punishment as the communication of collective anger and indignation at the infliction of suffering or loss is that this was an attempt to ground punishment in human reactions which, however natural, are also non-moral and are therefore insufficient by themselves to warrant the imposition of suffering and loss. This therefore suggests that a better account might be found by looking to an explicitly moral feeling, one whose content includes moral judgements which

---

[9] J. F. Stephen, *General View of the Criminal Law of England* (London, MacMillan, 1863), at p. 99.

can contribute to the justification of the hard treatment which the account suggests is rightly consequent upon the communication of this feeling. Butler famously appropriated the term "resentment" for such a feeling, precisely distinguishing it from anger and indignation by taking it that we feel resentment at injuries (*iniuriae*—wrongdoings) rather than the mere hurts or losses which give rise to anger.[10] Yet what remains to be clarified here is the relationship between resentment at wrongdoing and the thought that those who have done wrong should suffer some penalty. For Butler, it is clear that resentment includes this latter thought because he takes it that justice requires that wrongdoing should be punished. But if this is the way the role of resentment has to be conceived, then it clearly makes no fundamental contribution to an account of the justification of punishment, but simply assumes one—in Butler's case a broadly rule-utilitarian one of punishment as minimal deterrence. Within such a position the importance of resentment appears to be that it serves to internalise within the community the feelings and motivations requisite for the practice of punishment. It provides no justification of punishment, but by redirecting "the passion of revenge" into calmer and more rational channels—"the cool consideration of reason"[11]—it helps to secure the broader practice of justice within a community.

Butler's position falls short of that to which the communicative theorist aspired, since the communication of resentment appears to contribute nothing to the justification of punishment but only to its implementation. The dilemma for the communicative theorist which it clarifies is therefore that while no acceptable justification of punishment is to be found by looking to the communication of non-moral feelings such as anger, the introduction of a specifically moral feeling of resentment does not help either, since its moral content is such that an independent justification of punishment has to be assumed. Although one can represent punishment as the communication of collective resentment, so conceived, this representation is an implication rather than a foundation of a theory of retributive justice.

Is there a tenable position which somehow escapes this dilemma? I think myself that any discussion of the institution of punishment has to start from a recognition that the central role of the state in protecting the life, liberty, and property of its citizens brings with it a commitment to ensuring that those who are convicted of injuring others should be liable to suffer some penalty. For otherwise the state would be condoning acts whose perpetration runs directly contrary to the expectations that underlie its own existence; and in thus condoning them it would be indicating to its citizens either that these acts are not really prohibited within its jurisdiction or that it simply lacks the power to protect its citizens. Either way, the state's authority would be fatally compromised. So the state's authority necessarily includes the authority to punish.

---

[10] J. Butler, *Fifteen Sermons* (London, Bell, 1969), at p. 125.
[11] *Ibid.*, at p. 131.

I shall call this the "political account" of punishment. The issue therefore is whether acknowledgement of these considerations leaves any space for the thought that punishment is to be understood as the communication of collective resentment, on the part of citizens, at wrongdoing. The suggestion I want to make is that in two respects it does.

The first concerns the importance of the distinction between deliberate and accidental wrongdoing. It is notoriously difficult from within the rule-utilitarian reasoning characteristic of the political account of punishment sketched above to provide an adequate rationale of this distinction, since the infliction of penalties on some accidental wrongdoing may well have appropriate deterrent consequences for others. But, as Butler observes,[12] when the situation is conceived from the perspective of the victim of wrongdoing it is obvious that this distinction is of great importance: it is one thing to have someone stumble and accidentally trip one up in a crowded shopping street; it is quite a different thing to recognise that one has been deliberately tripped up by someone. One feels resentment in the latter case at the other person because their action manifests a settled determination to do one harm, which is altogether absent in the case of an accident (though accidents that manifest inexcusable casualness are again a ground for resentment); and what applies to resentment felt by the victim applies equally to the vicarious resentment felt by others. Hence the fact that the punishment is a way of communicating resentment, and is not just an instrument of social control, affects its scope. The political account of punishment under-determines the details of its application which are only filled out when punishment is conceived as the communication of collective resentment by citizens towards wrongdoing within their own state. These citizens can be conceived of as having internalised the political account of punishment; but the way in which their own feelings are then informed by it brings a crucial distinction to the practice of punishment which that account does not by itself motivate.

The second respect in which reference to resentment fills out the political account of punishment is that this account assumes that citizens will accept that under certain circumstances other citizens should be made to endure suffering or loss. But this thought could not commend itself to people unless they were antecedently disposed to think it appropriate that those who cause harm should be made to suffer for doing so. I have argued that the desire for retaliation is not an appropriate basis for a theory of punishment; it is only the moralised form of this desire, resentment, that can have a role within an account of punishment. But although this moralisation has to include some independent account of the way in which punishment can be just, for which I have offered the "political account", there is a degree of interdependence here. For this account is one which is to be implemented by citizens and it cannot of itself create wholly new motivations among them. What it can do is to educate and redirect existing

---

[12] *Ibid.*, at p. 127.

motivations in the pursuit of justice alone, and it is precisely this which constitutes the transformation of revenge into resentment. This transformation, however, is not simply an external implication of internalising the political account of punishment: its achievement is integral to the viability of the political account itself. So in this respect too the conception of punishment as the communication of collective resentment helps to fill out the otherwise impersonal details of the political account.

My suggestion, therefore, is that although the conception of punishment as the communication of collective resentment cannot have a fundamental role in the account of the justifiction of punishment since resentment itself has to include a judgement to the effect that wrongdoing merits punishment, it does make an essential contribution to the scope and practice of punishment. One way to understand this is to think of Strawson's famous distinction between the "objective" attitudes characteristic of impersonal social control and the "reactive" attitudes characteristic of personal relationships.[13] Strawson famously included resentment, in precisely Butler's sense of the term, among the latter and argued that our commitment to such reactive attitudes is so deep that we cannot soberly imagine ourselves abandoning them. Whether his argument is this respect is altogether conclusive is, I think, debatable; but the contrast that he draws between objective and reactive attitudes, and the centrality of resentment among the reactive attitudes characteristic of personal life, does help to clarify the way in which the theory of punishment needs to take account of the feeling of resentment. For it is precisely by recognising that punishment is the communication of resentment that we can see that punishment is not just a matter of "objective" social control but belongs instead to the practice of civil society by persons who recognise each other as persons. Another way of putting much the same point is this: punishment inescapably involves considerations of deterrence, as the political account implies; but punishment is not just minimal deterrence, as its critics urge, and the way in which it is not is explicated once the practice of punishment is understood to be the communication of resentment by persons towards persons.

---

[13] P. F. Strawson, "Freedom and Resentment" in G. Watson (ed.), *Free Will* (New York, Oxford University Press, 1982) 59–80.

8

Albert Speer, Guilt, and "The Space Between"

ALAN NORRIE[1]

1. INTRODUCTION

This chapter seeks to develop themes from my recent work about criminal law and moral responsibility[2] in relation to some reflections by Anthony Giddens on the nature of guilt in conditions of "high" or "late" modern society.[3] It seeks to relate these themes to discussion of one particular case study of the nature of guilt, the case of Albert Speer, as interpreted in the recent book by Gitta Sereny.[4] The chapter is of a preliminary and investigative kind, drawing on disparate sources.

Broadly the argument takes the form of an insistence on the *dialectical relationship* between *questions of judgement* and *questions of responsibility*, between the *expectations of moral communities* and the *attitudes of moral agents*. In particular, I argue that the possibility of moral judgement emerges from the dialectical intersection of the *conflicts of modern communities* and the *ambiguities of modern selfhood*, leading to an essential ontological *ambivalence* in judgements about guilt. This is not to say that responsibility, or judgements about responsibility, are impossible, far from it, but it is to point to the historical emergence, the instability, and the dialectical character of processes of judgement in modern society.

The chapter has three main sections. In the first, I introduce the argument by considering certain passages in the work of Anthony Giddens on the nature of self and community in "late" or "high" modernity. From these, I highlight questions about problems of moral judgement and agency stemming from the nature of the modern self and community. In the second section, I develop these

---

[1] I would like to thank all those at the Morrell seminar who commented on the paper on which this chapter is based, and Robert Fine and Rom Harré for their perceptive criticism.
[2] A. Norrie, "The Limits of Justice: Finding Fault in the Criminal Law" (1996) 59 *Modern Law Review* 540–56; and, A. Norrie, "'Simulacra of Morality'? Beyond the Ideal/Actual Antinomies of Criminal Justice" in A. Duff (ed.), *Criminal Law: Principle and Critique* (New York, Cambridge University Press, 1998), p. 101–55.
[3] A. Giddens, *Modernity and Self Identity* (Oxford, Polity, 1991).
[4] G. Sereny, *Albert Speer: His Battle with Truth* (London, Picador, 1995).

arguments by drawing on themes in my own recent work concerning selfhood and community. That work, drawing on the social psychology of Rom Harré[5] and the dialectics of Roy Bhaskar,[6] asserts the relationality of the self, its "in betweenness", or co-mediation by the individuated agent and his or her communities. Individual identity exists within an overall, *totalising*, context and its nature is radically affected thereby:

> "To grasp totality is to break with our ordinary notions of identity . . . It is to see things *existentially constituted,* and permeated, *by their relations with others*; and to see our ordinary notion of identity as an abstraction not only from [its] existentially constitutive processes of formation (geo-histories), but also from [its] existentially constitutive inter-activity (internal relatedness) . . . When is a thing no longer a thing but something else? . . . [I]n the domain of totality we need to conceptualise *entity relationism*".[7]

This position on relationality is explored through an analysis of Gitta Sereny's work of judgement on Albert Speer. My argument here is that there is a tension in Sereny's account, an ambivalence in her judgement, which stems from an ambiguity in her reading of the character of Speer. At various points in the book, Sereny refers to Speer's attempt in Spandau and beyond to become a "different man". Some of the difficulties of judging Speer stem from the different meanings that can be given to this idea. Was Speer attempting to become another person in a deep moral sense, or was he, more calculatedly, seeking just to reinvent himself as a person who could evade the condemnation on his head? Or, a third possibility, did the post-war Speer occupy some intermediate position between these two possibilities, and, if so, what was the nature of that position?

Put another way, was his sense of guilt "real" or was it cultivated; or, was it both real *and* cultivated? More broadly, what does it mean to be a "different man" and what is the relationship between attempts at development of the self and one's existence across time in societies with very different public and private moralities? These questions are all posed by Sereny's account of Speer, and my suggestion will be that answers to them reside in the sense of the relationality of the self and community that I will first develop. The dilemmas Sereny finds in judging Speer are real dilemmas in the sense that they reflect real issues about what it means to be a person in modern society.

2. Guilt, Community, and the Self in Late Modernity

I begin with certain themes developed by Anthony Giddens, and in particular with his discussion of the erosion of guilt as a moral category in late modernity. For Giddens, guilt is "anxiety produced by the fear of transgression" where the

---

[5] R. Harré, *Personal Being* (Oxford, Polity, 1991).
[6] R. Bhaskar, *Dialectic: the Pulse of Freedom* (London, Verso, 1993).
[7] *Ibid.*, at p. 125.

"thoughts or activities of the individual do not match up to expectations of a normative sort".[8] Guilt concerns things done or not done, it concerns wrongdoing, and it has as its obverse reparation. It concerns "discrete elements of behaviour and the modes of retribution that they suggest or entail":

> "Guilt carries the connotation of moral transgression: it is anxiety deriving from a failure, or an inability, to satisfy certain forms of moral imperative in the course of a person's conduct".[9]

So far, this sounds like a modern version of Kant, albeit one mediated by Freud, but for Giddens, there is a social link between the expression of particular moral emotions and the nature of historical periods. He relates the experience of feelings of guilt to the periods of "early", "mature" and "late" modernity. In this last phase, he accepts that "guilt mechanisms persist",[10] but their significance is substantially diminished. The reason for this is the erosion of established normative communities in late modernity. The individual lives less "by extrinsic moral precepts but by means of the reflexive organisation of the self",[11] so that the "characteristic movement of modernity, on the level of individual experience, is away from guilt".[12] For Giddens, late modernity marks a further qualitative individualisation of the experience of the self so that its inward reflexivity is at the same time a cause and a result of the erosion of the moral communities that previously held the self in check.

This argument raises three questions. The first is whether Giddens is correct to identify a diminution of issues of guilt in late modernity. The second concerns the relationship he posits between the decline of guilt and the diminution of community. The question here is to what extent it is correct to speak of an *erosion* of community, or to what extent, rather differently, one should speak of an emergent, or just more visible, *fragmentation* of communities. The third question concerns the nature of the self, guilt, and responsibility in Giddens' account: can we conceive of the self in Giddens' terms as self-reliant and reflexive to the extent that issues of guilt and responsibility concern it less and less?

First question: the diminution of guilt in late modernity?

At certain levels of society, Giddens may be correct to identify a trajectory of the diminution of guilt, but he is surely also right to hedge his bets—against his own argument—by recognising that "guilt mechanisms persist". But this is not just a "throwback" to an earlier period, for late modernity itself continues to generate questions of guilt, and questions of what guilt means. For example, one of the

---

[8] Giddens, n.3 above, at p. 64.
[9] *Ibid.*, at p. 153.
[10] *Ibid.*
[11] *Ibid.*
[12] *Ibid.*, at p. 155.

features of late modernity is the risk of the "rise of totalitarian superstates",[13] and this, together with the breakdown of such states, throws up some of the most poignant and important questions about the nature of human responsibility and guilt. Think for example of the war crimes trials in the Hague, the "Commission for Truth and Reconciliation" in South Africa, or the trial of East German border guards after reunification. The issue of guilt remains one of the most compelling questions in a world in which individual and collective atrocities are commonplace and late modernity remains as fascinated by such questions as any earlier period. Beyond violence associated with globalising phenomena, think also of the concern, which includes but goes beyond prurience, with the guilt of individuals like Rosemary and Fred West, of the two boys who killed James Bulger, of Mary Bell, or of Myra Hindley.

Now it might be argued to the contrary that these cases support Giddens' argument. Perhaps the very fascination with guilt here indicates in Durkheimian fashion the need to hold on to a moral reaction that is going out of currency. On the other hand, pressing Durkheim into service, perhaps these cases reveal a continuing need to create the values of moral community and to mark the boundaries of the unacceptable. The need to know how a person could have transgressed such boundaries is part of understanding how it is that communities exist within which most people would not do such things. Of course in these cases, there is often more going on than meets the eye. The demonisation of the two boys in the James Bulger case, or in that of Myra Hindley, suggests that, beyond the horror of the crimes, these cases are asked to carry other social and political baggage such as the populist political agendas of the tabloid press. Still, I believe these cases do involve a continuing focus on moral transgression as a late modern concern and this is so even if we say that it is precisely the breakdown of moral communities in late modernity that leads to an *increased focus* upon the worst kinds of normative transgression. Whichever view is taken, Giddens points to the significance in general terms of the existence of moral communities as a crucial factor in the creation of individual guilt. It is impossible to feel guilt without feeling that one has transgressed a norm, and impossible to feel that one has transgressed a norm without some sense of a relationship to a community to which a norm pertains.

Second question: the diminution of community in late modernity?

This brings us to a second question concerning whether we are witnessing an absolute erosion of community in late modernity or whether we are witnessing its fragmentation into a number of communities, or a greater visibility of the same. There is a difference here. While Giddens suggests that the individual is thrown back on her own reflexive devices, the alternative suggests the continu-

---

[13] *Ibid.* at p. 4.

ing existence of a variety of conflicting, perhaps overlapping and intersecting, sub-communities rather than their overall absence. For example the rise and fall of super-states brought about by "globalisation" has often led to a "balkanisation" of very strong and conflictual communities rather than to a reflexive individualism. In making this point, we pick up—on the "domestic" front—continuing themes in sociology about the significance of social, class, and gender conflict as structural and relational features of late modern societies, features that are of course present in Giddens' argument, but in a subsidiary position *vis-a-vis* his argument about the modern self and his/her guilt. The problem with community may be not so much that it has gone away, but that conflicts between communities have either become sharpened or more visible or both. It is very important to hold onto this different notion of the nature of moral community(ies) when we think of the conflict between, for example, a liberal democratic and a fascist community, an issue that underlies many war crimes trials from Nuremberg onwards, and which is directly relevant to thinking about, as we will, Albert Speer.

Third question: the reflexivity of the self in late modernity?

Giddens writes of the negotiated and changing nature of selfhood in late modernity. Self-identity increasingly is "reflexively" maintained by individuals apart from moral communities. They maintain a biography about themselves through the "capacity to keep a particular narrative going".[14] This is an essentially fragile activity "because the biography the individual reflexively holds in mind is only one 'story' among many other potential stories that could be told about her development as a self".[15] This ability of the individual to shift reflexively from one account to another fits with the idea of the erosion of guilt in late modern conditions. To avoid feelings of guilt, individuals simply reinterpret life events. This account of the self generates a sense of both its fragility and its ambiguity: if Giddens is correct, we might look to pin responsibility to a site whence it has fled. The agent responsible for a particular act may resist responsibility by reinventing herself as a "different person" with a different story to tell as to why an action occurred. For example the move might be from a confession that "I was to blame for 'X'" to "you (society, 'my parents, teachers', etc.) made me do 'X'. I was a victim. The person who did those things is now no more for I have overcome what you did to me".

Giddens does acknowledge however that at one and the same time, the self is both fragile *and* robust: fragile for the reason just stated, robust because "a sense of self-identity is often securely enough held to weather major tensions or transitions in the social environments within which the person moves".[16] What is

[14] *Ibid.*, at p. 54.
[15] *Ibid.*, at p. 55.
[16] *Ibid.*

the nature of this "robust" aspect of the self and what is the precise connection between these robust and fragile aspects? Giddens says less about the robust than the fragile side of selfhood. It seems to involve a minimum content, sufficient only to maintain the basic attributes of personhood and to fend off the most serious pathologies such as mental illness. If the robust side of selfhood underpins the fragile side, does it produce the possibility of a unified "metanarrative" of the self? It is hard to see how it could given Giddens's diagnosis of the late modern condition of reflexivity, for it must be sufficiently minimalist to lead to the conclusion that guilt is under attack in conditions of late modernity. It cannot be so robust as to undermine the question: how would we hold a person responsible, in the sense of looking for a feeling of guilt within a person who has transgressed the rules of a moral community, where that person has reinvented herself to evade the blame associated with her transgression? This is Giddens' question of the reflexive self under the declining conditions of moral community in late modernity.

My aim in raising these questions is to challenge Giddens' thesis about the nature of late modernity but still to pick up the following from his account: his thematisation of the fluidity of selfhood, the ability of the self to shift between narratives, and the significance of moral communities as syncategorematic to the idea of guilt. To summarise, Giddens gives us a start in our exploration of ideas of guilt and community. He points importantly to the ambiguous nature of selfhood and the significance of community in the construction of guilt. More contentiously, he claims that selves are able under late modern conditions to avoid the inner sense of guilt by freeing themselves from the receding claims of community. Giddens' image of late modern individuality has shorn his initial "Kantian-Freudian" conception of guilt of both its affective and its morally imperatival qualities.[17] But how far must we follow this thesis and accept that the decline of community and the reflexivity of the self lead to an erosion of the concept of guilt?

My suggestions are (1) that questions of guilt are alive and well in late modernity; (2) that this may be linked to the fragmentation of communities in conflict rather than a trajectory of absolute community breakdown; and (3) that if the self's "fragility" does permit the evasion of responsibility, this observation has to be synthesised with its obverse: the continuing ability of communities to instantiate senses of guilt and responsibility under late modern conditions, and for individuals to *feel* guilty. To put this last point more concretely, the evasion of responsibility by the apparent reinvention of the self may be a strategy that is adopted by a *guilty* individual. Or at least, as I shall argue with regard to Speer, denial and acknowledgement of guilt may compete for the soul of the modern individual.

---

[17] Though later, I will argue that there still remains a close affinity with the Kantian subject in Giddens' position.

3. Ambiguity about Guilt, Ambivalence about Judgement

In this section I continue to investigate the ambiguity of selfhood and the conflictual nature of community and how the relationship between the two affects notions of responsibility and judgement. I begin with the question of selfhood and relate this to the issue of moral responsibility and how a community (a social audience) comes to blame a person for wrongdoing. My argument is that audiences' reactions to a person who has done wrong reflect an ontological ambiguity in selfhood, which ambiguity in turn arises from its dialectical relationship with a community. This argument retains the emphasis found in Giddens on the relationship between self and community, but insists, in a context of the continuing existence of community, or more accurately, communi*ties* subject to fragmentation and conflict, on the continuing situation of the self within his or her communities.

In earlier work,[18] I suggested that people often have an *ambivalent* attitude to the attribution of fault stemming from an *ambiguity* in the nature of what it means to be an individual agent. This ambiguity feeds into moral judgements of wrongdoing and the sense of what it means to do justice. In ordinary moral life, i.e. in relation to judgements of matters that do not concern crime and punishment, we often follow a two-phase approach. At first we may be angry at what has been done and seek to blame the person who has done wrong, but then later we may proceed to judge the person "in the round", taking the context of their actions into account. We interpret what was done as part of a person's history and situation. We "explain" what they have done and, so doing, come to excuse or forgive them.

Consider, for example, in a non-punitive context the ways in which we judge what we regard as the reprehensible conduct of those we like with that of those we do not. In the latter case, we are likely to accuse, to insist on the wrongful agency of a "bad" person, to condemn. In the former case, perhaps initial irritation or anger at the bad act gives way to empathy, sorrow, explaining, and excusing. This illustration depends, I would suggest, not just on the emotional orientation to the individual, but on two possible ways of regarding agency. In one, agency is *personalised* or *individualised* to achieve an immediate sense of responsibility; in the other, agency is *contextualised*, which has the effect of questioning the immediate sense of responsibility that comes from personalisation. Importantly, the "duality of judgement" observed in this discussion reflects a duality in agency itself: human beings are both acting persons and persons who act in contexts.[19]

---

[18] Norrie, n. 2 above.

[19] This argument is informed theoretically by Bhaskar's account of the "duality of structure and agency". Under his transformative model of social action, agency "reproduces and/or more or less transforms, for the most part unwittingly, its conditions of possibility", which include "social structures and their generative mechanisms . . ., the agent herself and, generally, what was given, the *donné*, . . . which has now been reproduced or transformed" (Bhaskar n. 6 above, at p. 155). This

To illustrate the link between "personalising" and "decontextualising" judgements and the nature of the agency that is judged, this time in a punitive context, take an example I have used elsewhere.[20] In the United Kingdom in the 1970s, a climate of what was later labelled as corruption developed in local government. Council officials and local developers became involved in relationships that were too close and involved the acceptance of hospitality and gifts by officials. These were later seen as bribes, but at the time they could be seen as simple emollients or "just the way things are done". When these officials were eventually tried and convicted for accepting bribes, they were held to be guilty of corrupt acts, yet for many at the time, it probably seemed normal activity within a particular culture. At the same time, is it not possible that, at the back of their minds, a part of them also knew that there was "something wrong" in what they were doing? The point is that individual subjectivity is not fixed with regard to a moral code, but rather shifts between vocabularies of right and wrong *which social contexts provide and agents mediate*. Agents do things that can be interpreted in different and contradictory ways. We can either view the convicted councillor as a corrupt agent "in control of his actions" and operating with a conventional moral vocabulary of right and wrong (a personalising strategy), or as a "victim of the times" (a contextualising strategy). Most appropriately, we should see *both* sides of the question, but if we do, we recognise not just the *ambiguity* in our sense of individual responsibility, but also the *ambivalence* in judging that goes with it. The important point is that the ambiguity of responsibility and the ambivalence of judgement are dialectically related. They feed off each other symbiotically in order to resolve what is essentially irresolute, the judgement of individual responsibility.

The two-sided character of agency gives rise to ambivalence in how an audience judges conduct. Ultimately, ambivalence about judgement is "resolved" according to the general social, political, and moral standpoint of the onlooker. How does the onlooker view the actions of the friend or enemy, the actions of the local government officer? Such questions involve general and particular aspects. A friend's actions are judged as responsible or irresponsible in part on the basis that one is judging a friend, local government officers in part on how one feels about such people. Consider for example the likely different judgements of one who believes that local government officers generally "mean well and try to do their best in difficult circumstances" and one who sees them as a "drain on local resources". What comes out is a judgement about individual responsibility for an act, but this is context-driven because personal agency is context-emergent. They cannot be separated.

---

implies a duality of structure and agency, "dual points of articulation" which are the "differentiated and changing *positioned-practices*" within structures which agents occupy, reproduce, and transform. These constitute the system of social relations in which intentional human activity occurs.

[20] Norrie, "'Simulacra of Morality'? Beyond the Ideal/Actual Antinomies of Criminal Justice", n. 2 above.

The guilt of council officials is one thing, but surely the example is an easy one. What about the most serious crimes involving horrible violence? Does a similar ambivalence and ambiguity operate there? I would argue that even in the most demonised cases, like those of a Rosemary West or Myra Hindley, we do come to wonder how they could have done what they did and to question the personalising strategy that establishes their guilt. We do not do this in order to deny their wrongdoing, but we are led to wonder about their ultimate responsibility for what they did. Nothing makes us excuse or forgive their acts, but looking at what they did, we seek to understand contextually how they could have become the sort of person who committed such crimes. We also come to see the refusal to understand by those who persist in unthinkingly condemning as itself a failure of human being.[21] Thus, our initial reaction of anger and condemnation is followed by a sense that the criminal was also, in a different sense, and one that does not diminish the horror of what she did, a victim. So doing, we move from the sense of the individual as an autonomous responsible agent to that of the person as a constructed social phenomenon. We place the criminal wrongdoer in her context.[22]

Personalising and contextualising involve contradictory responses, yet I would argue that both are in a sense appropriate. Both are evoked by one facet of individual being and agency. Condemnation is relevant for acts over which the individual has control, while empathy and excusing are relevant for acts over which the individual has not. The point, however, is that *both* standpoints are one-sided because they reflect only one aspect of an ambiguous phenomenon, that is, the individual operating *between* agency and context. This is evidenced in a further third stage that is particularly significant and remarkable with regard to serious crimes. After the initial sense of anger and condemnation, and the second stage of contextual interpretation, we go back to the question of responsibility in a more considered way. How many are really satisfied, for example, with the sense that can be drawn from Myra Hindley's essay,[23] that the person who committed her crimes was "another person" from the Hindley of today? There remains a sense of moral reckoning that corresponds to neither the immediate sense of responsibility (the personalising sense employed by the law), nor the diffuse, contextualising approach to which I have also referred. It

---

[21] One must distinguish the reaction of families of homicide victims from the knee-jerk reaction of those who follow the tabloid press, although it seems to me that families are not helped to live with their loss by the views of the latter.

[22] If retributivist philosophy is the theoretical home of a personalising attitude to guilt, it is instructive to observe a leading modern retributivist's acknowledgment of, *and* discomfort in relation to, the contextualising strategy. Michael Moore writes that "Undeniably, many people soften their judgements about responsibility when they know more of the causal story behind a person's bad behaviour", but happily for the retributivist, this is no more than an example of "philosophically impure common sense [which] should not survive . . . insights into its philosophical impurity" (see M. Moore, *Placing Blame* Oxford, Oxford University Press,1997, at p. 512). In justifying a personalising strategy on the other hand, Moore is convinced that our feelings about wrongdoing are otherwise "our main heuristic guide to finding out what is morally right" (*ibid.*, at p. 115)!

[23] *The Guardian*, 18 December 1995.

is a floating sense of what doing justice means, one that is hard to pin down. It operates in the space between what a person did and the ways in which that person was herself created, a dialectical space between conflicting alternatives, but a sense that is central to our lives as moral individuals and agents.

Part of this sense involves living with and coming to terms with events in our pasts, even those that are long past. This deeper sense of responsibility is accordingly particularly seen in the case of serious crimes committed many years ago, by someone such as Myra Hindley, and also in the current interest in prosecuting former Nazi war criminals. The past may be "another country", occupied by "other people", yet the sense of injustice that a denial of past responsibility evokes, or the sense of justice that demands the trial of serious crimes done long ago is linked, I suggest, to the complexity in understanding what individual life is as both a socio-historical and a personal phenomenon. But the very way of expressing this issue already reveals that a crucial mediating factor in "fixing" responsibility is the role played by the social audience—the community— making judgements.

4. THE TWO SPEERS OF GITTA SERENY

In her book on Albert Speer, Gitta Sereny sought to understand the "origin of Hitler's evil" and "Speer's realisation of—and participation in—it". Part of Hitler's genius was to corrupt others, and corruption is insidious, so that "Speer, in the course of his growing relationship with Hitler, inevitably became— though for a long time unwittingly—a part of it".[24] This is how Sereny describes Speer at the beginning of her book:

> "Speer, I was already convinced, had never killed, stolen, personally benefited from the misery of others or betrayed a friend. And yet, what I felt neither the Nuremberg trial nor his books had really told us was how a man of such quality could become not immoral, not amoral but, somehow infinitely worse, morally extinguished".[25]

If he became "morally extinguished", then his "struggle with the truth" (the title of Sereny's book), must have been a struggle to recover that which had been lost. At the very end, Sereny writes as follows:

> "I came to understand and value Speer's battle with himself and saw in it the re-emergence of the intrinsic morality he manifested as a boy and youth. It seemed to me it was some kind of victory that this man—just this man—*weighed down by intolerable and unmanageable guilt . . . tried to become a different man*".[26]

Sereny summarises the process from moral extinction to awareness. She details Speer's growing recognition of "Hitler's madness" through two formative war-

---

[24] Sereny, n. 4 above, at p. 9.
[25] Ibid., at p. 10.
[26] Ibid., at p. 720. My emphasis.

time experiences. The first was at Posen, where in a speech in October 1943 Himmler directly confronted all the top Nazis with what had been done to the Jews, the second concerned his own personal visit in December 1943 to the "Dora" project, the underground rocket factories built with slave labour, where Speer was again directly confronted with what was happening. After the war, Speer was subject to the "revelations of Nuremberg" and was confronted "with the reactions of the civilised world". He came to realise the "horror of what had been done" and to experience "feelings of personal guilt" which were illuminated by, most importantly, a pastor at Spandau, Casalis, and his daughter, Hilde. In the context of the solitude of a twenty-year sentence at Spandau, Speer experienced a "continuing and tormenting awareness of guilt" and "out of all this, there came to be another Speer". This is Sereny's summary (with a crucial part of one sentence missed out) of the "other" Speer, a man who sought with all seriousness to come to terms with his past:

> "In this Speer, obsessed with a history he understood perhaps like no other man, I found a great deal to like over the four years I knew him. This, I feel, had become the real Speer [. . .] This was a very serious man who knew more about that bane of our century, Hitler, than anyone else. This was an erudite and solitary man who, recognising his deficiencies in human relations, had read five thousand books in prison to try to understand the universe and human beings, an effort he succeeded in with his mind but failed in with his heart. Empathy is finally a gift, and cannot be learned, so, essentially, returning into the world after twenty years, he remained alone.
>
> Unforgiven by so many for having served Hitler, he elected to spend the rest of his life in confrontation with this past, unforgiving of himself for having so nearly loved a monster".[27]

In this account, Speer sought resolution with his guilt, but remained essentially solitary. He could not ultimately get there, but his effort in seeking to do so was what Sereny admired. In a newspaper interview, she states that "to me, there was one extraordinarily redeeming thing, that his sense of personal guilt was so deep" and that through this guilt, he regained "some of his morality".[28] This is a compelling and sympathetic account of Speer, a man whom Sereny admits she "grew to like".[29]

It rests, however, alongside another story she tells. In the long passage I quoted above, I missed out part of one sentence. Just after Sereny has spoken of the "real" Speer, there is a line in which she notes that for a brief period before he died, Speer discarded his moral seriousness, but she states that she is convinced that he would have rediscovered it "after the euphoria of his late-life passion had passed".[30] Sereny refers here to an affair Speer conducted in his final

---

[27] Ibid., at p. 719.
[28] The Guardian, interview of Gitta Sereny by Megan Tresidder, September 1995.
[29] Sereny, n. 4 above, at p. 3.
[30] The full passage omitted, which belongs where I have placed the square brackets in the quote, is as follows: "the one I am convinced—after the euphoria of his late-life passion had passed—he would have become again, had he lived on".

years with a woman much younger than himself. In Sereny's estimation, this affair jolted Speer into a different moral outlook. The woman with whom he became involved bestowed upon him "unlimited and uncritical acceptance" which was to "free him from the questioning self he had been for so long".[31] The fruit of this was observed in a phone call Sereny took from Speer shortly before his death in which he reflected self-satisfactorily on his life. She quotes him:

> "'What I wanted to tell you' Speer said happily, 'was that after all I think I haven't done so badly. After all, I *was* Hitler's architect; I *was* his Minister of Armaments and Production; I *did* serve twenty years in Spandau and, coming out *did* make another good career. Not bad after all, was it?'".[32]

Was this just a final deflection from contrition, as Sereny has it, or did it reflect another side to Speer that Sereny's positive moral image of him downplayed? Compare her account of the end of his life with her assessment of its beginning. We have already seen Sereny comment on "the re-emergence of the intrinsic morality [Speer] manifested *as a boy and youth*" (my emphasis) but this can be contrasted with what she says, only on the previous page, that Speer "felt nothing" for the Nazi slaughter:

> "There was a dimension missing in him, a capacity to feel *which his childhood had blotted out*, allowing him to experience not love but only romanticised substitutes for love.
> Pity, compassion, sympathy and empathy were not part of his emotional vocabulary".[33]

These are two deeply opposed accounts of Speer's youth, which offer crucially different lenses for the interpretation of his later moral behaviour. At varying points in the book, this "other" Speer, lacking in significant moral experience, makes himself felt. The same Speer could write letters from Spandau that acknowledged something of his responsibility, but were ultimately evasive, and could acknowledge feelings of guilt, but also consider his position in coldly calculating and strategic ways. In this context, it should not be forgotten that Sereny's whole interrogation with Speer had to negotiate his continuing *denial* of direct knowledge of what was happening to the Jews under the Nazis, so that his entire post-Nazi life involved the living of a lie. Even his final apparent acknowledgement of a form of direct complicity he challenged later himself.

Sereny encountered this "other" Speer during her conversations with him, when she would occasionally trip a circuit in Speer's mind which would replace his sympathy and urbanity with something threatening and violent:

> "Here was not the reasoning Speer, my urbane host. Here was Hitler's great Minister who had ruled Germany's economy and the lives of millions ... I was suddenly keenly and somewhat frighteningly aware ... of the authority coiled inside this man, which

---

[31] Sereny, n. 4 above, at p. 715.
[32] *Ibid.*, at p. 781.
[33] *Ibid.*, at p. 719. My emphasis.

manifestly suppressed with constant deliberate effort, only burst out at moments of disappointment, intense irritation or weary anger".[34]

Again, at the very end of the book, Sereny counterposes the guilt-feeling Speer to the pragmatic Speer who gave up every consideration to satisfy his own ambition, and who "manipulated, cajoled, intrigued against and threatened those who interfered with his power and his aims".[35] In her *Guardian* interview, counterposed to the image of Speer's deep sense of personal guilt was Sereny's acknowledgement that "Speer was a man of such multi-personalities and if you didn't understand that, you could not deal with him".[36] Thus at one level, Sereny recognised Speer's morally schizophrenic character, but the picture that dominates her analysis is of a man who "once was lost but now is found", one "weighed down by intolerable and unmanageable guilt" who "tried to become a different man".

5. Guilt: The Space Between

In the light of Sereny on Speer, let us now return to Giddens' observations about the nature of guilt and community in late modernity. As regards the self, Giddens suggested that an increasing individual reflexivity erodes normative boundaries and leads to a diminution of the sense of transgression that underlies guilt. The self is able more and more to create and recreate itself through the fashioning of changeable narratives that position and reposition it according to the needs of the moment. Reflexivity undermines transgression, which undermines guilt. The reflexive self reinterprets its biography to suit the context, so that a sense of a unified self becomes increasingly fragile. At the same time, however, there is a minimal level at which this self remains quite robust, able to weather major transitions or tensions in the social environment.

If we consider Speer in this light, one could interpret his conduct during and after the Second World War in terms of the "fragile" aspect of the Giddens self. Relying on the minimal "robust" side of selfhood to get him through the transition from Nazism to liberal democracy, Speer would simply be a person who reinvented himself to suit the changing times. But what then of his sense of guilt, on which Sereny focuses? As we have seen, Sereny's image of a "morally continuous" Speer, seeking to come to terms with his past, is undercut by the "other" Speer who irrupted into her narrative and consciousness from time to time. Perhaps we might be inclined to dismiss Sereny's view and say that Speer was just a cynic, manipulating Sereny and anyone else prepared to listen to him. Perhaps, then, we would say that Giddens is right. But I think we have to grasp the post-war Speer in a more complex way than saying *either* that he was a

---

[34] *Ibid.*, at p. 222.
[35] *Ibid.*, at p. 718.
[36] *Guardian*, interview with G. Sereny, n. 28 above.

moral being *or* that he was a cynic and manipulator. The truth seems to involve capturing a sense in which both aspects could be true, and so doing, to move beyond both.

A way into this complexity comes from the second aspect of Giddens' account, the idea of the erosion of community. I suggested that another interpretation of late modernity might involve us looking as much at the fragmentation and conflict between communities as at the erosion of their moral influence. This seems to me particularly important in thinking about Speer. The post-war process from Nuremberg onwards represented a confrontation between the moral values of two quite different communities, the fascist and the liberal democratic. When Speer was charged with crimes against humanity, when he was confronted by the pastor Casalis at Spandau, when he was asked by his daughter what he had known and done, when he was interrogated by Sereny herself, when he wrote explaining for a post-war society what Nazism had meant, he was confronting in each case a different moral outlook from the one of which he had been a part. What we get from Sereny's analysis of Speer is the sense of a *moral dialogue* between two political communities in which an individual, who passed historically from one to the other, was confronted with *and was genuinely engaged by* the condemnation of his past, and from which he developed, *at least at one level of his being,* feelings of guilt. It seems to me that Sereny is not wrong to recognise his feelings of guilt, but these always coexisted with careerist calculation. He both felt guilt and was "a man of such multi-personalities". This sets up an ambiguity and an ambivalence in her analysis. While recognising both sides of Speer, Sereny cannot synthesise her account. She gets drawn too close to the Speer she liked, while remaining both too acute not to note his other, deeply unattractive, side *and* unable to reconcile this with her liking of him. The ultimate problem she faces is how to judge this level of conflict and complexity in one man. It is this that causes the tension in her book.

This problem of complexity takes me to my own argument about the ambiguity of the self and the ambivalence of judgement in modern society. The post-war liberal democratic communities established, at one significant level at least,[37] different public and private norms and judgements to those of fascism. Nuremberg, Pastor Casalis, Speer's daughter, and Sereny all approach Speer from the judgement of the utter wrongs of the Nazis, so that they impose a judgemental context upon Speer with which he became engaged. Post-Nuremberg involved a process of dialogue between one who had been a fascist and a liberal democratic community, and whatever feelings of guilt occurred within Speer's individual moral life were invoked by that dialogue. The point seems an obvious one, but its impact on Speer is significant. Recall the two images that Sereny provides, one of his morality, the other of his cynicism. My

---

[37] Any full assessment of the gap between post-war morality and that of the Nazis would have to absorb the lesson of the ways in which, as Tom Bower puts it, a blind eye was turned to murder in the post-war denazification of Germany (see Bower, *Blind Eye to Murder* (London, Warner, 1997).

suggestion is that he was both these things, that these were both life stories that one could tell about Speer. Speer was both the calculating careerist who knowingly turned his back on the consequences of his action and endorsed Nazism, and a man who evolved moral responses to what he had done in his later years. The transition, however, was never such that the later Speer completely subsumed, or sublated, the earlier. Speer's life spanned two different socio-political periods, and accordingly so too did his personality and his morality. Speer the individual was really two Speers spread out across two historical contexts. Dialogue with Sereny, Casalis, and his daughter contextualised his subjectivity in the liberal democratic context, setting up a profound conflict with what he had been. This led to genuine feelings of guilt, but feelings that were not strong enough to lead him to draw a clear line against what he had been.

The escape into a romantic and sexual affair in his last years can thus be seen not, as Sereny sees it, as a moral "blip", but as the creation, as it were, of a "moral micro-community" with his girlfriend sealing Speer off from the broader liberal democratic context, in which his guilt was set aside and his earlier amoral egotism and pride in his fascist achievements resurfaced. Similarly, the occasional irruption of his violent Nazi persona through his urbane liberal democratic self, which so shocked Sereny, was an indication of the different selves co-existing in the later Speer.

Where does all this take us in relation to the questions of guilt and responsibility? I have been trying to get at the relationship between the individual and the community as a nexus within which responsibility and guilt are established. Individuals shift between registers of self-accounting, so that it is socio-political contexts that "fix" responsibility. War criminals provide a particularly vivid illustration of this issue because they move historically between quite different moral contexts of judgement. In the process their responsibility for their crimes, as a matter of individual guilt, is something that they ambiguously and ambivalently negotiate with their interrogators. Individual guilt and responsibility are thus real categories which we need to understand, but contextually and dialectically, as processes, by individuals, of symbiotic engagement within different socio-political communities.

They do not as a result, however, possess a complete fluidity, so that no judgement becomes possible. Recall that in my reference to Myra Hindley, I suggested that beyond an immediate finding of guilt and a contextualisation of personhood, there was a further third step, at which it was possible to ask whether, taking into account what was done and the context within which it was done, there could be an acknowledgement by a person that it was he or she who had done the wrong, even taking into account a context that was different and distancing from the here and now. Such an acknowledgement, in dialogue with a community, is possible even, *pace* Giddens, under conditions of late modernity. The evidence of Sereny's account is that Speer had such a dialogue—with his daughter and with Casalis—but that he never took the third, morally totalising, step of fully acknowledging *for himself* his guilt. The ultimate problem was not that he "lacked empathy",[38] but that he lacked a full sense of his own guilt. He felt guilt but insufficiently to overcome a competing impulse to denial.

6. Beyond "Individual" and "Community" in the Philosophy of Punishment

I want to end by locating the foregoing in the context of problems within the philosophy of punishment. The dominant tradition here is broadly Kantian in the sense of a reliance on "notions of personal agency, responsibility, and the moral law".[39] Such a sense of individual responsibility informs in different ways the analysis of guilt in both Giddens' and Sereny's work. With Sereny, the idea of a man coming to terms with his guilt is plainly Kantian in this broad sense; but the same is true *mutatis mutandis* with Giddens' emphasis on the isolated, reflexive individual of late modernity. Indeed one might say that Giddens' individual, freed of the norms of a community, is living out the solipsistic quality that Hannah Arendt finds in Kant's failed moral law, the categorical imperative. The categorical imperative requires the rational individual to agree with himself because it "is based upon the necessity for rational thought to agree with itself".[40] Such an unconnected individualism is not so far from the "reflexive organisation of the self", but it clearly misses the continuing linkages I have sought to demonstrate between individual morality and the community(ies) of which it is a part.

If much modern philosophy of punishment proceeds in this broadly Kantian mode,[41] there have been attempts to link issues of responsibility to questions of community, and a sense of dialogue between individual and community. For example, Antony Duff[42] has written of punishment as a process of communication between individual and community. However, I have argued elsewhere[43] that Duff retains an essentially Kantian notion of the responsible subject which he himself undermines by his attempt to locate that subject within a broader community. At the same time, he fails to recognise fully the moral effect on issues of guilt and blame of acknowledging what community means in modern Western societies with structural social conflicts. In this regard, Duff's move is not a new one, bearing a strong resemblance (though there are important differences) to the work of the late nineteenth century English Hegelians, T.H.

---

[38] Sereny, n. 4 above, at p. 719.

[39] G. Bird, "Kantianism" in T. Honderich (ed.). *Oxford Companion to Philosophy* (Oxford, Oxford University Press, 1995) pp. 439–41; cf. J. Gardner, "On the General Part of the Criminal Law" in A. Duff (ed.), *Philosophy and the Criminal Law*, n. 2 above, pp. 205–56.

[40] H. Arendt, *Between Past and Future* (London, Faber, 1961).

[41] See e.g. A. von Hirsch, *Censure and Sanctions* (Oxford, Oxford University Press, 1993); M. Moore, n. 22 above.

[42] R. A. Duff, *Trials and Punishments* (Cambridge, Cambridge University Press, 1986); R. A. Duff, "Penal Communications" (1996) 20 *Crime and Justice: A Review of Research* 1–97.

[43] Norrie, "'Simulacra of Morality'? Beyond the Ideal/Actual Antinomies of Criminal Justice", n. 2 above.

Green and Bernard Bosanquet[44] who were earlier initiators of a communitarian political philosophy.

Green and Bosanquet were Victorian inheritors of the idealist tradition of Kant and Hegel, and their work was designed to relocate what they saw as the too ideal individualism of the Germans in a more realistic sense of the nature of modern capitalist society. Viewed in this perspective, the past and present concerns of communitarian writers are really the other side of the Kantian heritage against which they frequently rail: they are still dancing to a Kantian tune. Indeed, if we follow Arendt's interpretation, Kant was himself an enthusiastic participant in the "individualist-communitarian *pas de deux*". She describes a striking philosophical contrast between Kant's critique of moral reason and his critique of aesthetic judgement. In the latter, she identifies a different relationship between the individual and the community in which, contrary to the categorical imperative, "it would not be enough to be in agreement with one's own self", but rather there would be a relationship which involved "being able to 'think in the place of everybody else'". Under what Kant called an "enlarged mentality", the power of judgement:

> "rests on a potential agreement with others, and the thinking process which is active in judging something is not, like the thought process of pure reasoning, a dialogue between me and myself, but finds itself always and primarily, even if I am quite alone in making up my mind, *in an anticipated communication with others with whom I know I must finally come to some agreement*".[45]

To be sure, Kant's target in the critique of aesthetic judgement is quite different from moral wrongdoing, but there are parallels. Arendt continues that aesthetic judgement is both impossible without, and limited by, the nature of community. As regards the necessity of community, judgement cannot function in strict isolation or solitude; it needs the presence of others "in whose place" it must think, whose perspectives it must take into consideration, and without whom it never has the opportunity to operate at all. As logic, to be sound, depends on the presence of the self, so judgement, to be valid, *depends on the presence of others*.[46]

As regards the limitation of judgement by virtue of its place in community, Arendt observes that it:

> "is endowed with a certain specific validity but is never universally valid. Its claims to validity can never extend further than the others in whose place the judging person has put himself for his considerations".[47]

She concludes that judgement "is a specifically political ability", the ability "to see things . . . in the perspective of all those who happen to be present". As such, it is "one of the fundamental abilities of man as a political being".

---

[44] See my *Law, Ideology and Punishment* (Dordrecht, Kluwer, 1991) ch. 5 for discussion of these writers.
[45] Arendt, n. 40 above, at p. 220. My emphasis.
[46] *Ibid*. My emphasis.
[47] *Ibid*., at p. 221.

I suggest that Kant, on Arendt's rendition, got at least as close to issues of guilt and responsibility in his discussion of aesthetics as he did in his moral philosophy. His emphasis on the role of community and its relationship with the individual, far from the solipsist bar of the categorical imperative, identifies the place where judgement occurs, and which generates the complexity, ambivalence, and ambiguity I have sought to identify here. Community, as I hope I have made clear, is not the whole story, but it is an integral part of it. It is only in a community that the floating stories of the self that Giddens identifies *theoretically*, and Sereny identifies *biographically* can be "fixed". My approach locates a "site" of judgement that is both within a community and a means of bringing to bear judgement on individuals for whom guilt is a possible moral sentiment. This involves a more complex, dialectical, understanding of individuals and communities than individualistic or communitarian approaches have been able to provide.

I want finally to anticipate one possible objection to the foregoing and at least to indicate how it might be met. The objection would be that in moving our debate beyond Kantianism and into an area where morality operates *between* an individual and a community, the force of an absolute morality is lost. Kant's categorical imperative might have proved empty in practice, but at least it marked a site where deontological issues were discussed as real moral possibilities. In locating guilt and judgement somewhere between individuals and communities, one may be committing oneself to the dangerously relativist view that all that exists morally is the morality of communities.

To do no more than identify one possible response to this objection, let us consider briefly Roy Bhaskar's discussion of an example provided by Isaiah Berlin.[48] Berlin contrasted four descriptions of what happened under Nazi rule in Germany: "the country was depopulated"; "millions of people died"; "millions of people were killed"; "millions of people were murdered". Language is the place where communities in conflict can seem to agree on "the facts", while disagreeing fundamentally on their moral import: think of "ethnic cleansing". But what Berlin's example shows is that, while all four of his statements are true, it is the last that is "not only most evaluative, [but] also the best (i.e. the most precise and accurate) description of what actually happened".[49] Bhaskar's moral realism relates the description of social phenomena to their truth content, and their truth as adequate descriptions, where relevant, to their truth as moral descriptions. The fourth statement's factual and moral truth "turns not on the subject's interest in the subject matter, but on the nature of the subject matter itself and criteria for its adequate description and explanation".[50] In the last sentence we could talk just as easily of the "community's interest" as the "subject's interest".

---

[48] R. Bhaskar, *Plato etc* (London, Verso, 1994), at p. 110.
[49] Ibid.
[50] Ibid.

This reference to a moral realist underpinning to the discussion of the historical and community mediation of individual responsibility, requires to be developed, but I will conclude on the main themes of my argument. The issue of legal or moral guilt is a complex one that defies the easy answers of those who assume the existence of a fixed, responsible subject, or argue for the late modern erosion or reflexivity of all subject positions. Central to the establishment of guilt is the dialectical relationship between a subject and his or her historically evolving communities. Speer's ambivalence concerning his guilt, reflected on but not fully understood by Gitta Sereny, illustrates such a relationship. When all was said and done, Speer had not decisively moved to acknowledge fully his guilt, and it is on that basis that he is to be judged. Yet he had felt guilt, and it is the phenomenal texture and possibility of this ambiguous subject position I have sought to explain, by a relational theory of rationality.

9

Penal Practices and Political Theory: An Agenda for Dialogue

NICOLA LACEY

The question of punishment forms an important object of analysis within a wide variety of disciplines. In moral philosophy, political theory, social history, sociology, law, theology, psychology, and social and legal theory, punishment has preoccupied scholars from the birth of the disciplines to the present day. Yet the extent to which the insights attained by these various analyses have been brought together, and to which the disciplines have found effective ways of communicating with one another, remains limited.

In this chapter, I focus in particular on penal philosophy and political theory on the one hand and on sociological and historical analyses of penality on the other. My object is to consider both the ways in which each of these broad approaches to punishment puts questions on the agenda of the other, and, to the extent that this is so, the degree to which the tools of each may either effectively accommodate those questions within their existing frameworks or draw on the conceptual resources and insights of the other approaches in order to accommodate them. In doing so, my aim is not to argue for a synthesis of political-theoretic and socio-historical analyses of punishment. Rather, it is to suggest that the ambition of normative theories of punishment is destined to founder unless those theories can find ways of adapting to the changing contours of punishment as a social practice identified by sociological and historical analysis. In particular, I argue that contemporary social theory generates certain conceptual tools which might usefully be adapted within a political-theoretic discourse and brought to bear upon the normative questions raised by contemporary penal practices, and that the primacy of state punishment within political theories needs to be modified in the light of contemporary socio-legal research.

1. Punishment and Political Theory

Within political theory, punishment occupies an important and in several respects distinctive position. Its distinctive treatment lies in the fact that punishment is typically dealt with by political theorists as a relatively discrete issue.[1] This stands in contrast to political theorists' treatment of what might be thought to be analogous and equally important social institutions such as taxation, reparations, compensation, or the welfare state. The tendency to take punishment as a discrete object of philosophical enquiry has certain weaknesses. For example, it entails a relative insulation of the debate about the justification of punishment from broader questions of political theory which are integral to a proper analysis of punishment. Thus while issues about moral responsibility and (somewhat less often) political obligation are regularly integrated with philosophical analyses of punishment, the nature of legal obligation, the moral authority of the state as the giver of punishment and the proper scope and functions of criminal law are frequently ignored or drawn as separable issues.[2]

This insulation of the question of how punishment is to be justified from questions about the standards breach of which justify the invoking of a penal response certainly simplifies the philosophical issue. Moreover, by directing attention away from the link between state punishment and brute political and administrative power, it enhances the rhetorical plausibility of an analogy (sometimes explicit but more often implicit in penal philosophy) between state punishment and the more obviously or "purely" moral or spiritual practice of atonement. But although some political philosophers, and notably Antony Duff, have made serious attempts to think about how punishment might be organised so as to make this analogy closer,[3] unless it can be articulated with a view about the genuinely moral content of criminal law—a view which sits unhappily with the modern realities of state punishment and of an extensive and increasingly regulatory criminal law—it tends to collapse under critical scrutiny. In the context of pluralistic modern societies, contemporary theories of punishment which seek to strengthen the moral case for punishment by emphasising its role as a form of communication among members of a political society, whether of a liberal-individualist or communitarian temper, raise intractable questions about who or what constitutes the body with the authority to punish. Who is the "we" in whose name punishment is enforced: is it a geographical, national, cultural, or normative order?[4] What are the conditions for membership in this moral-institutional order? And what gives it the moral authority to punish, in the name of the collective "we", even those who contest its norms?

While the scholarly tendency to isolate the question of punishment within political theory has undoubtedly limited our view of the complexity of the issue, the philosophical focus on punishment as a discrete or at least special issue in

---

[1] See for example H. L. A. Hart, *Punishment and Responsibility* (Oxford, Clarendon Press, 1968); T. Honderich, *Punishment: The Supposed Justifications* (Harmondsworth, Penguin, 1984); R. A. Duff, *Trials and Punishments* (Cambridge, Cambridge University Press, 1986); Nicola Lacey, *State Punishment: Political Principles and Community Values* (London, Routledge, 1988).

[2] See Lacey, n. 1 above, chs. 1, 3–6.

[3] Duff, n. 1 above, chs 2, 3, 9.

[4] cf. Duncan Ivison's chapter in this volume.

political theory also has certain advantages. Put simply, it affords the political theorist a distinctive focus which can claim attention as illuminating and providing a framework for critical reflection upon a significant social practice which presents a variety of pressing practical and ethical problems. Hence debates about how punishment should be defined are not mere quibbling with words: rather, they represent a crucial engagement with the question of how the social contours of the practice should be drawn.[5] We could argue, for example, that in focusing on the power to punish or the power to levy taxation, as distinct from "power" generally, political philosophers are, at least implicitly, acknowledging the need to produce what might be called a socially relevant or sociologically informed political theory. In other words, by focusing on actual—and normatively troublesome—social practices, the political philosopher commits herself to a certain view of the relationship between political theory and the social world. This commitment, however, is incompletely realised in the methodology to which most political theorists confine themselves.

In what follows, I set out to illustrate this limitation of penal philosophy's perspective by drawing attention to two issues explored in contemporary sociology, history, and social theory which raise questions relevant to political theories of punishment yet which have been ignored within penal philosophy. The first arises out of the work of Michel Foucault and in particular out of his differentiation between a number of conceptions of power. The second arises out of an empirical understanding of how penality actually functions in late modern polities such as Britain.

2. Sovereignty, Juridical, and Disciplinary Power

The work of Foucault is, perhaps significantly, difficult to classify in terms of the conventional disciplines such as philosophy and history. His writings ranged across a number of theoretical debates, social institutions and historical periods, and many of his ideas are of direct relevance to punishment.[6] In this chapter, my interest in Foucault is confined to his reflections on different forms and conceptualisations of power. Put simply, Foucault drew a distinction between sovereignty power, juridical power, and disciplinary power. Power as sovereignty may aptly be characterised as a form of property: it is something which people may have less and more of, which they can gain or lose, which they hold and exercise. Juridical power is rather a mode of power which operates by means of formal classification and distinction. Power understood as discipline is less tangible than either sovereignty or juridical power: disciplinary power inheres in particular discourses and practices, and operates (rather than being exercised)

---

[5] cf. Hart n. 1 above, ch. 1; Lacey, n. 1 above, ch. 1.
[6] See in particular *Discipline and Punish: The Birth of the Prison*, transl. A. Sheridan (Harmondsworth, Penguin, 1977); *Madness and Civilisation* (London, Tavistock, 1967); *The Birth of the Clinic* (London, Tavistock, 1973).

in a subtle and diffused way throughout the social body. It does so, typically, by means of practices of "normalisation": it makes and, in a real sense, enacts assumptions about "normality", distributing agents around its means. Furthermore, this disciplinary power operates at least in part—and this is perhaps the summit of its realisation—when agents become complicit in their own subjection to (and genesis as subjects within) its subtle force. Thus the "chosen" practices of therapy, religion, physical training, as much as our more obviously determined participation in social discourses such as gender or social class, are seen as being among the operations of power and hence as open to analysis in those terms.

Foucault's differentiated conceptualisation of power is, of course, tied up with a broad historical thesis about the decline of sovereignty and juridical power and the increasing importance of disciplinary power in late modern societies. Various objections might be (and have been) raised to this historical argument. One might question, for example, whether disciplinary power is as "modern" as Foucault implies and, conversely, whether sovereignty power has lost its importance in all spheres of the modern world. Moreover, it may be argued that Foucault's three conceptions of power can be mapped onto institutions in a somewhat different way than that which he envisaged: for example, contemporary legal theorists have suggested that modern law has long had an inevitably disciplinary aspect, and that the growth in importance of disciplinary power may therefore imply a change in the nature of law's power rather than a diminution of its scope.[7] For my purposes, however, it is not the historical or (as Foucault would have had it) genealogical thesis, but rather the conceptualisation which Foucault has developed, which is significant. This is because, whatever we make of Foucault's historical claims, it seems clear that the disciplinary power which he identified constitutes an important aspect of the social practice of punishment today. In other words, Foucault's conceptualisation of power as discipline can alert us to aspects of penal practice of which a narrow conceptualisation of the power to punish as the sovereignty-type power of the state obscures our view.

For example, Pat Carlen's striking study of the nature of women's imprisonment in Cornton Vale Prison in Scotland revealed that the meaning of a sentence of imprisonment cannot be grasped in terms simply of the order of the court and the executive that a person serve a sentence of a particular length in a particular institution. Rather, the operation of imprisonment involves the disciplining of prisoners within, for example, powerful discourses of gender—discourses which are an integral part of the state's penal practice.[8] And this discipline which is at the core of the modern power to punish inheres as much in the micro-details of prison regimes, uniform, staff attitudes and so on as in the formal sentence of the court and the other more obvious indices of state power. At

---

[7] See for example C. Smart, *Feminism and the Power of Law* (London, Routledge, 1989), ch. 1.
[8] See P. Carlen, *Women's Imprisonment: A Study in Social Control* (London, Routledge, 1983).

other stages of the criminal process, too, research reveals that discourses of masculinity, femininity, and family, alongside a host of other assumptions about "normality", structure the practices of sentencing, policing, and prosecution which, as its inevitable precursors, are integral to our understanding of punishment.[9] In short, Foucault's identification and conceptualisation of disciplinary power has generated a richer vision of the *modus operandi* and implications of social practices of punishment. If, then, penal philosophy is in the business of developing not only the best possible justification of punishment but also a framework for the critical assessment of something like the social practice of punishment, the phenomena of disciplinary power are ones which it cannot afford to ignore.

Ignorance or indifference remain, however, the typical attitudes characterising penal philosophers' response to Foucault's well-known arguments and to the conclusions drawn by sociologists about their implications for punishment.[10] Three strategies are, moreover, available to the penal philosopher who wishes to justify this attitude of indifference. In the first place, she may simply define punishment so as to exclude its disciplinary aspects. In other words, she may define punishment merely in terms of the sovereign and/or juridical power which sets the formal sentence to be served, conceptualising the hardships implicit in the sentence in terms of its impact on a standard set of human interests such as liberty and property. In adopting this strategy, the political philosopher need not, of course, imply that sociological analyses of the disciplinary aspects of punishment,[11] or analyses of modern punishment within the framework of governmentality and in the light of the decline of sovereign power,[12] are either unimportant or wrong-headed. Her attitude is far less arrogant than this, but it is similar in effect. For the consequence of this first philosophical response is that two very rich literatures—the philosophy and sociology of punishment—are destined to speak past one another (to the extent that they are spoken in the same place at all). Moreover this intellectual barrier is sometimes reinforced by sociologists, who often see normative questions as occupying an entirely different intellectual terrain from their own analytic and interpretive concerns.

---

[9] See for example H. Allen, *Justice Unbalanced* (Milton Keynes, Open University Press, 1987); M. Eaton, *Justice for Women?* (Milton Keynes, Open University Press, 1986); N. Lacey, "Unspeakable Subjects, Impossible Rights: Sexuality, Integrity and Criminal Law", in *Unspeakable Subjects* (Oxford, Hart Publishing, 1998), ch 4; C. Smart, *Law, Crime and Sexuality* (London, Sage, 1995), Parts I and II.

[10] For a rare example of a philosophically inspired treatment of punishment which is nonetheless informed by an analysis of the influence of economic and social power, see Alan Norrie, *Law, Ideology and Punishment* (Dordrecht, Kluwer, 1991).

[11] Carlen, n. 8 above.

[12] See D. Garland, "The Limits of the Sovereign State: Strategies of Crime Control in Contemporary Societies" (1996) 36 *British Journal of Criminology* 446; see also his *Punishment and Welfare* (Aldershot, Gower,1985); *Punishment and Modern Society* (Oxford, Oxford University Press, 1990). For other interpretive social histories of criminal law and punishment see M. Wiener, *Reconstructing the Criminal: culture, law and policy in England, 1830–1914* (Cambridge, Cambridge University Press, 1990); L. Zedner, *Women, Crime and Custody in Victorian England* (Oxford, Oxford University Press, 1991).

Foucault, for example, was famously uninterested in normative questions about power, and confined himself to a (notoriously underdeveloped) account of the way in which power calls forth resistance, without considering the conditions under which power might or might not be regarded as legitimate.

Is this academic partition really apposite to the nature of the issues at hand? While I certainly do not want to suggest that there is no difference between penal philosophy and the sociology of punishment, I do think that there is obvious scope here for dialogue between the two. On the one hand, the sociology of punishment—at least sociology of an interpretive rather than narrowly empiricist temper—inevitably engages with the norms, values, and ideals which are internal to the practice of punishment. Agents' understanding of what renders punishment legitimate and justifiable, in other words, are part of its social reality. Hence the world of ideas refined and articulated by the political philosopher, though it does not have the same meaning for the sociologist, is nonetheless of significance for her. More importantly for the purposes of this chapter, and notwithstanding Foucault's disclaimers, disciplinary power raises, from the point of view of political theory, a discrete and morally pressing set of normative questions. If, in other words, the concept of power as discipline illuminates aspects of practices of punishment, the justifiability of those practices arises as a question for political theory. Why should political theory turn its back on a conceptual innovation which potentially expands its terrain? Why should the practices best understood in terms of disciplinary power be the latest in a long line of phenomena "banished to another discipline" by operation of the famous "definitional stop"?

The second possible response available to the political theorist wishing to justify her failure to accommodate the notion of disciplinary power is more substantial. This is the deployment—familiar to all students of theories of punishment—of the distinction between ideal theory and non-ideal theory.[13] The argument, in essence, is that political philosophy is in the business of developing the best possible justification of punishment under ideal circumstances. Thus it assumes, for example, the general justice of social institutions, including the criminal justice system; the general legitimacy of state power; and the goodwill of those administering the system. Inevitable disparities between the real world and these assumed circumstances may be ignored in theory-construction, though they are of direct relevance to the application or implications of theory: for the moral assessment of punishment in the real world must take place not only by reference to the theory but also in the light of the gap between the actual and the ideal. This entails, of course, that the best theory of punishment may turn out not to justify a large proportion of—or indeed all—actual practices of punishment in a given social order. On the other hand, it is argued that ideal theory has a political relevance in that it provides not only a framework for critique but also a motivating horizon towards which we may work gradually

---

[13] See for example Duff, n. 1 above, ch. 10 ; Lacey, n. 1 above, ch. 8.

to move actual institutions of punishment. On this view, it could simply be argued that the disciplinary aspects of punishment are unjustified according to the most convincing theories of punishment, and are therefore features of social reality which we should try to eliminate from the practice of punishment.

This purported justification for ignoring the idea of disciplinary power is unsatisfactory for at least three reasons. First, from the point of view of political theory, it surely cannot be assumed, *a priori*, that all disciplinary aspects of the power to punish are unjustifiable. This is a conclusion rather than a premiss: as such, it requires argument, and the argument in turn requires the political theorist to incorporate the concept of disciplinary power within her analytic framework. Secondly, to the extent that sociological analyses suggest that punishment in certain kinds of social order inevitably implies the operation of disciplinary power—that penal power is implicitly, in part, disciplinary—the sidelining of this aspect of punishment looks much like an admission of defeat for the political theorist's aspiration to develop the best possible account of how punishment may be justified. If we are right, then, in arguing that the political theorist's focus on the particular question of punishment implies a commitment to developing a socially relevant theory, that commitment is inconsistent with the theorist's refusal to consider and incorporate aspects which sociologists can show to be central to the practice of punishment.

Thirdly, it might be argued that disciplinary power is irrelevant to normative political theory because, unlike sovereignty or juridical power, it is not a product of human agency and is hence, like the weather or contingencies of talent, beyond the scope of moral assessment or justification. This is an important argument. However, it cannot justify the political theorist's indifference for, just as the "natural" distribution of talents poses important questions for the operation of principles of distributive justice,[14] the "naturally" disciplinary implications of institutions of punishment designed and administered by human beings poses questions about the justice and justifiability of those institutions. The goal of eliminating or radically restructuring disciplinary power may be, in the strict sense, utopian, but the existence of such power (if we are convinced of it) nonetheless affects the implications of our normative principles.

To sum up, I have argued in this section that penal philosophers cannot, consistently with their theoretical aspirations, maintain their attitude of wilful ignorance towards the insights generated by social theory or by social histories of punishment. And to the extent that conceptual innovations such as Foucault's genuinely illuminate the shape of contemporary social practices, then political theory will have to incorporate them—even if this is merely a prelude to an argument about the illegitimacy of those contemporary social developments.

---

[14] See J. Rawls, *A Theory of Justice* (Cambridge Mass., Harvard University Press, 1971), pp. 12–15, 72 *et seq.*, 101 *et seq.*, 507 *et seq.*

3. POLITICAL THEORY AND THE FRAGMENTATION OF PENAL POWER

The second issue which I consider is more straightforwardly empirical than the first, though the two overlap in significant ways. This second issue has to do with the tendency in political theory to identify the political and the public with the state and, moreover, with a relatively simple, unitary conception of the nation state. In penal philosophy, this tendency realises itself in the assumption that the "central case" of punishment is state punishment, with other instances defined in relation to this statist paradigm. Hence treatises on theories of punishment pay lip-service to the existence of, for example, parental punishment or penalties imposed by associations such as clubs, companies, or educational institutions. But these instances do not present the key problem for political theory, and are mentioned mainly as instructive comparators which may help to sustain, by analogy or disanalogy, the arguments developed in relation to the paradigm of state punishment.

Is this primary focus on a certain conception of state punishment consistent with the political theorist's commitment to producing a theory of punishment which is of use in the moral assessment of actual social institutions? In at least two overlapping respects, this focus appears unduly narrow. First of all, neither today nor at many times in the past has punishment been administered or even determined primarily by the nation state. Even confining our historical purview to the period following the establishment of modern nation states, private or quasi-private practices of punishment have been a significant social phenomenon. To the extent that (by analogy with feminist arguments about the untenability of the public-private distinction[15]) "private" punishments have implications for subjects' "public" interests or status—for their physical integrity, their property, their social reputation, and so on—we can argue that these "private" punishments are of "public" significance and hence a proper object of political theory. Since many such punishments do indeed affect not only physical integrity but also, for example, employment opportunities, such a spill-over from private to public would seem inevitable, and the public-private divide in relation to punishment as problematic as in relation to, for example, the gendered division of labour.

Even, secondly, if we were to accept the appropriateness of a focus on state punishment, the particular conception of the state and of state power which is assumed in most penal philosophy looks increasingly simplistic in the light of recent developments in the configuration of state power in the criminal justice field. The privatisation of penal power is, of course, not a historical innovation, the nationalisation of the prison system, for example, being a relatively recent

---

[15] See N. Lacey, "Theory into Practice? Pornography and the Public/Private Dischotomy", in *Unspeakable Subjects*, n. 9, above ch. 3; F. Olsen, "The Family and the Market", (1983) 96 *Harvard Law Review* 1497; C. Pateman, "Feminist Critiques of the Public/Private Dichotomy", in her *The Disorder of Women* (Oxford, Polity Press, 1989) p. 118.

development. But over the last fifteen years, we have seen not only a resurgence of privatised penal institutions, along with the contracting out of a variety of services ancillary to "state" punishment, but also a diffusion of the very concept of state punishment itself.[16] By this I mean the development of a variety of "community justice" and "mediation" schemes, operating as alternatives or, occasionally, supplements to the formal state power to punish.[17] Not all of these institutions are genuinely supervised by the state, and many of them were not originally state initiatives. Thus while scholars concerned with criminal justice are quite rightly sceptical about a too-ready diagnosis of the "decline of the nation-state", we are also witnessing a genuine growth of legal (and hence penal) pluralism which puts into question the assumption that crime and punishment are exclusively or even primarily matters of state power.[18] Furthermore, there is a link between this development in the contours of social practice and the argument of the previous section of this chapter, in that our grasp of the development's significance becomes deeper once we have added to our analytic toolbox the concept of disciplinary power. This is because many of the relevant institutions operate not primarily in terms of instrumental penalties or by means of sovereignty or juridical power but rather by mobilising pre-existing norms and discourses within which it is sought to reintegrate or rehabilitate offenders or "at-risk" groups.[19]

I would argue that both the diffusion of state penal power into the hands of a wide variety of private—voluntary and commercial—and quasi-public agencies and the fragmentation of penal power beyond the state places four very important questions on the agenda of political theory. Each is a question the relevance of which political theory implicitly acknowledges, yet which it fails currently to address because of its puzzling lack of interest in the actual social phenomena of punishment.

First, these developments alert us to the ways in which state penal power is inevitably mediated via social power. To take a simple and long-standing example, the decisive influence of the popular interpretation of behaviour as criminal in shaping penal enforcement—the fact that ordinary people's reports to the police, and hence their attitudes and perceptions, are probably the single most important factor in socially defining crime—unsettles the political theorist's simple image of the state as applying penal power even-handedly to offenders.[20] The interpretive power not only of ordinary citizens but of a wide variety of

---

[16] See for example R. Matthews (ed.), *Privatizing Criminal Justice* (London, Sage, 1989).

[17] See N. Lacey and L. Zedner, "Discourses of Community in Criminal Justice", (1995) 22 *Journal of Law and Society* 93; A. Crawford, *The Local Governance of Crime* (Oxford, Clarendon Press, 1997).

[18] See for example B. de Sousa Santos (ed.), *State Transformation, Legal Pluralism and Community Justice*, (1992) 1 *Social and Legal Studies* (Issue 2).

[19] For one of the most influential defences of informal reintegrative strategies, see J. Braithwaite, *Crime, Shame and Reintegration* (Cambridge, Cambridge University Press, 1989), and "Shame and Modernity", (1993) 33 *British Journal of Criminology* 1.

[20] See N. Lacey, "Contingency and Criminalisation", in I. Loveland (ed.), *Frontiers of Criminality* (London, Sweet and Maxwell, 1995), p. 1.

officials—police, prosecutors, defence lawyers, social workers, probation officers—contributes to the overall definition of crime, and hence sets the scene for state punishment. To the extent that the power to define the norms of criminal law, and the legitimacy of such norms, are proper objects of political theory, these diffuse social practices are ones which the political theorist cannot afford to ignore.

Secondly, it is surely incumbent upon any theoretical justification of punishment to generate normative principles guiding the basis on which the power to punish or to determine penal norms may be delegated to non-state or quasi-state institutions. This, again, is a matter on which political theorists have been curiously reticent, perhaps because they are implicitly operating with an unrealistic conception of how the criminal justice system really works.

Thirdly, it seems equally obvious that the complex issues of accountability raised by the diffusion and fragmentation of the power to punish are ones to the analysis of which political theory ought to be able to contribute. Clearly, the penal power exercised by a private prison is still in some sense state power: it is power exercised at the behest of and under conditions set by the state. But how should this power be rendered accountable to democratic institutions, and what arguments can political theorists develop about the principles and structures of accountability which should be put in place to ensure the legitimacy of delegated penal power? Current social practice consigns this problem to the crude mechanism of the audit.[21] One would hope that the normative refinements of political theory might be combined with the practical insights of sociology to generate a somewhat more sophisticated conception. Similarly, one would expect political theory to generate some principles guiding our response to the fragmentation of state power and legal pluralism, as well as evaluating the appropriateness of "informal justice", mediation, and community justice in certain spheres. The complications of this task should not, however be underestimated: particularly once we add disciplinary power to the picture, accountability and legitimacy become very difficult questions. Once again we encounter the question of whether disciplinary power is to be regarded as an inevitable side-effect, beyond the scope of normative justification. But it is surely too soon to conclude that such power is entirely beyond human control. For example, it seems likely that the degree of discretion accorded to officials in determining and administering punishment has an important bearing upon the ambit of disciplinary power unleashed by penal practices.[22] The complexity of such issues is not an excuse for their marginalisation in political theory.

---

[21] See M. Power, *The Audit Society: rituals of verification* (Oxford, Clarendon Press, 1997); C. Jones, "Auditing Criminal Justice", (1993) 33 *British Journal of Criminology* 187; N. Lacey, "Government as Manager, Citizen as Consumer", (1994) 57 *Modern Law Review* 534.

[22] One could draw an analogy here with debates about the dangers of the rehabilitative ethic, which is often accused precisely of administering the "treatment" of offenders in relation to vague and unarticulated norms of "social health" or "reform" and covert assessments of "dangerousness": see Lacey, *State Punishment*, n. 1 above, at pp. 30–5.

Finally, we are faced with an important dilemma arising from research into the fragmentation of penal power and the blurring, in important respects, of punitive and social welfare power aimed at prevention, rehabilitation, and reintegration.[23] It has been argued that well-meaning attempts to soften the harshness of state punishment by developing alternative practices, often educative or preventive in intent, in fact operate under certain circumstances to thin the mesh of social control and, over time, to pull ever larger groups of citizens within the ambit of formal criminalising power. The particular significance of this argument for political theory is that it highlights once again the interaction between punitive and criminalising power: the power to punish, indeed the power to attempt to prevent crime, are themselves influential in shaping the interpretation and development of the norms against which the potential subjects of punishment are judged. We touch here on fundamental questions about the nature of political community and the kinds of power which social and political institutions are justified in wielding or acquiescing in their pursuit of social order. It would be astounding to conclude that these are not questions of penal philosophy and hence of political theory.

4. In Conclusion: A Plea for Dialogue

In short, both conceptual innovations in historically informed social theory and the insights generated by contemporary sociology in the criminal justice field place pressing questions on the agenda of political theory. Political theory, both in the sphere of punishment and more generally, today stands at a fork in its modern path. Its trajectory since the eighteenth century has been shaped by a conception of the nation state and its relation to the domestic and international social orders, by an understanding of the nature of political power, and by a view of the relationship between the political and the personal, the public and the private, which are based on assumptions which have gradually been undermined by changing social, economic, and political conditions. While, for example, the political theories of the great thinkers of the seventeenth and eighteenth centuries were explicitly informed by a detailed conception of the nature of the emerging modern social world, and while those of nineteenth century thinkers were preoccupied with, among other things, the changing configuration of public and private necessitated by the growth of what was regarded as the proper scope of the state and by emerging views about the importance of regulating markets and providing welfare, the theories of their twentieth century counterparts have too often been content to start out from a set of largely unexamined assumptions. Locked in a time capsule, penal philosophy is in danger of sauntering down a sideroad punctuated by intense and intellectually stimulating debates which have little relevance to the late modern world. It is always pos-

---

[23] See for example S. Cohen, *Visions of Social Control* (Oxford, Polity, 1985).

sible to cut across and back to the intellectual highway. Here lies a far less stable terrain, and one which will doubtless cause perplexity and confusion. But here also lies the audience for socially informed political theory: political institutions, policy-makers, citizens, those working in particular fields such as criminal justice—people who engage on a daily basis with pressing ethical and political questions. Among political philosophers, those who grapple with questions of punishment are addressing a range of questions which concern every member of the political community. Only if the philosophers can expand their view so as to theorise punishment not as an idea but as a real social practice, developing theories which proceed from a deep understanding of what kind of social order we live in, will they be able to meet their ambition of explicating the (possibly limited) potential for making that social order less unjust.

Index

Alexander, L. 40 n.31
Allen, H. 156
Ardal, P. 48 n.2
Arendt, H. 148, 149, 150
Ashworth, A. 76 n.13, 76 n.14, 77 n.18, 78 n.21
Austin, J. L. 127
autonomy,
 and communicative theories of punishment 54–60, 68, 97–102, 124–6;
 and Kant 24–7

Barry, B. 3 n.9, 118 n.17
Bell, M. 136
Berlin, I. 150
Berndt, R. M. 96 n.28
Bhaskar, R. 134, 139 n.19, 150
Bird, G. 148 n.39
Bird Rose, D. 96 n.28
Blackburn, S. 121, 122
Blocker, H. G. 3 n.8
Boldt, M. 105 n.49
Bosanquet, B. 149
Bottoms, A. 71 n.6
Bower, T. 146 n.37
Braithwaite, J. 2 n.6, 49 n.5, 76 n.14, 88 n.1, 98 n.35, 113 n.11, 114 n.12, 160 n.19
Bulger, J. 136
Butler, J. 130, 131, 132
Byron, Lord 42

Carens, J. 101 n.39
Carlen, P. 155, 156 n.11
Casalis 143, 146, 147
Clark, M. 33 n.12
Clinton, R. 93 n.18
coercion,
 and Kant 11–17, 22–3;
 and penitence 54, 55, 58, 59, 74, 83–4, 100 n.37, 102, 104;
 see also hard treatment
Cohen, S. 162 n.23
communitarianism 54, 57–60, 62, 83–5, 88–91, 149–50;
 and self understanding 97, 99–102, 118
condemnation 114, 141
consequentialism 52, 97
 and communicative punishment 49–50, 98 n.35, 113–14;
 and rights 29–31;
 see also utilitarianism
Cotterrell, R. 97 n.30
Cragg, W. 53 n.11

Dagger, R. 112 n.9
Daniels, N. 42 n.37, 120 n.20
Danto, A. 44
Davis, G. 101 n.39
Davis, M. 49 n.3
Denning, Lord 33, 34 n.13
Derathé, R. 43 n.41
desert 2, 48, 77, 97
deterrence 49, 55–6, 66–7, 70, 113–14, 130–2
Dodson, M. 95 n.26
Donziger, S. 2
Dolinko, D. 48 n.1
Dostoevsky, F. M. 125
Dreier, J. 122 n.29
Duff, R. A. 1 n.1, 34, 40 n.31, 69–81, 88 n.1, 89 n.3, 90, 91, 98, 100 n.37, 102 n.40, 104, 106, 108 n.1, 112 n.9, 124–8, 148, 153, 157 n.13
Durkheim, E. 136
Dworkin, R. 42 n.37, 43, 116, n14, 119–22

Eaton, M. 156
Estlund, D. 122 n.29

Faine, J. 96 n.28
Falls, M. M. 51 n.8
Feinberg, J. 49 n3, 50 n.7, 108 n.3, 125, 128
Foot, P. 33 n.11
Foucault, M. 154–8
Freud, S. 135

Garland, D. 1 n.1, 111 n.7, 156 n.12
Gewirth, A. 35 n.15
Giddens, A. 133, 135–8, 145–6, 150
Goldman, A. 36–7
Goodin, R. 30 n.6
Goot, M. 92 n.13
Green T. H. 148–9
Guest A. G. 32 n.10
guilt 133–150

Habermas, J. 62
Hampton, J. 45 n.46, 51 n.8
Hardin, R. 30 n.6, 91 n.10

The editor is deeply indebted to John Maynor for his help with the preparation of this index.

hard treatment 33
  and communicative theories of punishment
    50–1, 54–60, 67, 69–73, 75–6, 83, 86, 98,
    114, 123, 124–30
Haring, S. 93 n.18, 94 n.21
Harré, R. 134
Hart, H. L. A. 43 n.39, 69 n.1, 108 n.3, 153
  n.1, 154 n.5
Hegel, G. W. F. 29, 38, 44, 46, 54, 56, 149
Hill, T. 20 n.19
Himmler, H. 143
Hindley, M. 136, 141, 142, 147
Hitler A. 142, 143, 144
Hobbes, T. 16–17, 22, 40, 44
Hoekema, D. 3 n.8
Hoernle, T. 78 n.23
Honderich, T. 40 n.31, 48 n.2, 50 n.6, 148
  n.39, 153 n.1
Honoré, A. M. 32 n.10
Hudson, B. 64 n.27, n.28
Hume, D. 41–2
Husak, D. 48 n.2

imprisonment 32, 37, 50, 56, 60, 77, 96 n.28,
  155
incapacitation 1, 77, 82
Ivison, D. 109 n.5, 153 n.4

Jareborg, N. 79 n.24
Jones, C. 161 n.21
justice 61, 120, 130, 141–2
  distributive 3, 63–4, 80–1, 158

Kant, I. 10–27, 42 n.36, 44, 46, 50, 56, 97,
    99–102, 135, 138, 148–50
  and coercion 11–17;
  and Hobbes 16–17, 22–3;
  and justification of punishment 17–23;
  and motivation to obey the law 17;
  and public and private crimes 17, 19–21
Kleinig, J. 51 n.8
Korsgaard, C. 12, 13

Lacey, N. 49 n.5, 58 n.19, 88 n.1, 91 n.11, 93
  n.19, 103 n.43
law,
  Aboriginal 92–6, 101–7;
  function and scope in communicative theory
    49–50, 54–6, 58–9, 74, 84–5, 108–9;
  and community 62–4, 89; 92–6;
  and disciplinary power (Foucault) 155;
  interpretive account of 114–22;
  Kant's account of 11, 16–27;
  liberal account of 91;
  and moral theory 108–12, 115–23, 153;
  utilitarian account of 30–4
liberalism 11, 23, 54–6, 58–60, 62, 74–6, 88–91,
  105

Locke, J. 29, 35, 36–7, 44, 126
Long, J. A. 105 n.49
Lucas, J. R. 51 n.8
Lyons, D. 30, 34

McHugh, P. 101 n.39
MacIntyre, A. 64
Macklem, P. 92 n.15
Maddock, K. 96 n.28
Mason 94–5, 103
Matthews, R. 160 n.16
Mildren, J. 104
Mill, J. S. 30, 46
Miller, D. 101 n39, 118 n.17
Miller, F. D. Jr. 44 n.43
Moore, M. 108 n.2, 109–110, 141 n.22, 148
  n.41
moral theory 110, 114–23
Morris, H. 112 n.9
Mullin, C. 34 n.13
Mulqueeny, K. E. 95 n.24
Murphy, J. G. 4 n.10, 42 n.36, 52 n10, 57 n.17,
  61 n.23, 112 n.9

Nagel, T. 24 n.27, 46 n.47
Narayan, U. 53 n.12, 70 n.3
Nietzsche, F. 28 n.1, 29 n.4, 127
Nino, C. S. 38–41
Norrie, A. W. 61 n.23, 64 n.27, 133 n.2, 139
  n.18, 156 n.10
Nozick, R. 36 n.20

Olsen, F. 159 n.15
O'Neill, O. 24 n.26
Orwell, G. 25

Pateman, C. 42, 159 n.15
Patton, P. 103
Paul, E. F. 44 n.43
Paul, J. 44 n.43
Pearson, N. 92 n.13, n.16
Pettit, P. 2 n. 6, 49 n.5, 76 n.14, 88 n.1
Philippson, N. 103 n.42
Pocock, J. G. A. 101 n.39, 103 n.42
Power, M. 161 n.21
Primoratz, I. 49 n.3
punishment,
  Aboriginal 95 n.28;
  and contractarianism 42–46;
  communicative theory of 2, 24–5, 49–61,
    65–9, 71–3, 75–87, 88–90, 97–107, 108–23,
    124–132, 148;
  and consent 2, 38–42;
  expressive theory of 49, 108 n.3, 109, 123,
    128–32;
  and fair play 4, 112–3;
  and hard treatment see hard treatment;
  and interpretivism 114–22;

Kant's theory of 11, 17–27;
and moral standing 57, 61–5, 73–4, 84–5;
and proportionality 59, 78–80;
and prudential reason 17, 53–7, 70–1, 75–6, 123;
retributive theory of 1–3, 17–27, 48, 73, 130, 141 n.22;
and social deprivation 1 n.3, 62–3, 80–1, 94;
and the state 58–9, 75–80, 84–7, 88–107, 153, 159–162;
utilitarian theory of 1–3, 31–5, 76, 113–14, 130–1;
see also autonomy, coercion, condemnation, desert, deterrence, hard treatment, imprisonment, incapacitation, law, reform, rehabilitation, repentance
Ratnapala, S. 95 n.24
Rawls, J. 3, 24 n.25, 30, 33, 45, 62, 90, 119 n.20, 120 n.20, 158 n.14
reform 80, 125–28
rehabilitation 1, 76–7, 80, 82 n.30, 98–100, 101, 162
repentance 51–3, 57–60, 67, 71–3, 75–6, 83–4, 99–100, 124–7
retributivism, *see* punishment
Rex, S. 76 n.13, n.15, 77 n.17
Reynolds, H. 92 n.14
rights 22, 28–47, 59
Rosen, A. D. 22 n.23
Ross, R. 106 n.50
Rousseau, J. J. 38, 43, 44–5
Rowse, T. 92 n.13

De Sousa Santos, B. 160 n.18
Sadurski, W. 3 n.8, 112 n.9
Scanlon, T. 45–6
Sen, A. 46 n.47
Sereny, G. 133–4, 142–8, 150
Shapiro, I. 103 n.43
Sheridan, A. 154 n.6
Simmonds N. E. 48 n.2

Skillen, A. J. 49 n.3
Skinner, Q. 103 n.42
Smart, C. 155
Smith, E. 3 n.8
Snare, A. 79 n.24
social contract 2, 11, 42–6, 56–7, 91
Speer, A. 133–4, 137, 142–7, 150
Speer, H. 143
state of nature 11, 15, 16, 18–19, 25–7
Stephen, J. F. 109 n.3, 129
Stephenson, M. 95 n.24
Strawson, P. F. 132

Thomson, J. J. 35 n.16
Travis, C. 65 n.30
Tresidder, M. 143 n.28
Tully, J. 105 n.48
Turpel, M. E. 106 n.50

utilitarianism 30–35, 46, 76, 122, 130–1
and punishing the innocent 33–4
see also punishment

von Hirsch, A. 48, 51, 53–6, 60, 64 n.27, 67, 83–6, 112 n.9, 148 n.41

Waldron, J. 32 n.10, 45, 101 n.39
Walzer, M. 101 n.39, 117 n.16, 118 n.17, n18, 119–20
West, F. 136
West, R. 136, 141
Wiener, M. 156 n.12
Williams, B. 46 n.47
Williams, H. 22 n.23
Williams, N. 96 n.28
Williams, R. 93 n.18, n.20
Wittgenstein, L. 62 n.24, 65 n.30
Wolff, J. 34 n.13
Wood, A. W. 38 n.23

Zedner, L. 156 n.12, 160 n.17